Kindergarten in Canada

A Play-Based Approach
for Educators

Kindergarten in Canada

A Play-Based Approach for Educators

Nancy Maynes
Nipissing University

PEARSON

Toronto

Vice-President, Editorial Director: Gary Bennett
Editor-in-Chief: Michelle Sartor
Editor, Humanities and Social Sciences: Joel Gladstone
Marketing Manager: Ann MacDonald
Supervising Developmental Editor: Madhu Ranadive
Project Manager: Ashley Patterson
Manufacturing Manager: Susan Johnson
Production Editor: Vasundhara Sawhney (Cenveo Publisher Services)
Copy Editor: Barbara Kamienski
Proofreader: Jennifer McIntyre
Compositor: Cenveo Publisher Services
Permissions Researcher: Karen Hunter
Art Director: Julia Hall
Cover Designer: Julia Hall
Cover Image: Getty Images

Photographs by Jennifer Straub

Credits and acknowledgments for material borrowed from other sources and reproduced, with permission, in this textbook appear on the appropriate page within the text.

10 9 8 7 6 5 4 3 2 1 [EB]

Library and Archives Canada Cataloguing in Publication

Maynes, Nancy A.
Kindergarten in Canada: a play-based approach for educators/Nancy Maynes.
Includes index.
ISBN 978-0-13-257202-6
1. Kindergarten—Canada—Methods and manuals. 2. Play. I. Title.
LB1241.M39 2011 372.21'80971 C2011-906576-2

PEARSON

ISBN 978-0-13-257202-6

To John and the many supportive family and friends who have listened and guided me as this book developed; with thanks for the inspirational places in my life, especially the cottage. With special appreciation to Jennifer Straub for the photography that has enriched this book. Appreciation is extended to Gina Tullio for her role in facilitating the acquisition of these pictures in the classrooms of the Sudbury District Catholic School Board.

Brief Contents

Contents

Preface

Kindergarten in Canada: A Play-Based Approach for Educators has been designed to support courses for teacher candidates in teacher training programs, experienced teachers upgrading their qualifications, and early childhood educators engaged in college programs. Throughout this text, I use the term **educator team** to refer to the combination of adults who will serve early learners in their JK/SK program. In some jurisdictions, this combination of adults may be a teacher and an ECE educator; in others, it may be a teacher and an educational assistant; still other contexts may use a teacher and parent volunteers. There are many references in this text to how these adults, whatever their background in early learning, need to come together as a united team in their work in the classroom.

As the Council of Ministers of Education for each province and territory continues to meet and to make early learning a priority in their ministries across the country, we can anticipate greater similarities in delivery models across Canada. This book addresses a team-delivery approach that can be adapted to any of the existing and evolving contexts.

Kindergarten in Canada: A Play-Pased Approach for Educators has many design features that support course work through traditional face-to-face teaching modes or through online course delivery. Main features of this textbook include the incorporation of educator team learning activities into the text; the inclusion of several templates and organizers that will help educators with organization and planning tasks in the JK/SK classroom; photographs that demonstrate key points in the text; chapter openers and quotations designed to keep the reader focused and challenged; figures and tables that present data and conceptual models, to support educator understanding of key ideas and present information in easy-to-access formats; reflection points throughout each chapter, designed to encourage professional thought about the implications for professional practice of the ideas in the chapter; Thinking Ahead sections at the end of each chapter, designed to move the reader from theory to practice (praxis); and finally, an extensive glossary to assist readers with understanding the complex vocabulary of education.

As well, the book is supported by two supplements. An extensive and detailed Instructor's Manual provides examples of ways to teach with this text that support the philosophy of learning espoused in the text. Each chapter is also accompanied by detailed PowerPoint notes that will help course participants review and summarize key points about each chapter.

It is my hope that early learning JK/SK educators will find the book informative and full of ideas about how they can provide rich and rewarding learning experiences for young children.

N.M.

Acknowledgments

Pearson Canada and the authors would like to thank the following individuals for their reviews during the development phase of this book: Janet Buchanan, University of Ontario Institute of Technology; Taunya Laslo, Mohawk College; Kathryn Lockwood, Humber College; Larry Prochner, University of Alberta; and Mary-Louise Vanderlee, Brock University.

SUPPLEMENTS

The following supplements are included with this book:

Instructor's Manual (ISBN 978-0-13-289175-2)

Written by Nancy Maynes, the Instructor's Manual covers topics that are important to educators in and out of the classroom. The manual details how to prepare for class, provides goals for both the instructors and the student, and includes activities to assist in the pre-assessment of teacher/ECE candidates. Lesson outlines are explicit, promote active engagement with ideas, and provide approaches that move the learner from exposure to new ideas to increased ability to use the ideas in their professional practice.

PowerPoint Presentations (ISBN 978-0-13-289174-5)

Created by Nancy Maynes, the PowerPoint Presentations offer over 35 slides per chapter and include summaries of key ideas in the text, in an easy-to-access format. This supplement provides a comprehensive selection of slides highlighting key concepts featured in the text to assist instructors and provide summaries for students.

CourseSmart for Instructors (ISBN 978-0-13-257301-6)

CourseSmart goes beyond traditional expectations—providing instant, online access to the textbooks and course materials you need at a lower cost for students. And even as students save money, you can save time and hassle with a digital eTextbook that allows you to search for the most relevant content at the very moment you need it. Whether it's evaluating textbooks or creating lecture notes to help students with difficult concepts, CourseSmart can make life a little easier. See how when you visit www.coursesmart.com/instructors.

CourseSmart for Students (ISBN 978-0-13-257301-6)

CourseSmart goes beyond traditional expectations—providing instant, online access to the textbooks and course materials you need at an average savings of 60%. With instant access from any computer and the ability to search your text, you'll find the content you need quickly, no matter where you are. And with online tools like highlighting and note-taking, you can save time and study efficiently. See all the benefits at www.coursesmart.com/students.

Technology Specialists

Pearson's Technology Specialists work with faculty and campus course designers to ensure that Pearson technology products, assessment tools, and online course materials are tailored to meet your specific needs. This highly qualified team is dedicated to helping schools take full advantage of a wide range of educational resources, by assisting in the integration of a variety of instructional materials and media formats. Your local Pearson Canada sales representative can provide you with more details on this service program.

Pearson Custom Library

For enrollments of at least 25 students, you can create your own textbook by choosing the chapters that best suit your own course needs. To begin building your custom text, visit www.pearsoncustomlibrary.com. You may also work with a dedicated Pearson Custom editor to create your ideal text—publishing your own original content or mixing and matching Pearson content. Contact your local Pearson representative to get started.

MyEducationLab

The moment you know.

Educators know it. Students know it. It's that inspired moment when something that was difficult to understand suddenly makes perfect sense. Our MyLab products have been designed and refined with a single purpose in mind—to help educators create that moment of understanding with their students.

MyEducationLab delivers proven results in helping individual students succeed. It provides engaging experiences that personalize, stimulate, and measure learning for each student. And, it comes from a trusted partner with educational expertise and an eye on the future.

MyEducationLab can be used by itself or linked to any learning management system. To learn more about how MyEducationLab combines proven learning applications with powerful assessment, visit **www.myeducationlab.com**.

Introduction

Research into early learning and its benefits provides overwhelming evidence of its immediate and long-term advantages for children and society. The advantages of full-day learning experiences—in contrast to half-day structures—are also evident in recent studies. In many jurisdictions, kindergarten is optionally available, at the parents' choice, for children who would turn four by January of their JK year.

Early learning experiences are structured very differently across Canada. However, recent efforts to address the needs of early learners have set off a wave of exciting initiatives to support early learning for four- and five-year-old children in many areas of the country. During the next several years, coordinated early learning programs for four- and five-year-olds will be publicly funded in many provinces. Some jurisdictions are phasing in the implementation of these opportunities, in recognition of the space and resources, both human and material, that will be needed to support effective implementation of these initiatives.

Our schooling practices across Canada have their roots in the historical development and settlement of the country and in the cultural backgrounds of early settlers. Some early learning practices have their roots in both daycare and private schooling practices. However, recent early learning initiatives provide a coordinated and clearly conceptualized framework for early learning that may either support or cause us to question some current practices.

The conceptual frameworks supporting current early learning initiatives are consistent in their strong endorsement of learner-centred, play-based learning environments for young children. This text will examine the philosophy, instructional beliefs, and practices consistent with these frameworks. Samples of approaches in different Canadian provinces and territories and different jurisdictions around the world are used to illustrate ideas about programming for early learners. The influence of learning theories and research into brain development will be examined to inform the strategies that are recommended for early learning contexts.

Early learning initiatives are often conceived around the vision of a coordinated and specialized educator team with diversely trained professionals working cooperatively to plan, implement, and assess learning for young students. Some initiatives include a vision of coordinated community services to support the needs of young learners and their families. Developing conceptions include a vision of community support prior to formal early learning in JK/SK, to provide accessible, affordable, and coordinated community service from birth to age three.

Effective communication is an integral part of the evolving vision for full-day early learning environments. To be effective, program communication plans must include the identification of ways in which educator teams will communicate with young children, their parents or guardians, grandparents and elders, and the wider community. Accessibility of communications for the children of English as a Second Language cultures needs to be considered in program planning and communications. Culturally sensitive approaches must be learned by the educator team and practised as routines. Holistic approaches characteristic of Aboriginal learning must be incorporated into planning and practices. These considerations identify a few of the complex decisions that must be included in planning to establish an effective early learning environment.

Early learning programs must provide stimulating learning in an intricate and safe social environment, with learning that is responsive to many variables. Among these variables is the child's learning background. The educator team must be well equipped to assess the background, culture, social and physical development, interests, characteristics, and challenges of each early learner, and plan for supported progress to maintain high interest, personal growth trajectories, and proximal growth for each learner, while maintaining a supportive and congenial social context among learners.

The curriculum philosophy for full-day JK/SK learning environments is play based. This environment needs to support child-centred inquiry and active learning, and build age-appropriate social, personal, physical, emotional, and cognitive development. By using timely questions in child–adult interactions, the educator team members will build this supportive environment.

The assessment of early learning will involve all members of the educator team in observation based on their professional skills of seeing and interpreting during all phases of learning. A vision of assessment as embedded, non-intrusive, and growth oriented will create a foundational tenant of an effective early learning program.

Finally, the place of a full-day JK/SK program within a community context will need to be understood by all members of the educator team. Our communities want a system of support that is coordinated, centrally located, easily accessed, and readily available. Community support services that have at their centre a strong early learning program can support this evolving vision of community for early learners and their families.

It is my hope that this text can help readers understand the complexities and the subtleties of this vision for an effective learning environment for our youngest students.

1 The History of Early Learning Initiatives in Canada

"Mommy brushed snow from the car. She couldn't find the brush, so do you know what she used?"

(Friendly, Beach and Turiano, 2001)

1.1 *Overall, Canada does not have a national strategy for early childhood education and care.*

In this chapter, educator team members will learn about

- the history of kindergartens in Canada
- the various roles of early kindergartens
- the approaches to early childhood education that have been used across Canada
- the history of Montessori schools in Canada
- the history of private and alternative schools in Canada
- past and current legislation governing early learning across Canada
- the standards of care for early childhood educators in Canada

At the end of this chapter, educator team members can reflect on their personal growth through

- CHAPTER SUMMARY
- THINKING AHEAD: Opportunities for Professional Reflection
- ADDITIONAL READING SUGGESTIONS

The development of early Canadian kindergarten experiences for young children has been influenced by many historical factors and social movements. As we have expanded our understanding about the nature of early learning, the design and foci of kindergartens have evolved.

THE HISTORICAL ROOTS OF KINDERGARTEN IN CANADA

Early movements to include formal, school-based instruction and care for young children in Canada began with the move toward social responsibility for the poor in the mid-1800s. This movement reflected activity in European countries, most notably in Germany, to provide kindergarten experiences for young children. German educator Friedrich Froebel first introduced the term *kindergarten* in 1840 to identify the three-part focus for early learning he intended for the *Play and Activity Institute* established in Bad Blankenburg, Germany. The word *kindergarten* is translated as "children's garden," which reflected Froebel's vision for early learning and was intended to express the idea that early learning environments should be both gardens *for* children to learn through observation, stimulation, and interaction and gardens *of* children, nurtured in non-threatening, unified spaces that focused on the growth and development of the whole child. Froebel is credited with introducing play-based learning and the natural transition into **work play** in early learning environments.

The three-part focus for Froebel's kindergarten was directed toward

- providing toys that stimulated play and exploration,
- providing games and dance that promoted healthy activity, and
- providing experiences outdoors to stimulate awareness of the natural world.

In Canada, infant schools were opened in many provinces around this same time period, in response to the needs of a specific segment of the population. Later, in the middle of the century, privately owned and operated kindergartens began to open, in response to the growing social belief that young children benefit from formal schooling. By 1870, larger towns and cities had commonly available access to kindergartens for the local population. However, these were still private operations and mostly addressed clientele from middle- and upper-class backgrounds, as fees were charged for access.

Later, kindergartens began to be offered to immigrants and poorer families, and access was free. They became known as "free kindergartens," espousing a social reform philosophy and pursuing social integration for children from all backgrounds (Prochner, 2000). These free kindergartens were sponsored by charitable and religious groups. It was not until 1883 that the first publicly funded kindergarten opened under the auspices of the Toronto Board of Education. By 1885, provincial funding was being provided to support the first

Canadian kindergartens. The next fifteen years saw the expansion of kindergartens across Ontario (Mathien, 2001). These early kindergartens were intended to serve children between the ages of three and five years.

The methods used in early kindergartens were rooted in (and influenced by) the schooling traditions of the early settlers in various areas of the country, most notably those of the French, English, American, and Scottish settlers (see Table 1.1). The schooling traditions found their ascendency and decline parallel to the political evolution of Canada as a nation.

Table 1.1 *Influence of Canada's Early Settlers on School Traditions*

Time-frame	French 1650–1700	English 1760–1840	American from 1776 on	Scottish 1760–1840
Historical Context	• ranged from Cape Breton to the Great Lakes • based on the traditions of the Roman Catholic Church	• reflected beliefs and attitudes of the British upper classes • "public" schools were reserved for wealthier classes • Puritan religious groups established some schools with a focus on Bible studies	• Loyalists settled in Canada during the American Revolution	• Scottish migration
Educational Approach	• boys and girls attended separate schools • taught by members of religious orders • curriculum focused on catechism, singing, arithmetic, reading, writing, and grammar	• education was considered a church responsibility • education was seen as a function of one's class in society rather than of academic merit	• a two-track system: one for the wealthy and one for the poor • lower classes studied reading, writing, religion, and arithmetic • upper classes attended Latin grammar schools for a college preparation education • both tracks stressed religious instruction	• all children attended • schools had pupils from all classes of society mixed together • boys and girls attended the same schools • both elementary and secondary education were widely available • science and art were taught in addition to classics, fundamentals, and religious concepts
Funding	• Catholic Church • parents who could afford to contribute	• Church of England funded schools for the lower classes • charitable schools were provided to teach basics to the poor • dame schools were run as home-based schools with small fees collected from parents	• religious orders • Anglican church • parents of upper-class pupils	• parish • town (burgh)

In Quebec, education systems evolved to reflect the practices established in France. Schools were usually run by religious orders and taught by nuns and priests, with some lay staff. These schools were financed by contributions from the Catholic Church, the French monarchy, and the students' parents. Civil laws did not influence educational issues in Quebec until after 1760. The curriculum in Quebec schools focused on rudimentary reading, writing, and arithmetic skills. Schooling was usually available only to children in settled urban areas.

THE VARIOUS ROLES OF EARLY KINDERGARTENS

Early kindergartens did not share a common pedagogical approach, a common mission, or a common clientele in terms of age. Some served as daycare and supported opportunities for mothers to take employment during the days; some provided care for infants; and many were run by charitable groups with a focus on support for women. Because they started in areas of Canada where population density and settlement patterns created needs, key events in the development of early learning in the early years of Canada's history are mainly related to the areas of eastern and central Canada.

1.2 *New legislation has provided for more universal access to early learning support across Canada.*

Source: Hemera/Thinkstock

By 1942, the Canadian government passed legislation for some coordination of early kindergartens through an order-in-council. This order established the Dominion-Provincial Wartime Agreement for parents in Ontario and Quebec. The agreement provided a 50% funding subsidy for mothers employed in wartime essential industries. However, as a wartime measure, this subsidy agreement had a short lifespan and was discontinued when the Second World War was over. Following the turbulent times for early childhood care that characterized the years between 1995 and 1998 (see Table 1.2), several gains in early childhood care have been made. In 1998, the Ontario Child Care Supplement for Working Families was introduced. Families were provided with financial assistance of up to $1100 per year per child if the family needed care for children under age seven and the parents were working, in school, in job-related training programs, or caring for a young child at home. An Early Years Challenge Fund provided incentives to businesses to promote early childhood development and parenting programs, because parenting demands were found to be a major disincentive for people on welfare to look for work.

Table 1.2 *Early Learning Initiatives in Canada between 1881 and 2010*

Key Events in Early Learning Initiatives in Canada 1881–2010	
1881	The Crèche (now the Victoria Day Care and Family Services) is established in Toronto.
1883	Toronto Board of Education establishes Canada's first public kindergarten.
1887	The Education Act (Ontario) recognizes kindergarten for three- to five-year-olds in legislation.
1926	St. George's Nursery is established as a laboratory school with the opening of the Institute of Child Studies at the University of Toronto; its purpose is to train nursery school teachers.
1942	Ontario and Quebec sign the Dominion-Provincial Wartime Agreement to share the costs of nursery school; the Day Nurseries Branch of government was established to administer funds, license, and inspect. This was Canada's first childcare services regulation.
1950	Establishment of the Nursery Education Association of Ontario (now the Association of Early Childhood Educators Ontario) is established.
1950s	Kindergarten as a transition to school for immigrant children is introduced in Toronto.
1966	The Canada Assistance Plan provides early childhood care subsidies for low-income families in Ontario.
1974	The "welfare service" concept becomes part of Canada's first major policy statement on childcare services.
1978	Amendments to the Day Care Nurseries Act require licensing for private-home daycare agencies (amended in 1984 to set standards).
1980	The Ontario Coalition for Better Day Care (Child Care) is founded: it advocates universal, publicly funded, non-profit childcare services.
1987	Recognition of childcare as a basic public service, rather than a welfare service, is provided by a Liberal government policy called "New Directions for Day Care." A three-year, phased-in expansion of childcare programs becomes policy.
1991	NDP government policy encourages the expansion of non-profit childcare services and the conversion of private daycares into non-profit facilities; Wage Enhancement Grant is provided for childcare workers.
1992	Child Care Reform in Ontario is released by the provincial government: it focuses on childcare services that are affordable, of high quality, well managed, and universally accessible. Ontario Child Care Management Framework is released. It provides a "curriculum" framework for quality childcare programs; school boards can become licensed providers of childcare services. Fully funded childcare subsidies are provided to 8 200 parents who are either engaged in job retraining or looking for work.
1994	The Royal Commission on Learning recommends that the existing education system provide early childhood education for all three- to five-year-old children.
1995	The Early Years Program pilot project is proposed on an application basis to provide care for four- and five-year-old students. The program is never fully implemented because of a change in provincial government.

(*Continued*)

Table 1.2 Early Learning Initiatives in Canada between 1881 and 2010, continued

Key Events in Early Learning Initiatives in Canada 1881–2010	
1995	Many of the initiatives to support childcare (developed between 1987 and 1995) are capped or cancelled. **CANCELLED** • Program Development Fund • Capital funding for new childcare services • Cost sharing for Jobs Ontario subsidies (80-20%) • Funds for childcare services in new schools • Conversion to non-profit funding • Early Years Program • Limits on new subsidies to non-profit programs **CAPPED** • Pay-equity fund for childcare workers
1996	Changes in the Pay Equity Act are made so that childcare workers can no longer benefit. Report "Improving Child Care in Ontario" is produced. This report introduces "for-profit" childcare services and user fees in resource centres.
1998	Services Improvement Act is introduced to amend the Day Nurseries Act. First efforts to create a childcare services database (Child Care Data Warehouse) are introduced. These include an effort to centralize performance-related data as a monitoring mechanism.
1998	Legislation (A Workplace Tax Incentive) tries to encourage businesses to build and maintain on-site or community childcare services by offering tax deductions.
1998	Changes to the education funding formula cause many school closures and result in loss of in-school childcare spaces.
1999	A successful court challenge of 1996 legislation is achieved by the Equal Pay Coalition to provide the pay equity adjustment that was lost.
1999	Report of the Early Years Study (Dr. Fraser Mustard and the Hon. Margaret McCain) links early care with lifelong learning, behaviour, and health. Recommendations of the report include: • establishing early childhood development and parenting centres • making childhood supports accessible, affordable, and optional • focusing on the provision of supports from conception to Grade 1 entry

Used by permission of Nancy Maynes

In 2000, several new pieces of legislation supported improvements in childcare. First, subsidies for childcare services could be provided directly to parents under an amendment to the Day Nurseries Act. This allowed funds for parents of children aged 6 to 12, and up to 18 if the child had special needs, so that parents could enrol children in unregulated recreation programs. Second, the government encouraged partnerships between the public and private sectors and the use of volunteers to provide childhood supports for families. Third, applications for fee subsidies for childcare services were limited to times when parents were required to work or attend school. Finally, the Ministry of Education proposed full-day kindergarten for four- and five-year-old children in publicly funded schools to replace direct care payments to parents through the Education Improvement Commission.

Reflection Point

What factors might influence political decisions to make early learning opportunities available to Canadian families? What role has research played in making early learning possible more broadly across Canada?

The next nine years, from 2001 to 2010, saw a rapid expansion of the vision for services for early learners. These services continue to be made available at different rates in various jurisdictions across Canada. In the following chapters of this text, examples of services from different provincial and territorial jurisdictions will be used to illustrate key ideas that are emerging in many areas across Canada.

1.3 *Dr. James Fraser Mustard, a leading Canadian advocate of early learning.*

Source: © Richard Lautens/GetStock.com

In 2001, the government of Ontario produced an Early Years Plan based on the 1999 study of the early years. Early Years Centres were established throughout Ontario in each political riding. Funds were provided to support a wide range of family services, but remained limited in the direct services provided to early learners. Amendments to the Day Nurseries Act allowed fee subsidies for school-aged children's involvement in unregulated recreation programs. In 2002, phased-in funds were provided by the federal government for services across Canada to support early childhood development for First Nations and Aboriginal children through research, integration, and coordination of services. Also in 2002, the 1999 report by Dr. Fraser Mustard and the Hon. Margaret McCain was revisited in a second report which condemned the lack of action on its earlier recommendations regarding early childhood care. The second report resulted in the provision of a task force to review school funding formulas. Currently, the costs per pupil for school-based childcare are calculated at $6645 for JK classrooms and $6673 for SK classrooms. These funds support an Ontario provincial average class size of 22.2 in the primary division.

Early childhood care for children of Aboriginal origin is funded federally for First Nations, Métis, and Inuit children, and non-status native children both on and off reserve. Childcare initiatives for Aboriginal children emphasize services that are flexible, accessible, and sensitive to Aboriginal culture. On-reserve care facilities are typically administered by First Nations communities; this includes the administration of funds and coordination of services. In 1996, the Royal Commission on Aboriginal Peoples recommended improved coordination of services among levels of government to extend care to all Aboriginal children, regardless of location, to recognize growth needs across physical, social, intellectual, and spiritual development domains; to engage the Aboriginal community in

Reflection Point

What characteristics of early learning might you expect to be different in childcare environments offered in reserve settings as opposed to those offered off reserves? Why might these differences be established?

service design; and to administer programs, while respecting parental choice and involvement in services.

While specific details of the historical development of early learning vary across provinces, all Canadian jurisdictions share an on-again, off-again history in relation to their support of publicly funded early learning. Philosophies, approaches, accessibility, and funding have been varied and inconsistent, largely reflecting the social priorities and historical events of each jurisdiction. Research showing the long-term benefits of early learning and the long-term disadvantages of not addressing early learning has been the impetus behind the recent development of more supportive legislation to address the needs of young learners.

THE APPROACHES TO EARLY CHILDHOOD EDUCATION THAT HAVE BEEN USED ACROSS CANADA

In Canada, early learning environments in both private and alternative contexts are of four types. These environments are differentiated by the types of services they offer and the age group of children they serve.

Childcare These facilities may serve children from six weeks old to twelve years. Full childcare is available for preschool children, and before- and after-school care is available for school-aged children.

Daycare Daycare facilities may be publicly or privately operated. The size of a daycare facility may influence licensing requirements, and these can vary by provincial jurisdiction. Daycare hours may be set (i.e., 7 a.m. to 6 p.m.) or may be negotiated individually with the parent, who pays fees based on use.

Preschools These facilities are usually accessible to all children but are privately funded and may be aligned with particular social or religious affiliations. Preschools differ from childcare and daycare in that they have a more formal agenda for learning and generally provide service based on efforts to socialize young children in preparation for public schooling at age four. Preschools may have been called nursery schools in some jurisdictions.

Kindergartens Kindergarten facilities are usually tied to public and Catholic school systems and available only to four- and five-year-olds, with early entry available to those who will turn four before December 31st of their entry year. In many jurisdictions, kindergarten is optional for parents to choose, and mandatory school attendance is required only at age six. Kindergartens are governed by provincial school legislation and have provincially mandated curriculum guidelines.

The broad variety of approaches used for early learning across Canada, and the optional nature of all programs for this age group, have meant that children who enter schools at age six do so with a breadth of educational backgrounds. Some may have had no engagement in childcare, daycare, preschools, or kindergartens, while others may have had several years of experience with all of these early learning services. Some may have attended a Montessori preschool and kindergarten and have extensive formal learning experience.

A HISTORY OF MONTESSORI SCHOOLS IN CANADA

Montessori schools have been part of early learning across Canada for over a century. Approaches developed for the Montessori system of early education have added to our knowledge of how to address the needs of early learners.

Maria Montessori (1870–1952) developed an approach to early childhood education that evolved from her personal observations of children, as both an

1.4 *Maria Montessori (1870–1952)*

Source: The Canadian Montessori Education Institute, www.montessori-institute.ca

educator and physician. Montessori believed that educational opportunities should be structured so that the child's "true normal nature" could be developed. This approach was to be facilitated by providing materials in the learning environment that were designed to bring about, sustain, and support children's true, natural way of being.

Several pedagogical beliefs underlie the Montessori approach to schooling for early learners. Among these are the ideas that

- all children have their own perfect self-directed development innate in their being,
- the teacher serves as a director or guide who watches over the environment to remove any obstacles that might interfere with the child's natural development, and
- lessons are experimental interactions with children to either resolve misbehaviour or to show how to use various self-teaching materials that are provided in the environment for the children's free use.

The Montessori methodology differentiates between normal play, with toys and fantasy elements, and work play that extends conceptual understanding for the child that is realistic in the present moment. The Montessori methods are most prominently used with early learning for students between 2 and 6 years old but also have been applied to the learning approaches used with 6- to 12-year-olds. Schools that espouse a Montessori philosophy and pedagogical

1.5 *Montessori learning materials have special functions in early education.*

Source: The Canadian Montessori Education Institute, www.montessori-institute.ca

approach may differ in their interpretation of the Montessori methods, practical applications of the methodology, their in-house philosophy, and the age groupings they serve.

Reflection Point

How might you introduce the concept of work play to a young child?

Montessori schools in Canada are privately run and are not funded by public support. However, Montessori approaches and learning materials developed for Montessori environments are often used to support programs in publicly funded early learning environments. Montessori materials designed for early learning environments for infants to students up to six years old are identified in five categories. These include the following:

1. Practical life materials: These are items to help children learn self-sufficiency skills, such as physical coordination, care of self, care of the environment, and interpersonal socialization skills.
2. Sensorial materials: These are materials designed to help early learners experience the natural order of the physical environment by exploring attributes such as size, colour, shape, dimension, and position.
3. Math materials: These include concrete materials to help early learners understand basic concepts of mathematics related to numeration, place value, and number operations (addition, subtraction, multiplication, division).
4. Language materials: These include physical experiences to help students develop their use of a writing instrument, their basic skills of reading, and their ability to move from letter sounds to blended sounds to form words.
5. Cultural subjects: These topics include exposure to materials and concepts indigenous to subject areas traditionally addressed by schools. They include geography, science, music, art, and reading.

Reflection Point

Develop a learning material designed to address one or more of the five categories that are part of the Montessori program. In a peer group, demonstrate how that material would be used and the advantages of that material for early learning.

Montessori schools often use the "three-period lesson" (Lillard, 2005) to expose students to new learning in the curriculum categories. During three-period

Table 1.3 *Concepts that Guide Approaches to Learning in Montessori Schools*

Montessori Learning Concept	Explanation
Inner guidance of nature	The early learner is guided by inherent inner directives from nature, which guide normal development.
Prepared environment	By controlling the learning environment, adults can support the natural learning of the child rather than attempting to control the child.
Observation and indirect teaching	The child is free to choose to engage new stimuli, and the adult acts to guide rather than lead learning.
Normalization	This concept presents the belief that all learners will naturally move away from disorder, inattention, and attachment to fantasy to a state of perfect, normal being, which is characterized by spontaneous self-discipline, independence, love of order, harmony, and peace with others in a social situation.
Absorbent mind	The young child is receptive to learning and most open before the age of six.
Work, not play	The normal child's play of toys and fantasy is differentiated from the purposeful learning play that has a realistic context in the learning moment. This concept is often referred to as *play-based learning* in early learning contexts.
Multi-age groupings	The concept supports cross-age group exposure to other children to take advantage of one child's ability to learn from another child of a different age.

lessons, concepts are tied to language that names them. In the first lesson, the early learner is shown the material and it is named. The second lesson reinforces the naming of the object and may include a demonstration of its use to support developing understanding. In the third lesson, the teacher checks that the child understands by ensuring that the child can name and use the object. This sequence is comparable to **direct instruction** lessons that will be addressed in later chapters.

Several concepts (see Table 1.3) about how children develop are used to guide Montessori approaches. Many of the concepts have been used in public school and early childhood education contexts to guide and inform program development for early learners; these principles have become so engrained in the way adults work with young children that they have become cornerstones of primary and early learning classroom environments.

There is a body of research that supports the advantages of the Montessori approach for early learners. In comparing it to traditional school methods, researchers have found that students aged 5 to 12 schooled in a Montessori tradition display better social cognition, show stronger executive control, have more positive playground interactions, show greater development of a sense of fairness and justice, write more creatively and with more complex sentence structures, show more positive responses to social dilemmas, and report a stronger sense of community at school (Dohrmann, Mishida, Gartner, Lipsky, and Grimm, 2007; Rathunde and Csikszentmihalyi, 2005). The second study also demonstrated a higher level of student interest and motivation during high school for students whose early learning experiences were based on Montessori concepts.

A HISTORY OF PRIVATE AND ALTERNATIVE SCHOOLS IN CANADA

Private and alternative schools in Canada are typically provided for social or religious reasons. Both types of schools are privately funded, with the users paying full fees for access. While private schools may be designed to provide access to education with smaller class sizes and academically focused programs tailored to their clienteles' social class, alternative schools are often dedicated to instruction through approaches that are specialized for a particular type of learner, focus on learners with a particular background, or espouse an uncommon approach to learning or the learner.

Because of the fees that parents must pay, private and alternative approaches to early learning through childcare, daycare, preschool/nursery school, or kindergartens are not universally accessible. Government subsidies of various types provide additional support to allow broader access for many children, but subsidies are not stable and tend to vary, depending on the political climate and the social commitment to early learning in the face of competition for public support.

In the past, fragmentation of care in early learning environments reflected the social purposes and variations in accessibility of these resources for different children. The current services available for young children and their families evolved out of this mixture of various opportunities. A social-assistance approach to early learning continued into the 1970s when, as young women entered the workforce in greater numbers, the federally funded Canada Assistance Program (1966) provided more childcare facilities with funding from both federal and provincial sources. Regulated family childcare centres replaced day nurseries and were offered by social agencies and governments. These centres sometimes expanded to offer full-day programs. Early learning supports in the 1970s and 1980s were enriched by the availability of parallel supports for parents and caregivers through toy-lending libraries and parent-child drop-in centres, but the target groups and social roles of these supports continued to vary from jurisdiction to jurisdiction, and their goals reflected their funding origins.

As well, the lack of a coordinated public Canadian approach to early learning meant that the evolution of programs reflected the same jurisdictional variances and funding vagaries. The differing philosophies, beliefs, funding supports, and needs for early learning environments for young children during the last century in Canada have created a very diverse early learning environment across the provinces and territories. Childcare, early childhood education, and parenting/caregiver supports, with their histories of different funding sources, different purposes, and different goals for different populations, have left the country with different starting points for the introduction of full-time JK/SK for all children. Publicly funded, fully accessible, full-time JK/SK for young learners can be planned to coordinate the fractured efforts of the support programs that have, until now, been available across Canada.

PAST AND CURRENT LEGISLATION GOVERNING EARLY LEARNING ACROSS CANADA

The history of early learning initiatives across Canada is as diverse as the country's physical regions and the settlement patterns that have characterized each region. However, there is now sufficient research and social will to initiate a more broadly applicable national early learning environment for Canadian children. Canadian policy makers are realizing the importance of sound investment in opportunities for early learning for all children and recognize the need to realign current services to support efficient and effective delivery of services to young children and their families. While education has traditionally been the responsibility of provincial and territorial governments in Canada, as defined by the British North America Act (1867), the federal government is supporting provincial and territorial efforts through related policies and funding. Evidence of increased will to cooperate on service provision for early learners can be seen in policies and laws (see Table 1.4) that have taken effect over the last decade.

The recent National Children's Agenda, National Child Benefit, and Social Union Framework Agreement (Thompson, Maxwell and Stroick, 1999) provide national direction for the development of childcare policies and define desirable outcomes, but allow provincial or territorial discretion for specific approaches.

Table 1.4 *Policies and Laws to Support Early Learning 1998–2000*

Dates	Policy and Funding Initiatives to Support Coordinated Early Learning
1998	Implementation of the National Child Benefit (NCB), which provides a Canada Child Tax Benefit, a low-income supplement, and provincial reinvestment commitments, is coordinated between the federal and provincial/territorial governments.
1999	The Social Union Framework Agreement (SUFA) is signed by all jurisdictions, federal and provincial/territorial, except for Quebec; this agreement sets the parameters for Canadian social policy.
1999	The prime minister's speech from the throne calls for increased resources and supports from all levels of government for early childhood development, signalling this as a national agenda item.
2000	The annual premiers' meeting agenda includes discussion and support for early childhood development.

The Social Union Framework Agreement (SUFA) requires that the provinces/territories and the federal government work together on any new initiatives and ensures that, because of design input from stakeholders, the spending power of the federal government translates into the best impact locally. These frameworks can provide guidance for the evolution of early learning initiatives through mutual support of a comprehensive vision, followed by detailed development of responsible planning for service delivery. Beach and Bertrand (2000) suggest that the following principles should govern the interaction of the levels of government with new frameworks for childcare:

- Comprehensiveness: the services produced are child and family focused and broadly accessible for all children.
- Universal availability: costs for services are controlled and reasonable, so that all families have access to optional services.
- Accessibility: a child's aptitude, ability, or disability does not influence service availability; additional services with fees tied to income may be offered to those with unique socio-economic, biological, or psychological risks or needs.
- Integration: services are coordinated across service sectors to provide the most efficient service to children and families in the areas of social and health services as well as education.
- High quality: standards can be defined, to support high-quality service development with safety and health considerations that reflect current knowledge about young learners.
- Accountability: services must be accountable to their funding agencies and to those they serve; data, monitoring, and evaluation must be part of the accountability process.
- Community delivery: a local authority in the community where service is being delivered must be held accountable for seeing that the program of service meets locally defined needs.
- Coordination: early learning initiatives must bridge to formal schooling services for young children.

Moving a vision for coordinated services for young learners into action by providing full-time JK/SK schooling options is a major step in supporting young children and their families. Providing full-time JK/SK that is responsive to the wide range of backgrounds, both educationally and culturally, for Canada's children, is a challenge that can be served by developing a common vision of the young learner, the potential of a full-day JK/SK program, and the potential of a coordinated but differently skilled **educator team** to address learner needs throughout the school day and beyond to the extended-day option.

Holistic delivery of care services through full-time JK/SK programs within existing school infrastructures will help to alleviate the current mixture of policies that govern early childcare. The full-day option will mean that families

A Framework to Improve the Social Union for Canadians*
An Agreement between the Government of Canada
and the Governments of the Provinces and Territories
February 4, 1999

The following agreement is based upon a mutual respect between orders of government and a willingness to work more closely together to meet the needs of Canadians.

1. Principles

Canada's social union should reflect and give expression to the fundamental values of Canadians - equality, respect for diversity, fairness, individual dignity and responsibility, and mutual aid and our responsibilities for one another.

Within their respective constitutional jurisdictions and powers, governments commit to the following principles:

All Canadians are equal

- Treat all Canadians with fairness and equity
- Promote equality of opportunity for all Canadians
- Respect the equality, rights and dignity of all Canadian women and men and their diverse needs

Meeting the needs of Canadians

- Ensure access for all Canadians, wherever they live or move in Canada, to essential social programs and services of reasonably comparable quality
- Provide appropriate assistance to those in need
- Respect the principles of medicare: comprehensiveness, universality, portability, public administration and accessibility
- Promote the full and active participation of all Canadians in Canada's social and economic life
- Work in partnership with individuals, families, communities, voluntary organizations, business and labour, and ensure appropriate opportunities for Canadians to have meaningful input into social policies and programs

1.6 *The National Children's Agenda, National Child Benefit, and Social Union Framework Agreement provide legislation and frameworks for developing a national childcare plan for Canada.*

will not have to seek care that places children in conflicting circumstances as they move from part of the day or alternating days within a school, to care facilities with varying hours of operation, different licensing and standards, fees, different staffing requirements, changes in physical environments, mid-day travel, and possibly exposure to unsupervised time for part of the day. A full-time JK/SK placement that is available at the parents' option to all four- and five-year-old children will provide integration of services, standardize regulations that govern programs, facilitate planning and service coordination, and optimize the potential learning and socialization opportunities for children.

THE STANDARDS OF CARE FOR EARLY CHILDHOOD EDUCATORS IN CANADA

Care for early learners has been well established across Canada in many forms of service provision. Childcare is regulated through provincial or territorial laws, and implementation of the laws is outlined in detail in provincial or territorial regulations. In various provincial or territorial jurisdictions, the regulations that govern the specific details of childcare may include details about programs, staffing requirements, staff training, age, and qualifications, grants, fees, program materials, licensing requirements, governance provisions, and compliance with related regulations such as those required for health and safety. Early childhood educators are usually qualified under provincial or territorial statutes. Many training programs will teach a code of ethics for people who work with vulnerable sector clientele such as young children. Training programs will ensure that ECE workers understand their child advocacy role and the principles of fairness, equity, and diversity that characterize the universal standards for licensed childcare.

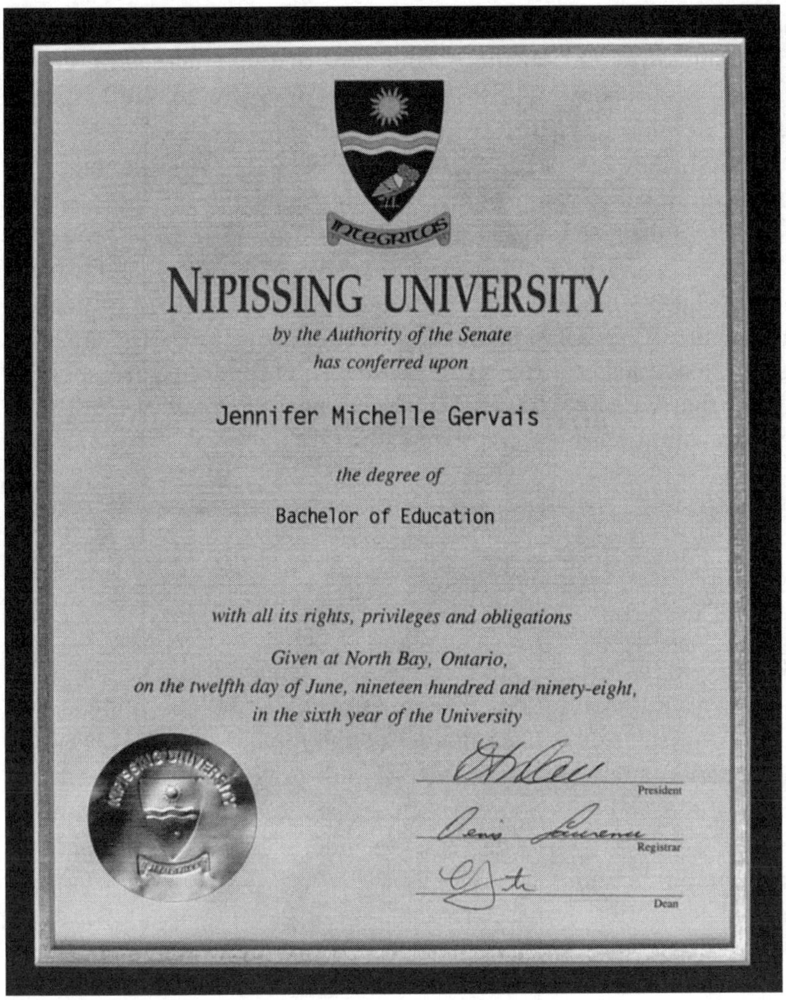

1.7 ECE staff receive a college diploma in recognition of their unique training.

Staff who work in childcare facilities may have early childhood education qualifications (ECE) certified by a college diploma. However, not all licensed facilities in all jurisdictions require ECE certification for childcare workers. As school authorities move toward the provision of full-day JK/SK programs for young learners and employ ECE staff to work alongside teachers to plan and deliver the program for JK/SK students, the **standards of care** that are subscribed to by ECE staff and those required of teachers will need alignment.

Since many ECE staff may be trained and experienced to work in small licensed facilities, where they provide all aspects of service for young learners, they may have expertise in areas such as materials hygiene that are not typically a specialized area of knowledge for teachers who have been trained through a Faculty of Education degree program. Conversely, teachers may provide expertise in areas of child psychology and curriculum program and evaluation that is learned in greater depth in their teacher preparation program.

The specialized areas of expertise and the standards of care for both teachers and ECE staff will enrich the partnership of these care workers as they come together in full-day JK/SK classrooms to provide kindergarten programming and extended daycare for young children. Each person in each partnership will need to work with their complementary staff member to develop a common vision for the program and design ways to optimize the expertise that each member of the educator team brings to the classroom to support early learners, including students from diverse cultural and educational backgrounds. Time and structure for team planning will be critical to making a strong team effort work most effectively. Care, integrity, honour, trustworthiness, inclusiveness, fairness, and respect for diversity are socially universal standards that will be essential values and traits of every adult who provides service for young learners and their families.

CHAPTER SUMMARY

The current practices across Canada for providing care and service for young learners and their families are largely unplanned. They grew as split services over time, as needs arose, and policies and regulations have developed across various jurisdictions. There is considerable overlap and duplication of services for young children. These services are provided by various provincial and territorial agencies. They may be in a variety of locations and may specialize in service to a unique age group of children or support a unique demographic. Some programs that exist outside of the publicly supported educational systems may serve an educational function.

In recent years, many provinces and territories across Canada have begun moving toward the provision of coordinated early learning services. Many jurisdictions are also responding to recent research about the advantages to the learner and to society of providing publicly funded, universal, full-day JK/SK for children in the four- and five-year age groups.

The quality of full-day JK/SK programs is critical to their success in reaching their potential as a Canadian standard for educational access. As universal access to full-day JK/SK programs expands across Canada, it will be valuable for parents, caregivers, educator team members, and policy makers to share a vision of the potential of these programs to start young children in their school careers in positive, productive ways.

THINKING AHEAD: Opportunities for Professional Reflection

The activities outlined below are designed to help you, as a potential educator team member, think about your role on the educator team. Opportunities to think about why you do what you do will support the development of your position as a reflective practitioner. Your course instructor may direct you to consider each of these reflective opportunities individually, in a partnership or small group, or in written or discussion formats. As you engage in each reflection challenge, you may find it helpful to maintain a journal to jot down ideas and thoughts to be revisited throughout your course.

- Historically, Canada's early learning services have been diverse and have developed as needs arose. What are the advantages and disadvantages of this situation?
- While specific details of a kindergarten curriculum will vary across provinces/ territories to reflect local priorities and regional differences, there are many similarities in programs for comparable age groups. Parents, caregivers, ECE staff, and teachers may assign different priorities to various curriculum areas. The list provided below outlines some JK/SK program elements that are typical for four- and five-year-olds. They are listed here in alphabetical order. Prioritize these program elements to show the ones you believe should receive most and least attention in full-time JK/SK programs in your jurisdiction. Be prepared to discuss your priorities with colleagues.
  - Art
  - Cooperating/sharing with other children
  - Creative activities
  - Fine-motor physical activities
  - Getting along with adults
  - Gross-motor physical activities
  - Group time
  - Learning to read
  - Learning to write
  - Making friends with other children
  - Understanding language
  - Using language
- After discussion with colleagues about your priorities, re-examine the list that is provided above. Add any priorities that you feel are important but have not been listed here.
- Focus groups of parents from a variety of Canadian provinces reached consensus about the principles that should govern programs planned for kindergarten aged children (Johnson and Mathien, 1998). Parents gave unanimous support to the following principles for kindergarten programs:
  - Programs must initiate children's acquisition of social skills outside of the home.
  - Programs must provide a learning continuum that prepares children to participate fully in grade one.
  - Children must feel safe and loved as individuals.
  - Children must be stimulated to enjoy learning, interact appropriately with their peers and authority, and strive for personal achievement.
  - Children's individual needs must be addressed by qualified and caring professionals.
  - Parents must be able to communicate readily with teachers and childcare staff about their children's individual problems, opportunities, and potential.
- Write an introduction of yourself to parents and caregivers through a classroom newsletter that will explain your views in relation to each of these priorities to parents new to your school and program.

ADDITIONAL READING SUGGESTIONS

To find out more about the history of education in Canada, read

Mathien, J. (2001). *Children, Families, and Institutions in Late-19th- and Early-20th-Century Ontario.* Toronto: Ontario Institute for Studies in Education, University of Toronto.

To find out more about early learning initiatives in Canada, read

Friendly, M., Beach, J. and Turiano, M. (2003). *Early Childhood Education and Care in Canada 2001* (5th edition). Toronto: Childhood Resources and Research Unit, University of Toronto.

To find out more about the three-period Montessori lesson, read

Lillard, S. (2005). *Montessori: The Science behind the Genius*. New York: Oxford University Press.

2 Knowing the Learner

"Children's central social structures change remarkably in the critical period between early and middle childhood."

(Porath, 2009)

2.1 *Children interact with other children in fluid ways as they play with and near each other.*

In this chapter, educator team members will learn about

- data relating to the achievement of learners
- the benefits of early learning through full-day JK/SK
- measuring early learning: analysis of early learning achievement scales
- learning exceptionalities in the early learner
- initiating learners into the JK/SK environment
- working with parents and guardians to understand the role of JK/SK in the schooling spectrum

At the end of this chapter, educator team members can reflect on their personal growth through

- CHAPTER SUMMARY
- THINKING AHEAD: Opportunities for Professional Reflection
- ADDITIONAL READING SUGGESTIONS

Education serves two distinct but related social purposes: It improves the life of the individual, and it improves the potential of the society. By investing in the growth and development of young children, a society invests in its future and has a hope of becoming that which it envisions for its citizens. Through strong education, we can develop citizens who share a vision of a world characterized by social justice, resource sharing, peace, disease control, and universally accessible medical attention. A strong foundation in education can increase each citizen's opportunity to participate in the common vision for a peaceful and just society.

DATA RELATING TO THE ACHIEVEMENT OF LEARNERS

A considerable body of sociological research has shown the correlations between early learning opportunities and the potential of an individual to become a positive member of society. The impactful events of the years between birth and age eight establish many of an individual's life patterns (Reynolds, Temple, Robertson, and Mann, 2001; Schweinhart, 2004; Schweinhart, Barnes, and Weikart, 1993). Correlations between opportunities for strong early learning experiences and a reduction in incidents of juvenile arrests, school drop-out rates, school failures, and the need for special education services are dramatic. High-quality early learning can affect the trajectory of a child's later life.

Evidence also links experiences with learning in the early years to many adult health issues, including obesity, high blood pressure, heart disease, some forms of diabetes, and mental health issues such as depression. Adult challenges with literacy and numeracy can be traced to early learning patterns (Hertzman and Irwin, 2007).

Recent brain research (see Table 2.1) has also shown the critical role of early learning in brain development (Healy, 1987; Jensen, 1998; Schore, 1997; Shore, 1997; Wolfe, 2001). Stimulation and nurturing in early childhood support the development of connections in the brain. These connections affect learning throughout life and are necessary for physical development, emotional and social development, personal abilities to express oneself, and the acquisition of knowledge. New ways to think about brain development inform new strategies for instruction with children. The physiology of brain development will be discussed further in Chapter 3.

Our expanding understanding of brain function has allowed for the development of theories that relate to how the brain can be nurtured and enriched as it grows. Neurosciences have expanded our understanding of how brain development affects learning. Allan Schore (1997a, 1997b) has proposed **attachment theory** through a synthesis of neuroscience (neurobiology, behavioural neurology, neuropsychology) and developmental studies. Attachment theory connects the brain physiology with brain-nourishing stimulation. Schore examined early infant studies to determine the impact of both pre-birth biological factors and early childhood nurturing factors to explain the importance of the interactions

Table 2.1 New Ways to Think about Brain Development

Old Thinking about a Child's Learning	Brain Research–Based Thinking about a Child's Learning
The genes a person is born with determine how the brain develops.	How a brain develops reflects a complex interplay between the genes a person is born with and life experiences, especially the early learning experiences.
The experiences a person has before age three have a limited impact on later trajectories for development, socially and physically.	Early experiences have a decisive impact on the architecture of the brain, and on the nature and extent of adult capabilities and physical health.
A secure relationship with a primary caregiver creates a favourable context for early development and learning.	Early interactions do more than create a context for physical, social, and emotional development: they directly affect the way the brain is wired.
Brain development is linear: there are prime times for acquiring different kinds of knowledge and skills.	Brain development is non-linear: the brain's capacity to learn and change grows steadily during physical development; there are prenatal biological and psychological impacts on brain development.

between the mother and child. Schore argues that his theory of attachment addresses nurturing from both the psychological and biological perspectives. The early social environment, mediated by a primary caregiver, influences the evolution of structures in the infant's brain. He shows how the maturation of the orbitofrontal cortex of the developing brain, the executor of the right cortex, is influenced by early interactions with the child's first caregiver (see Figure 2.1). This interaction is a critical determinant of the health of the individual, influencing their future capacity to self-regulate emotions, to appraise others' emotional state, and to manage stress.

Schore believes that internal biology influences psychological functions and that early interactions between human beings also impact that biology. In other words, the psychology between human beings alters a child's internal (biological/neurological/chemical) structure. As a result, the early social-emotional interactions between the primary caregiver and the infant impact the development of the baby's brain. This is partly determined by genetic factors and partly determined by early social emotional experience. Attachment theory explains that this interaction is the outcome of two factors: the infant's genetically encoded psychological and biological predispositions or temperament, and the quality and quantity of the caregiving. Prenatal health care reflects our societal investment in the relationship between the child and the mother at a cellular level.

In addition, the structure of and activities within a family have an influence on the development of the child, as do the quantity and quality of early interactions with the child. Single-parent families and families in which mothers participate in work outside of the home create different developmental conditions for children.

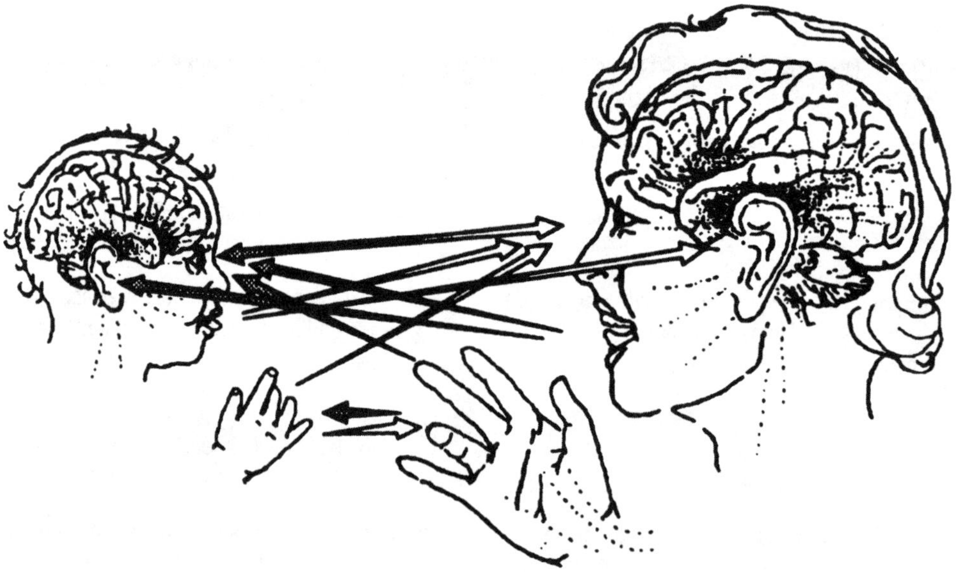

Figure 2.1 *Schore's Model of Right Brian Development to Explain Attachment Theory*

Used by permission of Dr. Allan N. Shore

Reflection Point

What interactions between the primary caregiver and the infant do you feel are critical to a child's social development? Emotional development? Physical development? Cognitive development?

There is also a trend in Canada toward first-time mothering at an older age. This is influenced by many factors affecting Canadian women, including the following:

- They are staying in school longer.
- They are participating in the workforce in greater numbers.
- They are more likely than previous generations of Canadian women to have jobs that require advanced skills.
- They enter the workforce later and are therefore more likely to delay having a first child.
- They have different expectations about life and family than previous generations did.
- They may have some responsibility for senior care, causing further delays in starting a family.

In 2006, 11% of first births in Canada were to women over the age of 35. In the same year, nearly half of all Canadian births were to women aged 30 or more, compared to only 23.6%, 15 years earlier. In the 1960s, the average age of women in Canada having their first child was 24. By 2005, the average age of the mother having a first child had risen to 28. In 2006, 9.75% of Canadian women between 40 and 44 years old had at least one preschool-aged child at home.

In situations in which children are born to older mothers, the mothers are generally better educated and live in stronger socio-economic conditions. However, women in Canada who are less well educated are twice as likely to have young children at a more advanced age as was the case 20 years ago. In 1986, 3.4% of less-well-educated Canadian women had young children, compared to 6.4% in 2006. Immigrant women in Canada are more likely (12.9%) to have a child born to them when they are older than are Canadian-born women (7.5%).

2.2 *Canadian women are having children later in life.*

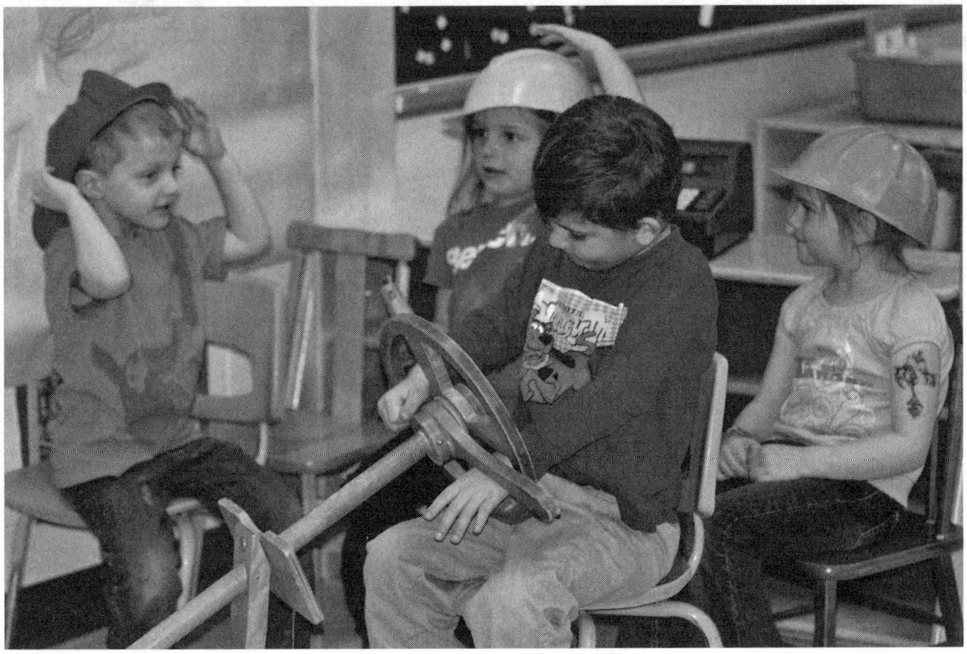

2.3 *Many children entering JK/SK are in transition from some form of day care.*

A Canadian Census (2006) found that a huge percentage (96.5%) of older Canadian mothers use childcare services and 44.3% of those mothers use childcare services for 60 or more hours per week. This provides a context for educators as they consider the issues of transition from childcare to formal schooling in the planning of their full-day JK/SK programs.

THE BENEFITS OF EARLY LEARNING THROUGH FULL-DAY JK/SK

Many parents across Canada choose some form of group-care interaction outside of the home for their preschool-aged children. The benefits of doing this may support the mother's career choices but also reflect the parents' concern for socializing the child. When parents are asked what they want early learning environments, including kindergarten, to provide for their children, socialization is high on their list of the benefits of schooling at this age. There is strong agreement among parents, teachers, and childcare workers about the purposes and goals of early learning kindergarten programs (see Table 2.2). On a ten-point scale, cooperation with other children rates highly as a program goal.

Table 2.2 *Parents, Teachers, and Caregivers Show Agreement on the Top Priorities for Kindergarten*

Top Ten Priority Objectives for Kindergarten Programs		
Parents	**Teachers**	**Childcare Staff**
Cooperating/sharing with other children 9.30	Cooperating/sharing with other children 9.59	Cooperating/sharing with other children 9.23
Understanding language 9.28	Making friends with other children 9.55	Making friends with other children 9.19
Using language 9.23	Understanding language 9.28	Using language 9.02
Making friends with other children 9.13	Blocks and other math activities 9.24	Creative activities 9.00
Getting along with adults 8.75	Using language 9.22	Free play 8.97
Gross-motor physical activities 8.65	Group time 9.00	Understanding language 8.94
Creative activities 8.58	Sand/water and other science activities 8.98	Getting along with adults 8.93

(Continued)

Table 2.2 *Parents, Teachers, and Caregivers Show Agreement on the Top Priorities for Kindergarten, continued*

Top Ten Priority Objectives for Kindergarten Programs		
Parents	**Teachers**	**Childcare Staff**
Group time 8.44	Getting along with adults 8.98	Space to be alone 8.92
Fine-motor physical activities 8.40	Creative activities 8.86	Gross-motor physical activities 8.85
Reasoning/ problem solving 8.27	Gross-motor physical activities 8.81	Dramatic play 8.60
Learning to write 6.67	Learning to write 6.67	Learning to read 6.03
Note: This objective was parents' 19th choice out of 20 options.	Note: This objective was teachers' 19th choice out of 20 options.	Note: This objective was caregivers' 19th choice out of 20 options.

Used by permission of Caldon Institute of Social Policy

Many school jurisdictions also see early learning kindergarten environments as a preparation for the transition to Grade 1. These jurisdictions may put more emphasis on the development of early literacy and numeracy skills to prepare students to engage in more academic tasks at age six.

2.4 *Learning to cooperate with other children and adults is a highly regarded outcome of the JK/SK school years.*

Many jurisdictions across Canada have provided kindergarten schooling for five-year-olds for many decades. Some have provided junior kindergarten for four-year-olds as well. Some of these offerings have been full-day placements, some have been alternate day placements (mainly responsive to mid-day bussing costs), and many have been half-day placements with the same classroom being shared by four-year-olds for half of the day and five-year-olds for the other half. In some jurisdictions, where the numbers of students are smaller, four- and five-year-olds may share the same time, teacher, and classroom.

In recent years across Canada, there has been an increased intensity of purpose to provide full-day JK/SK for every child because of our increased knowledge of the importance

2.5 Kindergarten experiences may help young children transition to the more formal learning experiences offered in Grade 1.

of early stimulation and its long-term impacts. With new health-based information, brain scanning capabilities, and data that correlates life trajectories with early learning opportunities (or the lack of these opportunities), the importance of providing publically funded JK/SK for full days for every child has become a national goal. Education is a provincial mandate, so various jurisdictions across Canada are managing this national goal differently, but the Council of the Federation, made up of all of the premiers of Canada's provinces and territories, has made this service a priority for Canada's children.

In many jurisdictions in the past, JK and SK placements have been made available at the will of individual school boards or authorities. This approach is problematic because of the lack of provincial or territorial funding to ensure the consistent availability of the program. During the last 50 years, kindergarten experiences for young children have come and gone as funding flexibility has varied. Only when the availability of fully funded, full-time JK/SK experiences in every province and territory for every Canadian child is ensured can educator teams provide the stimulation and social climate that research tells us is so critical for early childhood development. The poem "Everything I Really Need to Know I Learned in Kindergarten" is well known for its ability to capture much of the spirit and intent of early learning (see Figure 2.2).

Making friends and learning how to interact with others in constructive ways is a critical aspect of learning the JK/SK classroom setting (see Table 2.2). For this learning to be possible for young children, they need many opportunities to trust others, to test the impact of forays into independent action and exploration

Everything I Really Need To Know I Learned In Kindergarten

by Robert Fulghum

Most of what I really need
To know about how to live
And what to do and how to be
I learned in kindergarten.
Wisdom was not at the top
Of the graduate school mountain,
But there in the sandpile at Sunday school.
These are the things I learned:
Share everything.
Play fair.
Don't hit people.
Put things back where you found them.
Clean up your own mess.
Don't take things that aren't yours.
Say you're sorry when you hurt somebody.
Wash your hands before you eat.
Flush.
Warm cookies and cold milk are good for you.
Live a balanced life -
Learn some and think some
And draw and paint and sing and dance
And play and work every day some.
Take a nap every afternoon.
When you go out into the world,
Watch out for traffic,
Hold hands and stick together.
Be aware of wonder.

Figure 2.2 *Poem by Robert Fulghum*

Source: Robert Fulgham, 1988.

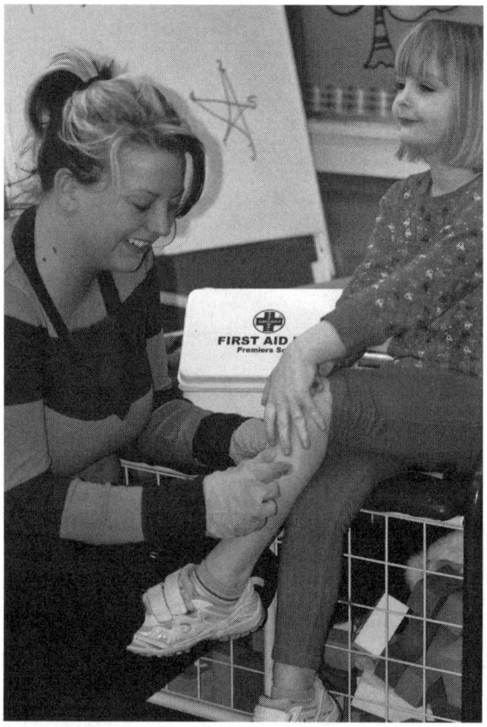

2.6 In the JK/SK school years, children learn to trust many adults who are there to assist them.

to seek their own **autonomy**, to show initiative when alone and when with others, to understand and show empathy, and to build self-confidence.

To develop trust, young children need opportunities to learn that others will provide support and encouragement, advice, and safety, as they explore and investigate. In the JK/SK kindergarten setting, young children need to learn to trust many teachers, the early childhood staff, school nurses, visitors, other parents, and school administrators.

To develop autonomy, young learners need to feel safe and welcome to take risks within the boundaries of safety. They begin to see options and make choices, while experiencing the impact of their choices. Opportunities to explore in new contexts, with new materials and self-identified problems, and in new relationships, support the young learner's sense of autonomy as an individual separate from their primary caregiver.

To develop initiative, young learners need many age-appropriate opportunities to make choices and decisions. Gradually they will come to understand options and planning as part of making choices with predictable outcomes. As children develop the language to describe their choices, their options, their plans, and their impacts, they begin to develop a sense of causality and responsibility for their actions and choices.

To develop empathy, children need many opportunities to interact with other young children and to experience a wide range of things. In these new contexts, a range of emotions can be experienced by the young children. Discussions can lead the children to be aware of the different language they can use to describe reactions—*happy, sad, excited*, and *scared*. Through language, children learn to express ideas about how they perceive the reactions of themselves and others. They come to understand that the emotions they experience are shared by other people, and they learn to display empathetic responses to the other children. Moreover, through interactions with other children, they also can learn that body language is another way of expressing feelings.

To develop self-confidence, young children need to experience successes with their explorations and experimentations with people, materials, and places. As young children develop their sense of accomplishment in diverse situations, confidence grows and helps them acquire coping skills that will support them when experiments and explorations are less positive. Research evidence suggests that success in interpersonal relationships and success in valued tasks create the two conditions needed for self-confidence (Curry and Johnson, 1990).

In addition to these personal skills, the JK/SK experience can provide young children with a wide range of contexts that help them to build a sense of the importance of routines, an understanding of symbols and their role in human communication, and metacognitive awareness or self-regulation skills as they face choices, make plans, act, and examine the impact of their actions. Young students can also come to understand the difference between *normal play* and *work play* and come to value work as part of the social interaction of humans. Educator team members support both types of play by helping young students link their daily learning with reminders of previous experiences or expressed plans to act.

2.7 Young children who have opportunities to learn in a variety of contexts strengthen their trust, autonomy, initiative, empathy, and self-confidence.

Reflection Point

With a group of colleagues, consider the term *self-regulation*. What do you think the term may mean in a social psychology sense? What might it mean in a cognitive psychology sense?

To create the optimal environment for young learners, educator team members need to share some beliefs about the learners and the learning environment before they begin to plan specific learning opportunities to stimulate exploration and investigation. Educator team members might start their work together by discussing where they stand on the following statements of beliefs and principles:

- Children are born with an innate desire to learn.
- Families are the primary caregivers of children and have the most important role in promoting their children's sense of well-being, learning, and development.
- Communities need to contribute to the growth and development of their young children.
- Play is vital to children's learning and to their healthy development.
- Consistency, responsiveness, and nurturing are essential to early learning.

2.8 Establishing a common set of beliefs about learners and learning will help the educator team establish an enriched learning environment.

- The physical, social, emotional, cultural, linguistic, and intellectual aspects of children's development are interrelated.
- Language is essential for children to connect thoughts and learning.
- Children need to learn through active exploration, with time and support to think about their explorations.
- Children's individual cultural and linguistic backgrounds need to be respected and integrated into early learning opportunities.
- The physical environment is an important variable in the quality of early learning opportunities.
- How I see the child as a learner influences how I support their learning.

By using these discussions to start the relationship building within the educator team, team members can start to develop a common vision for the direction of their early learning kindergarten program.

MEASURING EARLY LEARNING: ANALYSIS OF EARLY LEARNING ACHIEVEMENT SCALES

Children between the ages of zero and four have a vast array of early learning experiences. While many students may have experiences with daycare, nursery schools, or private school experiences such as a Montessori school, some will come to JK directly from a home environment with relatively little interaction with other children their age. Some, especially in urban settings, may not speak English in the home environment. For all of these children, educator teams need to determine what their previous learning has entailed and what skills they bring into this new context.

Many jurisdictions use an interview questionnaire with parents when they enrol their child in JK/SK. These questionnaires are designed to help educators understand the quantity and quality of the child's early learning, information that they can use as a starting point for the next steps in planning the child's learning experiences. This use of assessment is called *diagnostic assessment*. Observation of the child is the most useful diagnostic tool that educators employ with young children, but the input of the primary caregiver can provide very valuable insights into each child's current preferences, skills, interests, and concerns. Various jurisdictions have specific diagnostic questionnaires that are used within a board.

Many have adapted questionnaires that have a background in the *The Nipissing District Development Screen* (NDDS). The NDDS was developed in the early 1990s by a group of women who worked in the area of child development, including the areas of speech pathology, occupational therapy, nursing, and social work. In their occupations, these women were finding many young children with developmental delays that were not "caught" until age three or later. The NDDS was developed as a diagnostic survey to help identify these children at earlier ages and thereby maximize the effect of early interventions. In 1993, the NDDS was being used in many jurisdictions across North America as an easy-to-use checklist that parents could complete, based on their knowledge of their child's behaviours.

The NDDS survey helps educators and medical professionals consider the child's development in relation to 13 stages between the age of one month and six years. This survey provides a relatively quick and thorough analysis of the child's skills in relation to:

- Vision
- Hearing
- Speech
- Language
- Communication
- Gross motor
- Fine motor
- Cognition
- Social/emotional
- Self-help

In some jurisdictions, this survey is available free online to citizens. It can be purchased online in other jurisdictions. It can be accessed on the internet at www.ndds.ca/home.html.

The NDDS (see Figure 2.3) survey provides diagnostic descriptors of typical skills and developmental markers at key stages of a child's early development. These key stages include: 1 and 2 months, 4 months, 6 months, 9 months, 12 months, 15 months, 18 months, 2 years, 30 months, 4 years, 5 years and 6 years. A sample survey for the 4-year stage is provided on the next page:

ndds.ca
nipissing district developmental screen®

Child's Name: ____________________

Birthdate: ____________ Today's Date: ____________

The Nipissing District Developmental Screen is a checklist designed to help monitor your child's development.

Y	N		BY **FOUR YEARS** OF AGE, DOES YOUR CHILD:
○	○	1	Understand three-part related directions and longer sentences? *("put your toys away and wash your hands before lunch")**
○	○	2	Say rhymes *(cat-bat-hat)* or sing children's songs?*
○	○	3	Ask and answer a lot of questions? *("why?", "what are you doing?")**
○	○	4	Speak clearly enough to be understood most of the time without repeating or stuttering on sounds or words?
○	○	5	Tell stories with a clear beginning, middle, and end?
○	○	6	Show you four colours when asked? *("show me the red crayon")**
○	○	7	Tell what is happening in a picture when you ask?
○	○	8	Go up and down stairs alternating feet? *(with one foot on each step)*
○	○	9	Stand on one foot for one to three seconds without support?
○	○	10	Try to hop on one foot?
○	○	11	Catch a large ball with outstretched arms?
○	○	12	Snip paper with scissors? *(A)*
○	○	13	Draw a person with three or more body parts?
○	○	14	Hold a crayon or pencil correctly?
○	○	15	Undo buttons and zippers?
○	○	16	Use the toilet/potty during the day? *(toilet trained)*
○	○	17	Take turns and share with other children in small group activities?
○	○	18	Try to comfort someone who is upset?
○	○	19	Play near and talk to other children while continuing with own activity?
○	○	20	Look for adult approval? *("watch me" or "look what I did")**

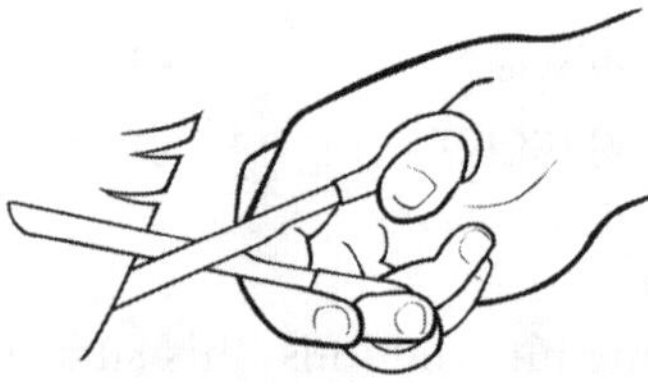

(A)

4
YEARS
English

* Examples provided are only suggestions.
You may use similar examples from your family experience.
** Item may not be common to all cultures.

Always talk to your healthcare or childcare professional if you have any questions about your child's development or well being. See reverse for instructions, limitation of liability, and product license. Nipissing District Developmental Screen © 2011 Nipissing District Developmental Screen Intellectual Property Association. All rights reserved.

Figure 2.3 *NDDS Developmental Screening Example*

Source: The Nipissing District Developmental Screen. NDDS and NDDS.ca are trademarks of the NDDS Intellectual Property Association, used under license. All rights reserved. Reprinted with permission.

Careful and thorough diagnosis of learning as an entry practice into kindergarten can support each child's unique way of learning. Katz (1998) emphasizes the need to ensure that students experience positive and solid school beginnings, as these establish the students' pattern of a "lifetime disposition to seek in-depth understanding" (p.28).

LEARNING EXCEPTIONALITIES IN THE EARLY LEARNER

It is a part of every educator's philosophy of education to recognize the uniqueness of each child. All children learn very differently and bring different predispositions to new learning experiences. When children are also challenged with special needs, their learning requirements are even more unique. When children have special learning needs, it is critical for JK/SK teachers to have a clear sense of the child's capabilities and challenges, so that the transition into kindergarten is successful.

Across Canada exceptionalities in learning are defined very differently, depending on the provincial or territorial jurisdiction. Many jurisdictions define exceptionalities in learning by both *type* of exceptionality and *severity* of the exceptionality (Janus, Lefort, Cameron, and Kopechanski, 2007). Special needs are not consistently defined by legislation across Canadian jurisdictions. Where they are defined, they may include categories of needs that are broad and so diverse within any category of needs that the educational needs are dramatically different for each child, even though their designation as "special" is the same. Over 93% of students with special needs attend schools, and over 62% of those students attend regular classrooms (Janus et al., 2007). JK/SK educator teams need to be skillful when serving the needs of these exceptional learners.

Recent research also shows that systemic services are not automatically available to families of children with special needs; parents must be skilled at identifying available services and prepared to advocate for their child in order to access these services (Janus et al., 2007). Educator teams need to be willing and able to accept parents of students with special needs in this advocacy role and support their prior experience with acquiring necessary services for their child. Parents may have varying levels of comfort in the role of advocate (Turnbull, Turbiville, and Turnbull, 2000), and discomfort with the role may be further exaggerated if they are recent immigrants and English is not their first language.

Depending on the jurisdiction, special needs of young students may be defined in any of the following categories, within the broader categories of physical, cognitive, and social/emotional/behavioural needs:

- Physically dependent
- Deaf and blind
- Moderate to severe/profound intellectual disability

- Physical disability/chronic health impairment
- Deaf or hard of hearing
- Autism/Autism Spectrum Disorder
- Behaviour intervention or support/mental illness
- Mild intellectual disability
- Gifted
- Learning disability

2.9 Assistive technology may be used to support the learning needs of young children.

Service of these young students is complicated by many situations, including the possibility that a student may have special needs in more than one defined category. Service categories within a jurisdiction may change over time, as the ability to diagnose and treat special needs for larger numbers of students evolves.

Using School Readiness Surveys

Some jurisdictions also use a survey that is completed by teachers after the teacher has worked with the child for approximately six months. The EDI (Early Development Instrument) is an example of a survey that would be used in a JK or SK context to provide the teacher with data about achievement and development milestones. The EDI (Janus and Offord, 2007) is neither a diagnostic nor an identification tool used for screening young children. Instead, it is designed to gauge a child's level of readiness for learning in a grade school context. The concept of **school readiness** is used to describe children's ability to tackle the demands of Grade 1 programs. Such surveys might be used within the system towards the end of a kindergarten program. The EDI survey asks educators to consider 120 items (see Table 2.3) that are indicators of school readiness (Doherty, 1997; Janus and Offord, 2007) related to:

- Physical health and well-being
- Social competence
- Emotional maturity
- Language and cognitive development
- Communication skills and general knowledge

Because the EDI survey is a readiness survey and can be used for examining population-based trends, it can provide guidance for program policy decisions to serve a population of students. This type of survey can provide information to

Table 2.3 *Early Development Instrument (EDI) to Determine School Readiness*

Domain of School Readiness	Includes
Physical Health and Well-Being	- Gross- and fine-motor skills - Motor coordination - Adequate energy levels for classroom activities - Independence in looking after personal needs - Daily living skills
Social Knowledge and Competence	- Curiosity about the world - Eagerness to try new experiences - Knowledge of acceptable standards in a public place - Ability to control own behaviour - Appropriate respect for adult authority - Cooperation with others - Ability to follow rules - Ability to play and work with other children
Emotional Health and Maturity	- Ability to reflect before acting - A balance between too fearful and too impulsive - Ability to deal with feelings at the age-appropriate level - Empathetic response to other people's feelings
Language and Cognitive Development	- Reading readiness - Age-appropriate reading and writing skills - Age-appropriate numeracy skills - Ability to participate in board games - Ability to understand similarities and differences - Ability to recite back specific pieces of information from memory
Communication Skills and General Knowledge	- Skills to communicate needs and wants in socially appropriate ways - Symbolic use of language - Storytelling - Age-appropriate knowledge about the life and world around them

report on strengths and deficits in populations of children over time, monitor groups of children over time, and predict how they will do in elementary contexts. More information about EDI can be obtained from the Offord Centre for Child Studies, McMaster University.

One issue that educator teams face with surveys completed by agencies on behalf of students is the inconsistency of collection, retention, and distribution protocols for data. Data may be unavailable to teachers from some agencies or may have been collected for purposes that do not meet the educational needs of a school. Inter-agency collaboration about services provided for young children and their families will promote the development of useful "data crosswalks"

(Goelman, 2008, p. 312) that will allow schools and researchers to get a better sense of the impact of services over time.

INITIATING LEARNERS INTO THE JK/SK ENVIRONMENT

Each child and their family approaches the first days of early learning in a kindergarten context with a set of hopes for success. The way the school structures the first contacts with parents and young children can have a lasting impact on their willingness to work closely with school personnel over time. The child's interests, readiness to learn, prior socialization, and preschool experiences influence their learning profile. Special needs and cultural differences from the dominant school culture also influence how the child manages the transition into an early learning kindergarten classroom.

Reflection Point

Locate a parent of a child about to enter kindergarten, preferably from among your acquaintances, so that the parent is familiar with you. Ask the parent what concerns they may have about their child entering kindergarten. Discuss their responses with a group of colleagues who made similar inquiries of their acquaintances. Consider what educator teams could do prior to the first days of JK/SK to address parents' concerns.

Parent–School Partnerships for Learning Success

Parents are willing to work with educators to get to know their child, but an invitational partnership must be established between the educators and the parents or family members for such a partnership to work. Establishing this partnership is one of the first tasks of the educator team.

Many jurisdictions begin the process of establishing such a partnership with parents by designing a kindergarten orientation that serves the information needs of parents and the socialization needs of early learners. Orientations may be held before the school year begins, even as early as the spring prior to entry into JK. Educators can anticipate that young children will have a long period of exposure to the idea of entering kindergarten, and giving them some physical exposure to the place they will experience can help to make their anticipation more concrete and their transition less anxious, because they have some prior knowledge.

2.10 *Orientation events can help children and their families prepare for entry into kindergarten.*

Orientations can take many forms (see Table 2.4). Successful orientations will provide something to engage both the parents and the children. Orientations should be designed to provide parents and children with knowledge about the classroom, the school, the program in kindergarten, and transportation systems that may be involved for travel to and from school. Orientations should also include activities that start bonding and trust building for the child, so that the child is less anxious about being left in the care of the educator team members when school starts. An example of the organization of a successful orientation is provided below.

During orientations to the early learning kindergarten program, parents want to leave feeling reassured about the safety measures being used to protect their child and want to learn initial information about what is expected of them. The educator team can provide quick reference sheets or booklets that parents can take away from orientation and that address commonly asked questions such as:

- What time should my child arrive at school each day?
- What should I do if my child is ill and will not be attending school one day?
- How do I let the school know what I want them to do if my child becomes ill during a school day?
- What should my child bring to school each day?
- Why and how do I need to label all of my child's belongings?
- Who will supervise my child before school, during outside time, and after school?

Table 2.4 *Sample of an Agenda for a Kindergarten Orientation Event*

TIME	The children will...	The parents will...
6 p.m.	Families arrive at the school and find the kindergarten classroom. It's easy to find because large clown footprints are taped to the hallway floor in brightly coloured paper. The doorway of the classroom is brightly decorated with streamers and balloons that say "Welcome to kindergarten." Two smiling adults are waiting at the doorway to greet each family as they arrive. Families are directed to the tables in the classroom, where juice, cookies, and a vegetable tray are set out for snacking while everyone arrives.	
6–6:15 p.m.	Children finish their snack and stay close to parents as the educator team introduces the kindergarten program to family members.	Family members are shown the various areas of the classroom, given a parent handbook to take home, and introduced to the overall structure of the program.
6:15–6:45 p.m.	Children are led to a centre(s) in the classroom where a special activity has been set up for them to try out. One educator team member stays to work with the children.	Families and the second educator team member talk further about the structure of the kindergarten program, including the curriculum, the timetable for a typical day, communication between the parents and educators, and resources children should have at school (e.g., snacks, packaging, labelling personal property, etc.).
6:45–7:00	Children rejoin parents and everyone gets onto the school bus for a short ride around the community. The bus personnel explain to parents what the rules for riding the bus are and ask parents to explain this to their children and speak about these rules often over the next months before they enter kindergarten.	
7:00–7:15	Children meet at a project table in the classroom, and each opens a take-home zip-lock bag that contains a specially made puzzle for him or her. The pieces spell out the child's name (and perhaps are accompanied by a colour photograph of the child). The children work with one educator team member to put their personal puzzles together.	Parents meet in a separate area of the same classroom, in sight of the children, and are introduced to a take-home survey that is designed to help the educator team find out more about the individual interests, skills, abilities, and challenges of each child. Parents are asked to complete the profile over the next week and return it to the school in the self-addressed envelope that is provided. Note: If families speak another language in the home and may have limited English, the questionnaire should be translated into the language of the parents when possible. Parents and family members have opportunities to ask questions as the children finish their puzzles. As the orientation comes to a close, parents are provided with a page of phone numbers, email addresses, and web page addresses where they can find out more details about the early learning kindergarten experience over the next few months as questions arise.

- How do I let the school staff know about my child's special needs?
- What communication will I get from the school about my child's progress throughout the year?
- Can I volunteer in the classroom?
- How do I arrange extended day care for my child?
- Aside from the educator team members we have already met, who else will work with my child during their school day? What is their role in my child's development?
- What does a normal day in JK/SK look like?
- What time does the school day end?

These information booklets should be readily available in print and electronic format and, if possible, translated into other languages that represent the makeup of the community. Written information should always be provided in clear, non-technical language, to facilitate broad accessibility.

Orientations are also opportunities to introduce families to strategies that will be used in school to teach social skills to young children. Read-aloud language development times during the kindergarten day also provide opportunities to expose students to the concepts of friendships, sharing, compassion, tolerance, and inclusion. There are many excellent books that can be read to groups of children and can launch discussions that will support students' learning about complex social concepts. Some examples of these books include:

- *Amos and Boris* (William Steig) — Two young friends with different abilities help each other.
- *Daddy Makes the Best Spaghetti* (Anne Grossnickle Hines) — Family roles are explored by considering tasks that Daddy does in the family.
- *Jamaica's Find* (Juanita Havill) — Girls of different ethnic backgrounds become friends and learn to be honest with each other.
- *Mrs. Katz and Tush* (Patricia Polacco) — Friendship spans age, ethnicity, and gender differences as a boy and a woman become friends.
- *Stellaluna* (Janell Cannon) — Lifestyle differences do not block friendship between a bat and birds.
- *The Paper Bag Princess* (Robert Munsch) — Role reversals and gender stereotypes are explored in this fractured fairy tale about a princess who rescues a rude prince from a dragon.
- *The Trees of the Dancing Goats* (Patricia Polacco) — Children and families of different religious traditions become compassionate friends.

2.11 *Fictional texts can provide touchstone stories that are revisited during the year to teach social skills to young students.*

Source: © Troels Graugaard/Istock

Early learning classrooms should have in-class libraries that have many of these types of books, which support character development. As children are exposed to them repeatedly and recognize that they present desirable social values, these books become *touchstone* books for the classroom and can be revisited as needs arise to support discussions of issues in the social environment of the classroom.

Once the school year starts, it may take some young learners much longer than their peers to become comfortable in the JK/SK environment. Activities should be initiated slowly, be optional, presented invitationally rather than being required, and be designed to pique the interest and natural curiosity of young children. Flexibility during the day to allow for considerable choice will help to ease young learners into the new environments. Opportunities to work and play with other children in configurations of their choice will help early learners to find a level of comfort and security that will support their progress. Later chapters will present more ideas about how to use *play* and *work play* in the classroom to support both socialization and learning. The kindergarten classroom is a busy, ever-changing, dynamic environment for learning. A clear sense of shared purpose, strong planning, and a welcoming invitational atmosphere will help young learners engage the learning opportunities fully in this environment.

WORKING WITH PARENTS AND GUARDIANS TO UNDERSTAND THE ROLE OF JK/SK IN THE SCHOOLING SPECTRUM

As our society changes, so do our aspirations for what early learning kindergarten classrooms can do to support children's development. In 1970, 76% of four-year-old children did not attend kindergarten. Today, that number is only 25% (Graue, 2009). Research showing the benefits of rich early learning experiences has supported growing awareness of the value of JK/SK for young children. Fully funded, full-day JK/SK will make it more affordable and manageable for families to provide this experience for young children. Extended days at the same site as JK/SK will make the full-day early learning kindergarten option a convenient one for working families.

As concern about meeting standards and making curriculum more competitive on a global scale puts pressure on the experiences of learning in Grade 1 and beyond, there is some pressure to make the early learning kindergarten experiences dip into what was formerly the aspiration for later grades, especially in the areas of literacy and numeracy. These are skills considered to be basic to school success. The pressure to have four- and five-year-old students learning to read and learning number concepts is called *back mapping*. It comes from the idea that kindergarten is about getting young children ready for Grade 1.

> High-quality kindergarten practice provides flexible instructional approaches with a planned set of content to help students grow across developmental domains. This program supports the child who talks and sings, writes and races, solves and causes problems, and makes and needs friends. ~ Graue, 2009

In contrast, many people envision kindergarten as a place where children should have time and support to explore, practise social skills, and build relationships among peers and adults who support their learning. This type of kindergarten is reflective of the needs of children with purposeful play at the centre of the program. Play is seen as valuable for its own sake and designed to build on children's experiences, cultures, needs, and interests. This kindergarten experience should provide play-based learning in a context that is supportive of a full spectrum of domains of learning (i.e., physical, social, emotional, cognitive) and foster the dispositions that will lead to successful learning in later grades.

Parents and guardians will need to understand the goals for learning in the full-day JK/SK context and be prepared to support extensions of that learning in the home context. The kindergarten experience may provide different instruction for different children at the same time. Parents and guardians will need to understand the reasons for this level of differentiation. They will need to understand that what each child learns, how and when they learn it, and how they demonstrate and extend their learning may look vastly different for one child than it does for others in the same-aged peer group. This type of kindergarten will be active, sometimes noisy, stimulating, and challenging. Well choreographed play-based learning, led by teachers who are mindful of their practice, will provide a rich backdrop for learners' diversity. Parents will need to understand that this diversity is a planned outcome of the kindergarten program and represents the developmental needs of each learner as they address the learning opportunities that will fill each day.

Educator team members can ensure that parents become familiar with the kindergarten program in many ways. The following are some strategies that can ensure a strong parent–educator vision for the type of kindergarten described throughout this book:

- A thorough orientation to kindergarten for both students and parents
- An inviting atmosphere in the classroom for parents to drop in and visit
- Meaningful ways for parents to volunteer in the classroom
- Clear procedures for routine communication with parents
- Predictable and well communicated short-and long-term plans for the classroom
- Classroom newsletters (paper and electronic)
- Celebrations of learning events to which parents are invited
- Parent participation on review committees
- Portfolios of students' work that are sent home for parents' comments
- Special classroom sharing days (e.g., grandparent day, literacy days)
- Translations of classroom news and communications into the language(s) that represent(s) the community
- Culturally sensitive inclusion of strategies for learning
- Regular program revision to improve the educator team's ability to meet the needs of young learners

Many of these strategies will be described in more detail in the remainder of this book.

CHAPTER SUMMARY

The JK/SK early learning experience has many benefits for children. School entry evaluations will help educator teams understand the child's prior learning and the skills and knowledge that they bring to their first formal schooling situations in JK/SK classrooms. Early comprehensive learning assessments will also provide information that may identify learning exceptionalities. Early identification will help educators provide appropriate supports for the child and family to ensure progress for every child.

For many parents, the routines and expectations of kindergarten contexts may be very different from those they have experienced in preschool contexts. Educator teams can help parents and children adapt to the new context by providing accessible information about the JK/SK program. By giving parents opportunities to visit the classroom before, during, and after the child's kindergarten program begins, educator teams ensure that parents become informed partners in the program.

THINKING AHEAD: Opportunities for Professional Reflection

- Work with colleagues in your class to develop a list of the characteristics of learners who are between the ages of three-and-a-half and six years old. Shade any characteristics on your brainstormed list that you think are more typical of the older children in this age spread. Create a four column chart and sort these characteristics under the headings "Physical," "Social," "Emotional," and "Cognitive."
- For the characteristics you have charted above, identify with a check mark those that you think might be the focus of early learning JK/SK instruction. Draw connecting lines between characteristics that you feel have an impact on each other.
- Observe in a JK or SK classroom for an hour or more. After the observation, add to the list of characteristics you have generated about this age group of learners.
- Observe an empty JK/SK classroom. Identify physical characteristics of the space or its resources that have been well planned to meet the needs of this age group of learners.
- Create a survey that you might use at an orientation event to ask parents about their personal priorities for their child's time in your JK/SK classroom.
- Interview other students who are now training to be in a complementary professional role to you in a JK/SK classroom (e.g., If you are training to be a teacher, interview an ECE student; if you are an ECE student, interview someone who is training to be a teacher). Ask this person to identify his or her priorities for programming in an early learning JK/SK classroom.
- Develop a system for "at-the-classroom-door" communication of routine information with parents. This should include any routine information that you want parents to have or that they may want you to have but that can be left at the classroom door for you to address later in the day when students do not need your full attention. Examples might include:
  - a student sign-in sheet,
  - specific directions about unusual pickup times for a student, or
  - a note from a parent requesting that you call them.

  Be prepared to show how this system will work to save time for the educator team while still respecting families' privacy, cultural and language sensitivities, and time.

ADDITIONAL READING SUGGESTIONS

This website provides data-based information about children's growth and development across Canada:

www.keepkidshealthy.com

These websites may provide further information about specific program components for early learners:

Early Literacy

www.reading.org
www.ciera.org

Mathematics

http://mathforum.org/teachers/pre-k/
www.aaamath.com/B/kinder.htm

Kindergarten Readiness Checklist

www.familyeducation.com/article/0,1120,21-14779,00.html

National Association for the Education of Young Children

www.naeyc.org/

3 Learning Theories

A constructivist learning environment is "... a place where learners may work together and support each other as they use a variety of tools and information resources in the guided pursuit of learning goals and problem-solving activities."

(Wilson, 1996)

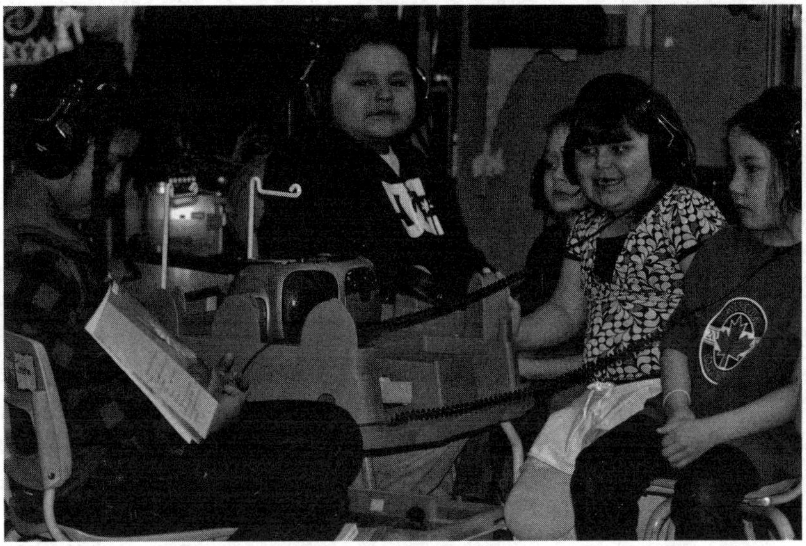

3.1 *Young learners use a variety of materials to make sense of their environment and to learn new ideas.*

In this chapter, educator team members will learn about

- cognitive development
- developmental approaches to learning
- constructivist approaches to learning
- neuro-research, brain anatomy, and building pathways
- play-based intentional learning: the basis in research

At the end of this chapter, educator team members can reflect on their personal growth through

- CHAPTER SUMMARY
- THINKING AHEAD: Opportunities for Professional Reflection
- ADDITIONAL READING SUGGESTIONS

How we address learning with young children is dependent on what we know about this stage of their development. The ages between three and six are typified by periods of rapid growth in all areas of development: language, cognitive, social/emotional, and physical. Children's level of independence during these years expands rapidly—although not always predictably, consistently across populations, or steadily for any single child. Knowing the types of development that can emerge during this age may help to support children's transitions towards being more confident learners.

3.2 Growth between the ages of three and six is rapid in all areas of development.

During the years between three and six, children's growth in language is rapid. They begin to develop **conceptual language** and can speak about abstract concepts, such as emotions and feelings. They love stories and have vivid imaginations. Their understanding of cause and effect in different contexts is developing, and they are beginning to experiment with ways to describe these observations. Print literacy skills are beginning to develop, and their understanding of print symbols is emerging. They show a keen interest in books and reading/pretend reading. They may overgeneralize language rules, such as how to form past tense words, e.g., "He putted on his hat."

Cognitive development in this age group is supported by concrete experiences. Young children learn by doing, with supported opportunities to attach language to their thoughts about what they observe through activity. Their ability to develop perspective and empathetic responses is evolving, but many need support to consider alternative perspectives. The ability to memorize continues to evolve, and they benefit from reminders and review that surface prior knowledge and experiences. Stories that provide opportunities to consider other perspectives help young children to navigate new ways of considering events. They benefit from manipulatives that support their conceptual understanding. Short-term memory is developing and the ability to respond to sequenced instructions is strengthening. They enjoy discussing and studying topics that have immediate relevance for them.

Children between the ages of three and six are beginning to expand their social connections and are starting to make true friendships. Empathetic responses are emerging. They will often choose **play configurations** that are reflective of developing social skills, sometimes choosing to play alone, sometimes in small groups, and sometimes in parallel play, where they do the same thing that their peers do but do it alone. They may function best in small groups and are responsive to problem-solving guidance in group social contexts. Feelings are easily hurt and their concept of self is fragile. Differences in strengths and preferences are emerging and may be accompanied by emotional and passionate expressions of preferences. Expressions of overconfidence and tentativeness may be extreme. They are very sensitive to both successes and failures and thrive on positive responses to their efforts. Young children often do not manage competition well and prefer cooperative play. They need models of ways to negotiate social interactions and strategies for disagreeing in agreeable ways.

3.3 Stories help young children understand their own thinking and help them to learn empathy and tolerance.

This age group benefits from physical activity as they learn. Fine-motor and gross-motor skills are still developing. Hand–eye coordination needs practice in short blocks of time. Hand muscles are still developing, and precise coordination of hand muscles may be sporadic. Many opportunities to work on activities that build manual dexterity are beneficial. Young children need alternative times to be highly active, but they tire quickly, so activity should be interspersed with quiet times. Interest in some types of school activities (e.g., writing, listening) will vary greatly in this age group. Regular breaks in the type of activity are necessary to help young children focus attention when it is required. Nutrition is essential to focus attention, so healthy snacks are necessary every couple of hours throughout the day.

Reflection Point

What books would be the touchstone or key books you would want to include in an early learning classroom? How would you go about collecting them? What storybooks were most memorable in your own childhood?

3.4 Play configurations evolve as students expand their social connections.

COGNITIVE DEVELOPMENT

Early learning kindergarten classes are unique in the formal schooling spectrum. While all school grades in elementary contexts have learning goals and aspirations for their students that include opportunities to learn in the cognitive, social, emotional, and physical areas, kindergarten is unique in the priorities it places on each category of learning goals. While all categories of learning goals are important to a balanced kindergarten program, this early learning environment provides a place to establish social and emotional security for young learners and use this security as a basis for learning in the cognitive and physical areas.

When young children feel secure and supported as they take risks, their engagement in learning opportunities is more likely to be ensured. They will try, experiment, try again, and gradually gain confidence in new understandings.

Young children's cognitive development may move ahead on a fractured front. They often will be at different levels of readiness for different opportunities to learn. One role of educator team members is to be aware of each child's interests, readiness to learn, and learning profile in relation to the new learning, so that opportunities to learn are provided at the most cognitively accessible time in the child's development.

Cognitive development can be accessed through either direct or indirect instruction. In **direct instruction**, the educator team members show, tell, demonstrate, name, and structure practice. In **indirect instruction**, children investigate, explore, examine, challenge, and discuss. Both of these approaches provide valuable learning of cognitive goals. Educator team members must decide which approach is best for each learning goal, based on their knowledge of the program and the children.

Reflection Point

What factors would you consider when deciding to approach a lesson through direct or indirect instruction?

When either approach is used to guide the learning of cognitive goals, the educator team will make choices about the following:

- How children will be motivated to learn something new
- Whether they will expose children to the new learning through modeling or through an indirect approach
- How practice with the new learning will be given
- How support for practice will be provided
- Ways in which children will have opportunities to use the new learning, so that it is internalized and applied
- Strategies that can be used to ensure that children know what they have learned (**metacognition**), so that they can access the new learning when it is needed in the future

All of these choices for organizing cognitive instruction for young children are displayed in the schematic that shows both direct and indirect instructional choices (Maynes, Julien-Schultz, and Dunn, 2010; see Figure 3.1).

Whether lessons with young children are approached through direct instruction or through indirect instruction with activity centres, the instructional plans that guide intentional actions for the instruction can be guided by the phases identified in this schematic.

DEVELOPMENTAL APPROACHES TO LEARNING

Developmental approaches to learning have a basis in the observed behaviours of young children. A developmental approach to learning draws our attention to the predictable skills and approaches that are most likely to develop at certain milestone ages in the majority of children. Jean Piaget (1896–1980) is closely aligned with our present notions of childhood development. Piaget was a Swiss biologist and psychologist whose interests included identifying the stages of intellectual development of young children. By analyzing patterns inherent in children's incorrect responses to questions, Piaget was able to build a theory about how children learn. Piaget's theory of intellectual development is supported by four main beliefs:

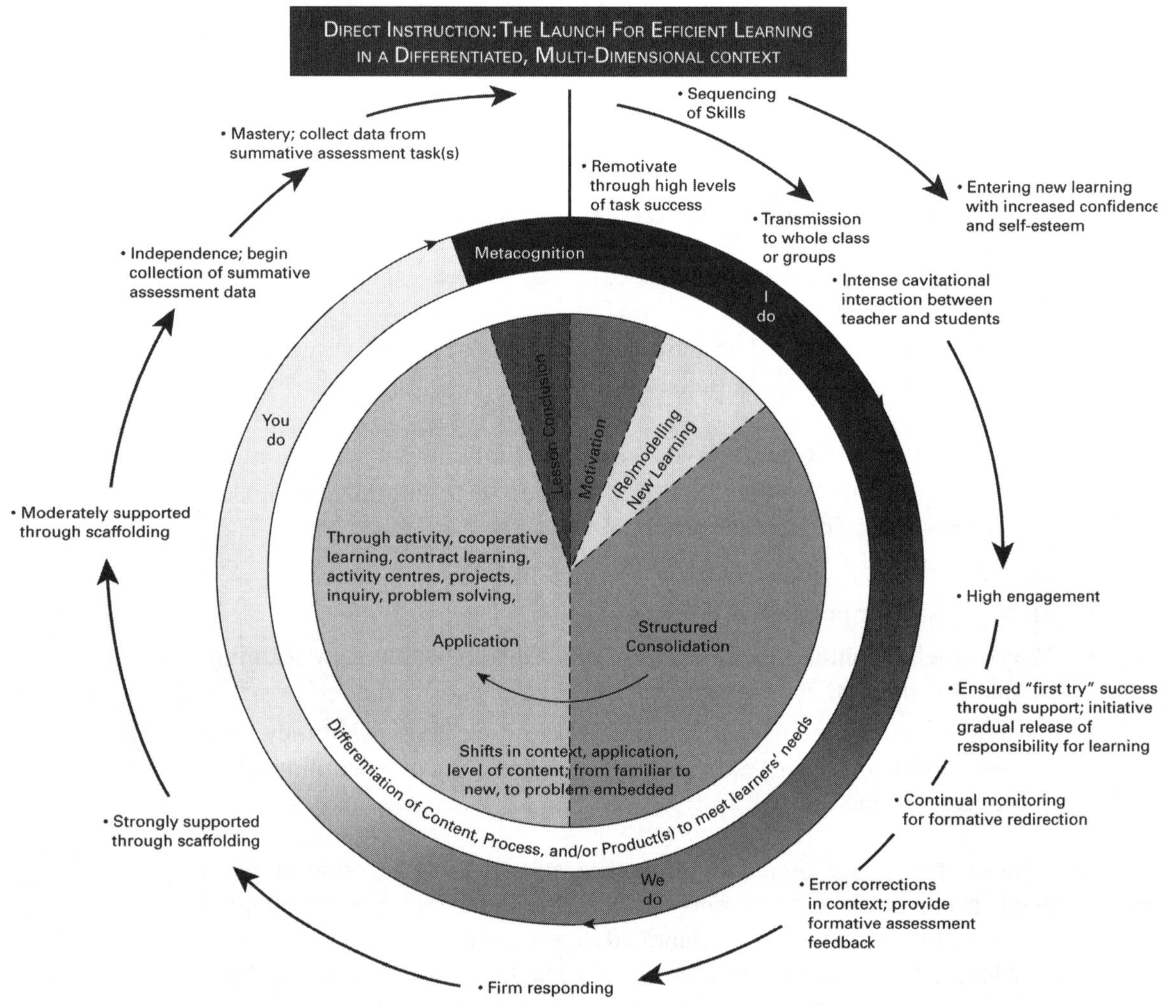

Figure 3.1 *Direct and Indirect Instructional Choices*

Used with permission of Nancy Maynes

- A child's mental development begins at birth.
- A child's cognitive structures are formed through encounters and experiences with the environment.
- The changes that occur in a child's mental development are cumulative.
- A stimulating environment can be constructed that supports the cognitive development of young children.

In 1962, Piaget wrote about his theory of development and provided vocabulary that explained his theory. Today, all of the concepts of Piaget's theory of intellectual/cognitive development are part of an educator's professional vocabulary (see Table 3.1). These concepts include: **adaptation, assimilation, accommodation, schema theory, equilibrium/equilibration** (or **self-regulation**), **stage theory**, and **play**.

Table 3.1 *Piaget's stages of intellectual/cognitive development*

Piagetian Concept	Explanation	Example
Adaptation	Environments put pressure on individuals to change what they do and how they perceive what happens around them.	Children may understand what wind is. Later, when experiencing a hurricane, they come to understand that there are different kinds of winds. Some winds will cause behaviours to change, as one must seek ways to protect oneself.
Assimilation	When people experience variations from prior experience, they can include this variation in the existing concept for the experience.	Children may consider the strength of the wind to be a factor in "windiness" (e.g., "It is really windy today" or "The wind is very light today").
Accommodation	When people experience variations from prior experience, they can change their existing concept to include more expanded criteria.	"This is more than just windy. This is a hurricane."
Schema Theory	Piaget believed that all people sought a sense of balance in their understanding of the things they experience in daily living. To achieve this balance, they either expand existing ideas to include new examples (assimilation) or develop new concepts to explain the new phenomenon (accommodation). **Schemas** are the mental images we hold about how something is or works.	"This is wind." but "This much wind is a hurricane (or tornado)."
Equilibrium (or self-regulation) Note: *Self-regulation* in the cognitive sense has a different meaning from *self-regulation* in the social science/behaviour sense, which will be introduced in later chapters.	When individuals face new experiences, they seek to make sense of the experience by either assimilating or accommodating the new information.	People experience a hurricane and know that the high winds, water, and destruction are different from previously experienced windy days. Naming this new experience a *hurricane* distinguishes it from other experiences with wind.

(Continued)

Table 3.1 *Piaget's stages of intellectual/cognitive development, continued*

Piagetian Concept	Explanation	Example
Stage Theory	Piaget's observations of young children led him to the belief that all children move through predictable ways of learning at fairly standard times in their life.	Piaget proposed four stages of development in cognitive thinking/intellectual development: • The **sensorimotor stage** (birth to age 2) • The **preoperational stage** (ages 2 to 6) • The **concrete operational stage** (ages 6 to 12) • The **formal operational stage** (starting around ages 12 to 14 into adulthood)
Play	Piaget thought that young children use play as recreational activity but also as sense-making activity or "work play," whereby learning about their environment and assimilating or accommodating their experiences is a major role of play. Piaget felt that play supported both cognitive development and symbolic thought in the child.	Children may make different forms of wind-driven objects and experiment with amounts of wind needed to move each object.

Piaget's stages of cognitive development are differentiated by the descriptions they provide about predominant ways that children learn at each stage of their development.

The Sensorimotor Stage: Birth to 2 Years

At this stage, young children use the senses of hearing, sight, smell, touch, and taste to distinguish objects and actions in their environment. Babies will often taste objects that an older child might know not to put in his or her mouth. Babies begin to "track" moving objects, respond to familiar sounds, and recognize comforting or rewarding smells, movements, and tastes. They begin to look for items or people who disappear from their line of sight.

The Preoperational Stage: 2 to 6 Years

At this stage, young children begin to understand symbols. They will use role play and alternative objects in their play. Naming and assigning roles is often seen in play. They begin to use pretend reading strategies and scribble writing in their efforts to communicate in the early preoperational stage. They start to develop relational vocabulary (e.g., *under, behind, beside*). Talk becomes an important part of meaning making.

The Concrete Operational Stage: 6 to 12 Years

At this stage, children may continue to use concrete objects as symbols for actions or a basis for their thinking. They are able to use one-to-one correspondence to make symbolic representations (e.g., maps). They develop reading, writing, and numeracy skills that symbolize thoughts and relationships they have considered in their thinking. The youngest children in this stage may rely on objects to help them manage processes such as mathematical operations. The ability to store mental images is expanding.

The Formal Operational Stage: Starting around Ages 12 to 14

At this stage, a person's ability to think abstractly is expanding, and reliance on concrete objects to represent thinking is reduced. Logical and deductive abilities are strengthening.

In addition to Piaget, other researchers and psychologists have studied early childhood and added some understanding to our present views of how young children develop. Behaviourism (Pavlov, 1849–1936; Thorndike, 1874–1949; Watson, 1878–1958) has developed our awareness of the need to reward desirable behaviours in the classroom, based on the behavioural theory that what is recognized and receives attention is repeated.

Reflection Point

What environmental factors might influence a child's stage of development? Which factors might cause extreme variations from the usual developmental patterns?

Developmental views of education for young children are also influenced by the work of Abraham Maslow and Arnold Gesell. Both researchers studied child development around the middle of the 20th century. Maslow (1954) proposed the theory of **self-actualization.** This theory identifies basic human needs and proposes that these needs must be met in a hierarchical order so that the next level of needs can be actualized. Basic needs were seen as preconditions to achieve higher-order needs. **Maslow's needs hierarchy** (see Figure 3.2) is a fundamental tenet of teaching. Many school-based services, such as health checks, immunizations, and breakfast programs, have a basis in Maslow's needs hierarchy.

Gesell (Gesell and Ilg, 1943) took a more biological view of childhood development, proposing that children had an internal developmental "clock" that genetically prescribed when certain developmental milestones were reached. Gesell's work led to the development of some of the benchmarks used to determine a child's developmental trajectories over time (see Chapter 2) and influenced our concept of **school readiness**. Gesell's work contributed to the discussion about nature versus nurture in early development.

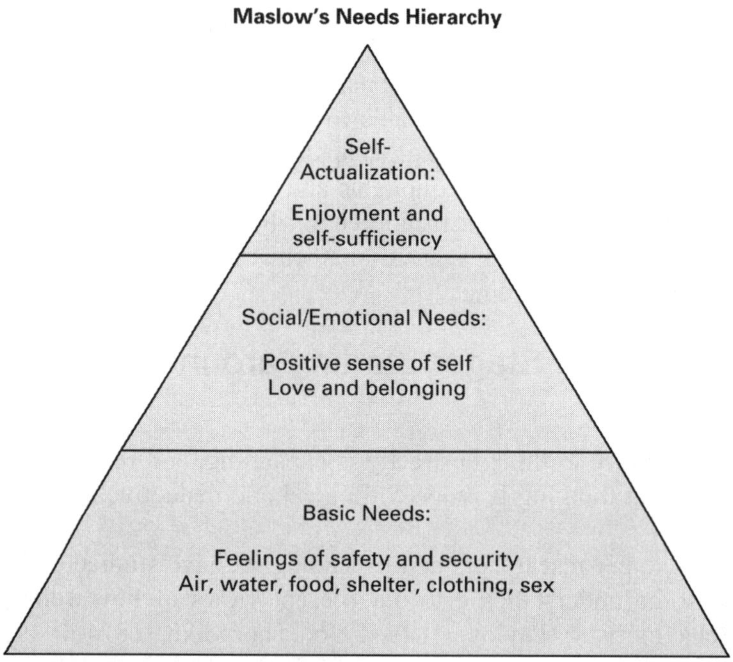

Figure 3.2 *Maslow's Needs Hierarchy*

Source: Adapted from Maslow, A.H. (1954). *Motivation and Personality* (2nd ed.). New York: Harper & Row. Used with permission of HarperCollins Publishers.

Reflection Point

What features of an early learning classroom could be put into place to ensure that every child's *basic needs* are met?

CONSTRUCTIVIST APPROACHES TO LEARNING

Constructivism is the belief that some essential experiences, accompanied by opportunities to make meaning of those experiences, are essential for learning. **Social constructivism** is the belief that these essential learning experiences and the meaning-making opportunities that are central to them are best accomplished through social interaction in which children can work together to learn and develop a shared sense of meaning.

As adults who guide children's development, we know that it is not safe to allow children to explore everything, because of the potential for harm in some situations. Through carefully guided experiences that are structured to provide latitude for safe exploration, educator teams use constructivist and social constructivist approaches to support students' safe but stimulating explorations within the framework of a carefully developed age-appropriate curriculum.

A Russian psychologist and teacher, Lev Vygotsky (1896–1934), added a great deal to our current theories of social constructivism. Vygotsky believed that the social environment had a strong influence on a child's development. Vygotsky is well known for his conception of the **zone of proximal development**. In Vygotsky's theory of socio-cultural learning, children learn through peer or adult support that helps them to transition between their current independent problem-solving capabilities and their level of potential development with appropriate guidance (Vygotsky, 1978 translation). In a classroom context, ideal teaching takes place in this zone of proximal development. The role of adults or capable peers in this setting is to help the learner bridge the zone of proximal development to attain new understanding.

Vygotsky's work also drew our attention to the shifts in learning ability as young children acquire language and start to consider objects symbolically. Before children develop language (preverbal stage), the meaning of an object affects how the object is used. For example, things are put into a box. The child sees the box as a container. However, as verbal skills develop, so does the child's ability to play with and manipulate objects and assign symbolic roles to them. At this verbal stage, young children may see a box as part of a fort, a new hat, the makings of a car ramp, or as an object to be put to other imaginative uses. As this ability to see symbolic uses of objects surfaces in young children, the nature of their play starts to become more complex.

3.5 *Educator team members provide guidance in each child's zone of proximal development.*

3.6 Common objects are assigned symbolic roles in imaginative play.

Constructivist and social constructivist beliefs about how learning occurs in young children are central to the development of school-based early learning JK/SK programs. In constructivist classroom environments, play is central to students' ability to make meaning from their experiences. Meaning-making experiences set the stage for strategic interventions in the zone of proximal development to introduce new learning. Educator team members have the roles of creating the environment, both materially and socially, to allow for safe and stimulating exploration through play and of interjecting in a timely and supportive way to help students build bridges from their present level of problem-solving to a new level by supporting them in their zone of proximal development. The support that is provided during this time of growth can take many forms: telling, showing, modeling, providing examples, adding language to help name objects or events, questioning, and many other responses, challenges, and extensions. A full range of these supporting behaviours is presented in Table 3.3. When an educator provides such supports, we refer to this as **scaffolding** (Wood, Bruner, and Ross, 1976).

Since the availability of Vygotsky's work through translation in the late 1970s and the work of other researchers and writers since that time, we have expanded our understanding of scaffolding and currently recognize its use in classrooms in four forms:

1. *Soft scaffolding* refers to the on-the-spot scaffolding that students receive in the form of comments and encouragement or redirection as they work on learning tasks (Saye and Brush, 2002). The type and amount of this feedback is responsive to the needs of each student (Van Lier, 1996).
2. *Hard scaffolding* refers to the support provided for students as they try a difficult task. When using hard scaffolding, the educator becomes the expert and provides guidance to support the learner's deeper understanding; the support is planned in advance to respond to the nature of the task (Van Lier, 1996).

3. *Reciprocal scaffolding* refers to the support that is available to learners as they work with peers collaboratively and support each other's understanding. Reciprocal scaffolding can be fluid, with support coming from any member of a group as a task progresses (Holton and Clark, 2006).
4. *Technical scaffolding* refers to the support students receive through the design of the learning materials. This concept was first applied to computer-support designs through weblinks, online tutorials, or help pages (Yelland and Masters, 2007), and later to the design of software itself (Lai and Law, 2006), but it applies equally to the design of any materials that support learning.

Regardless of the form of scaffolding used for early learners in a JK/SK context, its purpose is always the same: to provide the level and type of support needed to ensure that the learner is successful.

Reflection Point

How might educator team members organize their different roles in the early learning classroom to ensure that all four types of scaffolding are always available to support the learning of young children?

3.7 Collaborative work allows peers to provide reciprocal scaffolding.

During instruction in any classroom, educators will use a combination of more traditional and constructivist approaches to their role. The goal of understanding both approaches is to ensure that whichever approach is used, it is used with deliberate intent and full understanding of its value. The more consistent the approach in the early learning JK/SK classroom, the more effectively young students are able to start assuming some control of their own learning and to start the process of self-regulation of their learning and their social behaviours. A view of the more traditional and more constructivist approaches (see Table 3.2) can be seen on a continuum that presents these orientations in relation to the elements of a classroom that are affected by the approaches: the physical environment, the social interactions, the intellectual challenges, the role of language and other forms of communication in the classroom, and the design of and approach to the curriculum.

Table 3.2 *Constructs of Traditional and Constructivist Approaches in the Classroom*

Moving from a Traditional Classroom Approach to a Constructivist Approach				
CONSTRUCTS	ELEMENTS OF A CLASSROOM	CHARACTERISTICS	TRADITIONAL CLASSROOM "*Doing to* students" Characterized by a mixture of behaviourist and constructivist beliefs	CONSTRUCTIVIST CLASSROOM "*Working with* students" Predominantly constructivist beliefs
Importance of Children	Physical	• Organization	• Less use of students' past work	• Past work is prominent and used for reference
	Social	• Encouraging peer interaction • Facilitating children taking responsibility	• "the classroom"	• "our classroom"
	Intellectual	• Meeting students' needs	• Teacher provides solutions • Teacher nurtures	• Students participate in solving problems and making decisions • Teacher nurtures and challenges
Interactions among Classroom Participants	Physical	• The physical environment	• Teacher arranges furniture and resources • Desks	• Students use space flexibly • Tables
	Social	• The classroom communication system	• Teacher does most of the talking	
		• Student and teacher roles	• Talk is between teacher and students	• Most talk among the students
		• Classroom management	• Manage children's behaviour	• Children control own behaviour
		• Fostering cooperation	• Parents visit • Behaviour management	• Parents participate • Self-regulation
		• Fostering interpersonal understanding	• Respectful of children	• Respectful of children's ideas and feelings
		• Promoting moral values	• Lots of reminders, rewards, praise	• Fewer reminders
		• Maintaining a social-moral atmosphere	• Teacher controlled	• Shared control; class meetings
	Linguistic	• Language in use in the classroom	• Stress on quiet and calm	• Music is used for communication

(*Continued*)

Table 3.2 *Constructs of Traditional and Constructivist Approaches in the Classroom, continued*

Moving from a Traditional Classroom Approach to a Constructivist Approach				
CONSTRUCTS	ELEMENTS OF A CLASSROOM	CHARACTERISTICS	TRADITIONAL CLASSROOM "*Doing to* students" Characterized by a mixture of behaviourist and constructivist beliefs	CONSTRUCTIVIST CLASSROOM "*Working with* students" Predominantly constructivist beliefs
Interactions among Classroom Participants, (*continued*)	Intellectual	• How students interact with content	• Listening, participating and cleaning up	• Share in curriculum decisions
	Curriculum	• Student choice	• Mostly teacher orchestrated actions	• Shared responsibility for content, transitions, and scheduling
		• Assessing student learning	• Teacher assesses	• Portfolios and conferences; teacher helps students make connections
Engagement in Academic Activity	Curriculum	• Engaging students' interest	• Set curriculum	• Builds on students' interests and experiences • Shared experiences
			• Teacher knows learning goals	• Learning goals are shared
		• Encouraging active experimentation	• Distinct times for each content area • Children move at the same pace on similar work	• Ongoing project work and use of centres • Differentiation and choice
		• Facilitating students' constructions of meaning	• Limited choice • Centralized curriculum	• Encourage self-direction • Authentic opportunities
		• Promoting a technological environment	• Learning process is determined by the teacher	• Students choose how and when to engage in their work

NEURO-RESEARCH, BRAIN ANATOMY, AND BUILDING PATHWAYS

Early brain development is closely linked to lifelong capacity in humans (see Chapter 2). New technology has allowed scientists to examine the brain in ways that is markedly different from approaches used previously. We now know much more about both the circuitry and the neurochemistry of the brain and can make hypotheses about the impact of developmental conditions on the growth and health of brain tissue. We can expect that research in this area over the next several years will bring us even closer to understanding the intricacies of brain development.

Current research tells us much about the brain and its capacity for learning. We know that brain development begins prenatally and extends into adulthood. The brain is specifically designed to incorporate experience into its circuitry and rewires itself to connect new experiences within its developing structure. Environmental inputs need to occur early for brain development to proceed normally. This is especially true for premature infants in high-risk gestation groups. Without certain environmental inputs (e.g., sufficient amounts of iron) early in life, the brain becomes incapable of developing normally, and its capacity to do so decreases over time if deficiencies continue. Without early environmental inputs required for healthy development, the brain is decreasingly able to compensate. It appears however that, for most early deficiencies in environmental input, the young brain is open to compensatory experiences in the cognitive, social, and emotional development areas.

Converging areas of brain research provide scientific evidence that there is significant development in the human brain in its early years (Webb, Monk, and Nelson, 2001). Between birth and adolescence, the human brain increases in size by four to five times. This growth is caused by the increase in the growth of connections (synapses) within the brain. Synapses between neurons of the brain and between neurons and the insulating material, called *myelin*, expand with experiences. Myelin allows the brain impulses to be conducted rapidly among neurons (Craik and Bialystok, 2006; Webb, Monk, and Nelson, 2001). A richer learning environment and more learning opportunities increase both synapses and myelin (Thomas and Johnson, 2008; Knudsen, 2004). As the brain learns to create more efficient networks and connections, synaptic pruning occurs and decreases the number of neural connections in favour of the most efficient neural connections (Greenough, Black, and Wallace, 1987).

This ability of most young brains to recover and adapt, supports the efficacy of early intervention approaches to compensate for environmental deficiencies in prenatal or early childhood situations. In school settings, these interventions will occur as intentional, play-based learning opportunities. How such learning is structured in an early learning classroom should also be informed by what we know about brain development and compensatory brain growth. The educator team must be cautious not to misinterpret brain research as they apply this knowledge to planning for early learning opportunities. It is especially important to remember that the brain is remarkably resilient and that the early periods of rapid brain growth are not the equivalent of a limited window of opportunity for learning. While the early years are rich times for making connections that will support brain growth, all learning does not need to be packed into the first few years of a child's life. Early learning will create neural pathways in the brain that will support learning later in the child's development as well (Barinaga, 2000; Bruer, 1999).

PLAY-BASED INTENTIONAL LEARNING: THE BASIS IN RESEARCH

Current research shows us that the nature of play is a consideration for play designed to facilitate learning. Earlier in this book we differentiated between play and **work play**. Generally, *play* refers to a wide range of voluntary activities that typically are pleasant to engage in. Work play is associated with the intention that something is to be learned from the play experience. This type of play has also been called **play-based intentional learning**. There are many educational toys designed to, and sometimes claiming to, influence children's learning. While these may support learning, research shows us that interactions in real life with adults and other children, rather than with toys or other electronic devices, are the most effective means of learning.

Some researchers even suggest that some types of educational toys may actually hinder learning by discouraging young children's engagement in free or imaginative play or by limiting or replacing the time they might otherwise spend in interaction with adults (Paul, 2008). While there does not appear to be research-based evidence that certain toys can support extraordinary learning and development in young children, some toys chosen for early learning environments can capitalize on the natural motivation of young children to explore their environment. Unstructured toys such as blocks, balls, boxes, clay, sand, water, containers of different shapes and sizes, and costume pieces can support work play that has intentional learning purposes. Items that a child can manipulate or assemble in a variety of ways support imaginative, creative play and allow for educator team members to challenge and extend students' thinking as they play. Through these types of play, the young child has many opportunities to consider how things work and to construct connections, both cognitively and socially (Piaget, 1930; Schultz, Gopnik, and Glymour, 2007).

> "...toys should not command the child, but the child should command the toy"
> ~Kathy Hirsh-Pasek (2008)

Different types of children's play have been the focus of research for many years. Categories of play vary significantly, depending on the orientation of the observer of the play and the age group of children being observed. In the 1920s, Mildred Parten observed and categorized six types of play typical of children from ages two to five. She categorized play as follows:

- Unoccupied play: The child appears to be engaged in random movements without apparent purpose and is relatively stationary.
- Solitary play: Play is totally engrossing to the point that the child may not be aware of others around them.
- Onlooker play: The child is an observer of the play of other children but does not engage actively.
- Parallel play: The child may mimic the play he or she has previously observed, by using similar objects, repeating talk, or mimicking actions, but does not actively engage with other children.

- Associative play: Strong social bonds start to form, and the child seems more interested in connections with other players than in the object of play.
- Cooperative play: Play becomes more organized, and children may include rules, goals, and roles in the play.

Parten saw the development of play as a social process where children gradually developed the skills to play with others. Psychiatrist Stuart Brown (2009) identifies types of play in children from the perspective of the objects of play. Brown's system of categorizing types of play includes *body, object, social, fantasy*, and *transformational play*. To these categories, the National Institute for Play adds the categories *attunement* and *narrative play* (see Table 3.3).

"...the focus should not be on the toy itself, but on how the child interacts with the toy"
~ Canadian Council of Learning, 2010

Regardless of the framework used to guide the observation of children's play, it is an important aspect of early learning to include various forms of play as a central component of programming. Opportunities to play must capitalize on children's natural motivation to play as a way of making meaning. Such play opportunities should allow for ambiguous and unstructured use of objects, so that children can explore relationships and look for cause and effect. Observations of such play experiences should focus not on the object of play experiences but on how the child interacts with and explores with the object. As children mature,

Table 3.3 *Play Examples in Early Learning Contexts*

Form of Play	Skills and types of learning supported through play	What you might see children doing
Pretense Play	• Self-regulation • Communication • Role playing • Negotiating • Communicating • Investigating • Problem solving • Imitating • Comparing • Exploring relative social positions and power concepts • Evaluating • Extending • Combining ideas from various perspectives • Adapting resources • Planning	• Role playing • Scenario planning • Perspective taking • Visualizing • Organizing • Adapting • Extending • Challenging • Cooperating • Compromising

(*Continued*)

Table 3.3 Play Examples in Early Learning Contexts, continued

Form of Play	Skills and types of learning supported through play	What you might see children doing
Socio-dramatic play	• Self-regulation • Retelling • Story creation • Literacy acquisition • Communication through both oral and non-oral means • Making plans • Visualization • Creating • Planning • Differentiating between real and pretend situations	• Storyline development • Taking turns • Making plans • Adjusting plans via feedback • Printing to communicate • Creating resources • Setting goals • Achieving goals • Recognizing the achievements of others • Learning new print concepts • Accommodating and assimilating new ideas
Constructive Play	• Self-regulation • Resource acquisition • Using oral language • Negotiating • Using symbols (print, numbers, shapes, signs, signals, etc.) • Experimenting with written text • Developing fine- and gross-motor control • Using examples • Demonstrating • Explaining • Extending thinking through experimentation.	• Constructing • Searching for suitable resources • Communicating in many forms (drawing, painting, building, planning, coordinating) • Negotiating with peers • Managing time in relation to personal plans • Considering safety implications of actions
Problem Solving (Work) Play	• Self-regulation • Understanding the role of learning in one's development • Cooperating with adults • Reflecting in action and on action • Considering examples • Differentiating between explanations and examples • Understanding purpose • Understanding change processes • Understanding motivations • Negotiating conflict • Understanding cause and effect	• Using symbols • Choosing ways to display their knowledge • Planning with peers • Disagreeing in agreeable ways • Pooling resources to achieve a goal • Compromising • Using reflective language • Restarting • Making goal-specific resources

they are able to make imaginative use of play objects and will engage in sophisticated symbolic or imaginative play with both structured and unstructured play objects (Umek and Musek, 2001).

Play in early learning contexts might also be identified by local curriculum resource documents and may reflect a combination of research categories from other sources. In such documents, direction to teachers may include a wide variety of terms that relate the purpose of play.

CHAPTER SUMMARY

Educator team members develop their repertoire of strategies for observing, supporting, and reporting on children's learning through play as they develop facility with play variants.

The development of young children is rapid during the JK/SK school years. Their growth and development is supported and nurtured through exposure to concrete learning experiences in a play-based learning environment. In a stimulating environment filled with rich resources and stories, young children can continue to build their cognitive structures through experience.

Brain growth is supported by rich and stimulating experiences. Opportunities to engage in various types of play in a supportive and safe context provide situations in which growth opportunities are optimal and play-based intentional learning can be planned.

THINKING AHEAD: Opportunities for Professional Reflection

Use the following opportunities for professional reflection to consider what you have learned in this chapter:

- Start an observation log that you can maintain over the remainder of this course. For the first entry into your observation log, spend an hour watching a young child at play. In your log, create a web diagram and list the areas of this young child's behaviour that you would relate to the theories about child development addressed in this chapter (e.g., cognitive, developmental, constructivist, neuro-research). Beside each of these theories about learning, in point form, identify specific behaviours you observe that relate to each theory.
- With a group of peers, discuss the play-based approach to learning in the early years. Discuss the advantages and strengths you see in this approach. Also discuss any disadvantages you may consider.
- Consider how Maslow's Needs Hierarchy can be used as an initial planning framework for a new early learning environment. How might you use each category of the framework to ensure that each young child's needs are met in this new learning environment?

ADDITIONAL READING SUGGESTIONS

To learn more about creating a constructivist approach in your early learning classroom, read

Wilson, B. 1996. *Constructivist Learning Environments*. Englewood Cliffs, NJ: Educational Technology Publications.

To learn more about direct and indirect approaches to instruction, read

Maynes, N., L. Julien-Schultz, and C. Dunn. 2010. "Managing Direct and Indirect Instruction: A Visual Model to Support Lesson Planning in Pre-Service Programs," *The International Journal of Learning* 17 (2): 125–39.

Maynes, N., L. Julien-Schultz, and C. Dunn, C. 2010. "Modeling and the Gradual Release of Responsibility: What Does It Look Like in the Classroom?" *Brock Journal* 19 (2): 65–77.

To learn more about schema theory, visit

www.sil.org/lingualinks/literacy/implementaliteracyprogram/schematheoryof learning.htm.

To learn more about Maslow's Needs Hierarchy, visit

www.psychology.about.com/od/theoriesofpersonality/a/hierarchyneeds.htm.

To learn more about children's health and growth, visit

www.keepkidshealthy.com

4 Ages 0 to 3: Where the Community Serves Early Learners

"Base policy decisions on an evaluation of data that reflects all aspects of children's development – cognitive, emotional, social, and physical."

(National Institute for Early Education Research, 2004)

4.1 *Community resource centres can provide developmental assistance and resources for parents.*

In this chapter, educator team members will learn about

- preschool assessments
- an integrated model for community services
- school registration
- NDDS Developmental Screens and other resources as early school inventories
- working with community support services

At the end of this chapter, educator team members can reflect on their personal growth through

- CHAPTER SUMMARY
- THINKING AHEAD: Opportunities for Professional Reflection
- ADDITIONAL READING SUGGESTIONS

Community services that are available to young children and their families in the preschool years can support growth and development that will ultimately have an impact on school success. Coordination and integration of these community services is the goal. Such services may include preschool assessments.

PRESCHOOL ASSESSMENTS

The development of early childhood programs is informed by data collected to both describe and define limitations in current programming. High-quality programs rely on child-assessment data to provide direction. Such data provides both information about program effectiveness and background information to help childcare staff understand and support growth in young children. Preschool assessments are particularly difficult, because assessments are often based on forms of communication that in young children are only emergent.

Because children's performance may be influenced by their emotional state or factors related to the conditions of the assessments, the applicability and validity of assessments may be limited. Additionally, valid assessments need to consider all aspects of young children's development interdependently. Assessment tools that address cognitive, social, emotional, and physical aspects of the development of young children are rare, but necessary to provide reliable data to strengthen preschool programming and transitions into formal school contexts. Early testing is valued by preschool stakeholders, because it can provide answers to questions about program effectiveness; as well, testing is relatively economical as a means of acquiring a breadth of data in efficient ways.

4.2 Assessments help caregivers determine resources and stimuli needed to further a child's growth.

Assessments of young children can provide information for caregivers that would help to identify children who may need some form of special support or service to ensure their optimal growth and development. Valid assessments allow caregivers to plan instruction that will promote growth. Professional growth for community caregivers and personal growth for parents can be informed and directed by reliable assessment data. Such data can direct program revision or enrichment by providing information that assesses the alignment of programs with the identified needs of children.

For assessments to provide useful information, they must be both reliable and valid. Valid data will be achieved when the data is determined to be both accurate and effective for providing information about the needs of young children. To be both reliable and valid, preschool assessments must meet the following criteria (Epstein, Schweinhart, DeBruin-Parecki, and Robin, 2004):

1 Assessments should not make children feel anxious or scared.
2 The information should be collected over time, in order to represent a reliable data set that is not unduly influenced by the specific feelings arising in a single data-collection episode.
3 Many sources of data should be used, and overreliance on one form of data collection to make high-stakes decisions should be avoided.
4 The length of a single assessment endeavour should be planned with sensitivity to young children's attention and concentration spans.
5 When testing is being used for program accountability purposes, appropriate sampling measures need to be used to obtain reliable data.

Since language and conceptual limitations influence data obtained through many traditional forms of assessment, observation and portfolios of a child's work may provide many useful pieces of information for both program design purposes and individual progress assessment purposes. Portfolios of a child's work are valuable sources of information, because they provide rich information with observable samples that can be viewed by several adults. Because portfolios are developed over time, they include multiple sources of information gathered using many methods. Portfolios help caregivers and parents determine typical achievement for the child and are not subject to single episodic conditions that may give inaccurate views of the program or the individual's progress. Portfolios can provide easy storage of learning artefacts, chosen by the child or program personnel, that display evidence of growth and learning. As children mature and become more reflective, portfolios can also offer opportunities to engage children in self-assessment and planning.

Similarly, observations can provide sources of data about program effectiveness and about the achievement of individual children. Observation has the advantage of being unobtrusive. Learning does not need to be stopped to be measured. Through observation, caregivers can examine the interconnectedness of all areas of a child's development, including the cognitive, social, emotional, and physical aspects. Observation is also a culturally sensitive form of assessment, allowing caregivers and parents opportunities to partner in compiling data about an individual's achievement. Through careful observations, trained caregivers can use their professional judgment to make decisions about programs and next steps.

4.3 Observation, supported by carefully detailed notes, can provide information about a child's developmental needs.

AN INTEGRATED MODEL FOR COMMUNITY SERVICES

Most communities provide a variety of services to not only support parents and early childhood caregivers with advice but also to assist young children in their growth and development. However, for many parents, navigating the range of services available and finding out about the correct services to meet specific needs can be a daunting task. This is made more difficult in large urban centres, where long distances can reduce ease of accessibility. As well, urban areas tend to attract wide ranges of cultures and dialects through immigration; language becomes a barrier to accessibility when parents are not able to understand what is offered to support their parenting. Pelletier and Corter (2005) refer to the skill set of finding services as "negotiating the culture of schooling."

In some urban centers across Canada, moves are being made to develop more centralized early childhood services, with schools as the hub of services. Such integrated services may include access to public health nurses, library programs, toy-lending libraries, family resource drop-in centres, kindergartens, parenting groups, parks and recreation programs and facilities, childcare, home childcare access and coordination, and workshops on topics of interest to parents and caregivers.

Parents seek out these integrated services for a wide variety of reasons, in addition to the ease of access they provide. They may access integrated services to help their children meet other children, to help prepare their children for formal schooling, to become part of a group, to learn more about parenting, to learn more about the culture of their local schools, to gain access to pre-school readiness assessments for their children, to expose their children to official languages, to have their children learn additional social skills or empathy, to support their treatment of behavioural problems, to enrol children in summer readiness programs, to enrol their children or families in social events, or to access childcare. The wide range of services available in school-hub models of community services is economical in terms of parents' time and effort; they often allow parents to engage in employment when a lack of access to more scattered services might make employment less feasible.

4.4 Integrated school-based services help new Canadian families learn about supports available in their school catchment area.

> "Increasingly, we hear the need to build relationships among schools and communities (Beothel, 2003) and to provide seamless early learning and care for young children and their families (Brauner, Cordic, and Zigler, 2004; Johnson and Mathien, 1998)."
> ~ Pelletier and Corter, 2005

While a school-hub model of service integration may be diverse and broad based in large urban communities, it may take other forms in other contexts. In some communities, integration may be achieved through either a loose co-location of some services, coordination among some agencies, or coordination of referrals through a case-management approach, whereby many community stakeholders from different agencies come together to support families with young children (Gilliam, Zigler, and Leiter, 2000).

The school-hub model for integration of community services has the adjunctive goal of increasing parental involvement in education. Such involvement is sought in school contexts (Corter and Pelletier, 2005; Davies and Johnson, 1996; Epstein and Connors, 2002; Ho, 2000; Creemers and Guldemond, 2001) and in childcare and protection (Kamerman and Kahn, 1997) and health services contexts (Crowson and Boyd, 1995; Tinsley et al., 2002). The *Toronto First Duty* project has piloted such hubbed services and found that while initial use of several services was promising, service accessing rates varied greatly across service sites.

As parents develop awareness of available services and confidence in the service providers, it can be expected that service access will increase. Further research exploring the cultural and linguistic groups who access or do not access hubbed services will provide more information for sites about how to reach out to the communities they serve.

Reflection Point

Are hubbed services being offered in your local school catchment area? Investigate plans for improving coordination and integration of services for young children and their families in the school community where you live.

SCHOOL REGISTRATION

As children enter their fourth year of life, families start to make plans for formal school entry, and children are often reminded that they will start kindergarten soon. The experience of starting formal schooling is not the same for all young children and their families. When cultural and language differences challenge smooth communication, families may find the school registration process very stressful and may even choose to delay school entry. Creating transition plans and preparing both families and young children for school registration and the start of school may help ease the stress that is typical for this initial foray in formal schooling. Laverick (2008) provides a brief anecdote about a young boy who was not fully prepared for the days beyond the exciting first day of kindergarten:

> [A] child was surprised when his mother got him out of bed on the second day of kindergarten. All of the attention had been focused on the first day of school and he didn't realize that it was an ongoing commitment. "You mean I have to do this again?" he asked in surprise.

Thorough preparation for all aspects of early schooling can help to buffer the changes that this phase inevitably involves. A number of factors have been found to influence the ways that young children adjust to formal schooling. These include the following:

- the child's attitude toward school prior to attendance (Ladd and Price, 1987)
- the child's prior behaviour and familiarity with peers (Ladd and Price, 1987)
- the child's skills and prior school-related experiences (Maxwell and Eller, 1994)
- home lives and the child's interaction with parents (Maxwell and Eller, 1994)
- influences from the preschool (Maxwell and Eller, 1994)
- the kindergarten classroom characteristics (Maxwell and Eller, 1994)
- the amount of time spent in non-maternal childcare (NICHD, 2003)

However, many young children face school adjustment problems when entering kindergarten. A study by Rimm-Kaufmann et al. (2000) found that about one-sixth of all young children experienced general adjustment problems with school entry, while their peers reported being eager to go to school and liking their teacher, and praised the school itself (NCES, 1999). While this transition to formal schooling may be difficult for children, many parents also report that the move to kindergarten is a stressful transition for them as well. For many parents, this period is a time of realization that others will now start to influence the growth and development of their child. Parents indicate that this transition is difficult, because they realize that the child is growing up and starting a new period in their lives, that they will be following rules, acquiring new literacy skills, separating from some friends, and moving into an educational environment that may be less open to parents than the preschool environment (Corsaro and Molinari, 2000). Many parents may also feel that the start of school for a child may cause some level of "disequilibrium" in the family context (Pianta and Kraft-Sayre, 1999, p. 49).

Since the transition to formal schooling can produce stresses for both young children and their families, it is wise for schools to plan carefully for the anticipated challenges of transition. Many things can be done by the school and the educator team members to ease anxieties and smooth the transition for all concerned. Chapter 2 provided some ideas for JK/SK orientations. Many of these practices have become common ways of introducing parents and children to kindergarten in public school systems. However, educator team members may want to consider ways in which they can revitalize and advertise each strategy, to ensure that each one is optimized in the context of full-day JK/SK learning.

Transition strategies may include the following:

- making home visits prior to the start of kindergarten (e.g., personalized contact)
- providing school packets and reading books to families
- creating opportunities to discuss issues informally with parents (e.g., bus procedures, classroom routines, individual anxieties, food and break routines, social connections among children, length of the school day)
- establishing a variety of ways to communicate with parents including ways to communicate in native languages
- holding school orientation events (e.g., a kindergarten open house for parents and children prior to the start of the school year; see Chapter 2)
- providing summer curriculum options to address social and cognitive gaps in learning
- providing trial bus-travel events for children and their parent(s) prior to the first day of school

4.5 *When educator team members make preschool opening visits to the child and family, they are able to contextualize the child's development and learn about new ways to support and respect the cultural background of the child.*

Coordination of all of these opportunities will help the educator team support the transition of young children and their families into their new learning environment of the full-day JK/SK classroom. In some boards of education, coordination of these activities may be the role of a consultant responsible for the JK/SK program, but the more personalized the transition plan can be made, the better it is likely to be received by parents and children (Early et al., 2001). Educator team members should be fully involved in the planning for transitions to their program.

Once children are in the JK/SK program, several children's books (see Figure 4.1) can be used within lessons to help them understand the common feelings about transitioning to school, and to support their growing confidence in the program. Such books may also be recommended to parents during preschool visits and orientations. Many of these books can be revisited and can become touchstone texts for the early learning environment; they may be used often in the early weeks of the program.

4.6 *Children's books about starting school can help the child and family adjust to the transition.*

Source: © Mark Wragg/Istock

School readiness is a concept that has a long history in education. Contemporary understanding of school readiness includes all of the factors that may pre-dispose a student to initial success with the transition into formal schooling, including physical and health factors, social and emotional factors, language, motor skills, and cognitive development. **Ecological theory** (Bronfenbrenner, 1979) emphasizes the relationship between the biological factors (nature) that affect a child's development and the contextual (nurture)

Reflection Point

Do you have any memories of your own school starting experiences? Discuss the school starting experience with young children who have recently started kindergarten. What memories seem to have impressed them most? Did any early experiences with school leave negative impressions? Do the young students talk about the emotions, the people, the physical space, or all of these equally?

Ahlberg, J. & Ahlberg, A. (1988). *Starting school.* New York: Puffin

Bourgeois, P. (1995). *Franklin goes to school.* New York: Scholastic

Carlson, N. (2001). *Look out kindergarten, here I come!* New York: Puffin

Cohen, M. (1989). *Will I have a friend?* New York: Aladdin

Danneberg, J. (2000). *First day jitters.* Watertown, MA: Charlesbridge Publishing

Davis, K. (2005). *Kindergarten rocks!* New York: Harcourt

Hallinan, P.K. (1987). *My first day of school.* Nashville, TN: Ideals Publications

Himle, L. (2006). *Hands as warm as toast.* Ann Arbor, MI: Ann Arbor Media Group

Howe, J. (1994). *When you go to kindergarten.* New York: William Morrow & Company

McGhee, A. (2002). *Countdown to kindergarten.* New York: Scholastic

Penn, A. (1993). *The kissing hand.* Terre Haute, IN: Tanglewood Press

Pope, L. (2007). *Rullie and Joey's first day of kindergarten: The adventures of Rullie and Joey.* Charleston, SC: BookSurge Publishing

Rockwell, A. (2004). *Welcome to kindergarten.* New York: Walker Books for Young Readers

Rogers, J. (1999). *Tiptoe into kindergarten.* New York: Scholastic

Rose, D. (2003). *The twelve days of kindergarten.* New York: Harry N. Abrams

Ruhmann, K. (2002). *Who will go to kindergarten today?* New York: Scholastic

Senisi, E. B. (1994). *Kindergarten kids.* New York: Scholastic

Skarmeas, N. (2001). *My first day of school.* Port Washington, NY: Candy Cane Press

Slate, J. (1996). *Miss Bindergarten gets ready for kindergarten.* New York: Scholastic

Stiles, N. (2005). *On my very first school day I met....* New York: Milk & Cookies Press

Thompson, L. (2003). *Mouse's first day of school.* New York: Simon & Schuster

Wild, M. (2000). *Tom goes to kindergarten.* Morton Grove, IL: Albert Whitman & Company

Wing, N. (2001). *The night before kindergarten.* New York: Grosser & Dunlap

Figure 4.1 *Touchstone books. These help young children make a successful transition to full day early learning.*

factors that may determine or predispose outcomes. Contextual factors are much broader than the relationship between the child and the primary caregiver. These factors include such determinants as maternal depression, adolescent parenthood, stimulation level in the home, maternal education level, family structure, and socio-economic status (Dahinten and Willms, 2002; Field, 1998; Kohen, Brooks-Gunn, Leventhal, and Hertzman, 2002; McLoyd, 1998; Resnick et al., 1999).

Researchers have also found links between the child's neighbourhood and his or her developmental growth and well-being. Work done during the last decade shows that contextual influences, such as the neighbourhood interactions that the child experiences, actually become incorporated into the child's organic makeup and influence the child's development at the cellular level (Hertzman, 1999; Hertzman and Frank, 2006; Hertzman and Wiens, 1996). This concept is called **biological embedding.** If development can be influenced at the cellular level, there are tremendous implications for education; early learning environments can potentially prevent developmental difficulties by providing enriched learning opportunities in various contexts. If the school becomes the hub of social services available to a neighbourhood, the neighbourhood will have increased power and resources to address the needs of its residents.

As children start their learning in kindergarten contexts, the educator team members will need to remember that, although the children will be roughly the same chronological age, they will display a wide range of developmental characteristics. These differences will require a variety of supports to help each student make the transition from home or childcare to formal schooling successfully.

"Find a way to engage the heart in the problem and you are likely to see the child rise naturally to his own optimal levels of uncertainty, risk and relevance." ~ Richard Jones

As early registration for JK/SK shifts to daily contact with young children and their families, educator teams will need to maintain strong bonds of communication with parents and caregivers for every child. This can be done in a variety of ways and can be organized to take full advantage of the various skills each educator team member brings to the educator partnership. Many of the following communication strategies will be familiar in the school community and may have become the accepted and expected way of doing school business. Some strategies however, may require innovative approaches at the school and classroom levels as well as commitment from parents and other caregivers to be active participants in regular communications.

Strong communications from the JK/SK educator team will include

- an open policy that welcomes parents and close family members for informal visits; all participants will need to understand the primacy of the instructional mandate of the classroom, and visits should be welcomed but should not interrupt the flow of learning.
- providing a forum for parents and caregivers to act as supports for each other; this can be done through electronic messaging that is organized through a school site or can be done through facilitation of time, space, and talents.
- appropriate and timely translations of oral and written communications as needed; larger urban school boards may provide this service to schools from a central location within the board.
- promoting the active involvement of parents from all cultures; encourage parents and caregivers to participate on a voluntary basis and through more formal venues, such as school board committees or school advisory councils.
- making school and classroom events readily accessible to all parents and caregivers.

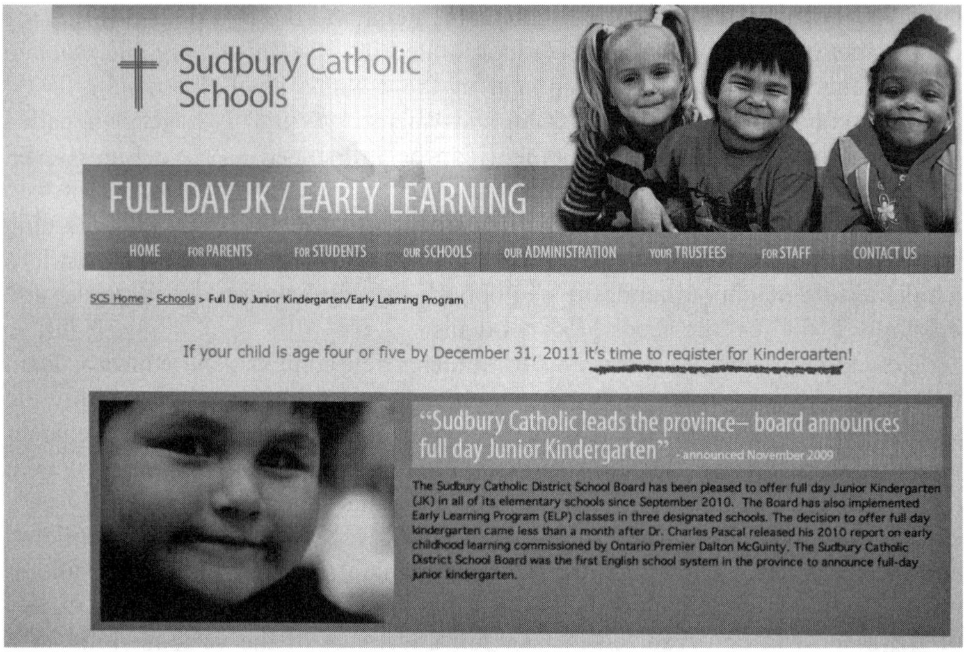

4.7 Educator team members can communicate with families through a classroom web page.

- systematic methods of communication with parents and caregivers about routine issues, such as special event days, family support requests, supplies needed by the child and other day-to-day communications; daily agendas, home bags, and web pages work well for these purposes.

In addition to maintaining day-to-day communications, the educator team can encourage and promote family involvement in the JK/SK classroom through strategies designed to celebrate learning and extend the child's academic and social growth milestones into family interactions. While educators must be mindful of privacy and confidentiality issues, they can invite participation in the life of the classroom by using many strategies that showcase the classroom's ongoing learning events. These approaches might include the following:

- Pajama Nights: Children come to school in their pajamas and engage in storytime activities and healthy bedtime snacks while educator team members meet with parents to explain the kindergarten curriculum.
- Grandparents' and Elders' Days: Grandparents or other older people of influence in the child's life are invited to the classroom to take part in learning activities that children are doing or support their learning through guidance.
- Learning Celebrations: Family members come to the classroom to see displays of children's work. The kindergarten students are trained to talk about the work and have displayed it in a format that is easy to see.

- Learning Bags and Book Bags: Educator team members can provide cloth bags for students to take home nightly or on a rotating basis. Bags may contain books, DVDs about a learning topic, activity booklets, parents' journals, and photographs of the child engaged in an activity. Information pages in the bag can direct parents as to how they can use each item in the bag to extend the classroom learning. These bags might also be Share Bags so that the students take the bags home for the purpose of showing parents work they have done in class.
- iMovies: In class, children can display their learning by creating a movie clip. Parents can be sent an email directing them to a secure spot on the class web page where the movie clip can be viewed.
- Blogs: Parents can participate in classroom blogs to respond to their children's learning, so that their supportive messages can be read to the children while they are at school.
- Digital Histories: Educator team members can create digital histories of special learning episodes in the classroom and provide these to parents electronically, so that they are able to see learning in action.
- Learning Scrapbooks: Educator team members can develop a learning scrapbook of each child's work and photographs of their activities. These scrapbooks can be provided for parents at the end of units, during interviews, when students move schools, or at the end of the academic year.

4.8 *Learning can be recorded using modern technology and shared with families through many means.*

Parents and caregivers should be included in these opportunities, because their involvement allows them to connect what the child is doing in the classroom with ways to enrich school learning in the home and community.

The National Network of Partnership Schools (1997) describes Joyce Epstein's framework of six types of involvement of community and family in school contexts. This framework can be used to develop programs that promote family and community partnerships such as:

- Parenting: Assisting families with parenting and child-rearing skills, and assisting schools in understanding their families.
- Communicating: Developing effective communication from home-to-school and school-to-home.
- Volunteering: Creating ways that families can be involved in the school or school programs and effective methods of recruitment.
- Learning at home: Linking families with their children's curriculum through learning activities that can be done at home, as well as homework.
- Decision making: Including families as decision makers, advocates, members of school councils, and committees.
- Collaborating with the community: Coordinating services in the community with family needs, and providing services to the community.

Collaborating with the community should be the focus of the coordination of services to preschool children. Early learners will benefit from this coordination of services as they enter kindergarten.

NDDS DEVELOPMENTAL SCREEN AND OTHER RESOURCES AS EARLY SCHOOL INVENTORIES

In Chapter 2, we looked at the Nipissing District Developmental Screen (NDDS) that is used by physicians and other health care professionals to help identify developmental delays in young children. We also examined the categories of the Early Developmental Inventory (EDI) which was designed to be used with children at about age five, when they are getting ready to enter Grade 1. The EDI is a school readiness inventory and can help determine the likelihood of a child's successful transition from kindergarten into formal schooling.

Each of these developmental inventories can support the learning process of young children by helping to identify cases of differentiated needs. This is especially important, since we have clear evidence of the very significant consequences of undetected and untreated developmental delays or disabilities (McCain and Mustard, 1999; Schweinhart, Montie, Xiang, Barnett, Belfield, and Nores, 2005).

The dilemma with these screening instruments is that they are underused by professionals who are in a position to detect developmental delays. Young children may be seen regularly by family physicians during the first years of life, but many of them do not perform routine screening for developmental delays, using objective measures such as the NDDS or EDI (Limbos, Joyce, and Roberts, 2010). Developmental disabilities are estimated to affect between 4% and 16% of children (Glascoe and Shapiro, 2008; Statistics Canada, 2001). However, only 30% of disabilities are detected before school entrance, and up to 25% of the children in whom they are identified have learning, health, and behavioural challenges that may interfere with their academic and social performance at school (Glascoe and Shapiro, 2008; Janus, 2006; Kershaw, Irwin, Trafford, and Hertzman, 2006; Wilms, 2002).

Instruments such as the NDDS provide a variety of touch points for screening between the ages of birth and six years and provide descriptors of expected growth across domains (e.g., vision, hearing, speech, language, communication, gross-motor, fine-motor, cognitive, social/emotional, and self-help). However, despite the easy availability of structured screening instruments, it has been found that only a small minority (16.5%) of family physicians use such instruments for early childhood screening (Limbos, Joyce, and Roberts, 2010). Physicians specializing in pediatric care are more likely to make use of them.

Many family physicians make use of the Rourke Baby Record for screening. This screening device can be accessed online at www.rourkebabyrecord.ca. This diagnostic system was developed to provide evidence-based health supervision guides for primary healthcare personnel. The system provides monitoring of nutrition, development, physical parameters, immunizations, safety, family, behaviour, and health promotion issues. The Rourke Baby Record is endorsed by the College of Family Physicians of Canada (CFPC) and the Canadian Pediatric Society (CPS). It is divided into four guides that contain components commonly addressed at the following ages:

- 1 week
- 2 weeks
- 1 month
- 2 months
- 4 months
- 6 months
- 9 months
- 12 to 13 months
- 15 months
- 18 months
- 2 to 3 years
- 4 to 5 years

Although it is in wide use in Canada, this instrument has a limited number of test items and has not been validated as a screening measure, unlike the NDDS instrument, which is recommended by experts in family medicine and child development (Limbos, Joyce, and Roberts, 2010).

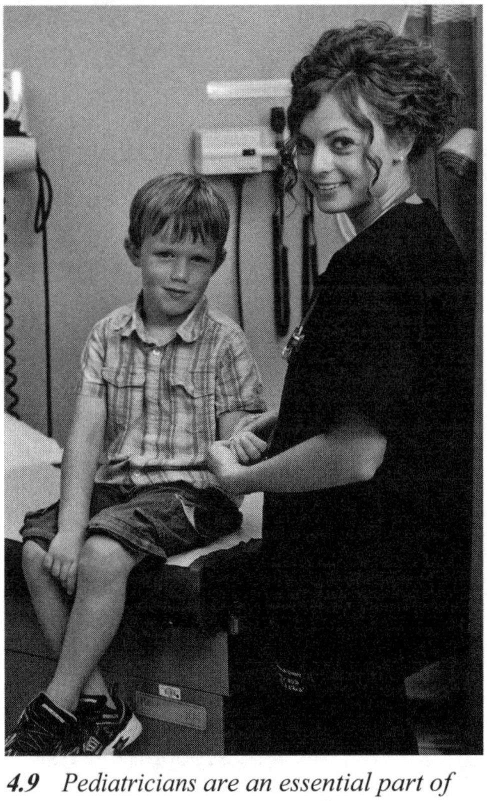

4.9 *Pediatricians are an essential part of the care circle for young children.*

As valid and reliable screening instruments become more readily available and family health care providers become well trained in their use for early detection of developmental delays, we can anticipate better systems of detection prior to school entry.

Reflection Point

Find out what early childhood development screening tools are being used in your school area by family physicians and by pediatricians. Are these two groups using the same developmental screening instruments? Why or why not?

WORKING WITH COMMUNITY SUPPORT SERVICES

The range and accessibility of community support services vary across Canada, based on location, population density, and the population-to-service ratio of each community. When services are fragmented and have different access points for families, it is likely that families will access the services less frequently. However, when schools, ECE facilities, early caregivers, physicians, and other parenting support workers can support families through regular and coordinated health care, we can anticipate that children's development will be optimized.

At present, most schools have a means of coordinating some health services such as dental screening, immunizations, and vision and hearing tests with the local school systems. By seeing early learning and early health care as seamless and interrelated aspects of development, schools can become the hubs of care in the community, supporting young learners and their families.

This type of coordination may be particularly beneficial for families of diverse linguistic and cultural backgrounds. Hubbed services based within the schools will help families know what services are available and help them negotiate access without having to know the intricacies of the health and knowledge sectors of the community and without encountering language barriers (Pelletier and Corter, 2005). Schools need to incorporate a strong emphasis on meeting the needs of families and communities into their mandate, with an emphasis on meeting the needs of diverse families in particular. As well, schools have a unique role to play in the provision of coordinated and integrated services because of their unique access to early learners. When parents feel valued and welcomed in the JK/SK context, we are setting them on the path to positive, productive school–parent relationships that can extend through the child's schooling years.

CHAPTER SUMMARY

Preschool assessments may help parents and educators provide appropriate supports to young children at different stages or touch points in their early development. Assessments may be offered by pediatricians. Research, policy and legislation supports, and new school practices may foster a cycle of continuous improvement in the care and services available to young children and their families. Making parents aware of the variety of community services available to help them support child development is important to all parents, but particularly important to parents new to the school community or new to the country.

Many factors affect children's successful adjustment to formal schooling as they enter JK/SK. Transition strategies that include touchstone stories can help children make smooth adjustments to a new school context. Educators can use many strategies to encourage parents' involvement in the school as children enter kindergarten. By coordinating services that parents may want or need to access, communities can support the navigation of services, especially for parents whose first language is not the language of the school.

THINKING AHEAD: Opportunities for Professional Reflection

- Visit the local health unit in your home area. Interview a staff member to find out what current services are being provided for families with preschool children and what plans may be underway to provide better coordination of services.
- Read the article "Toronto First Duty: Integrating Kindergarten, Childcare, and Parenting Support to Help Diverse Families Connect to Schools" (Pelletier and Corter, 2005). One conclusion of this article is that flexibility, willingness to share space, and roles are crucial to making coordinated services work for schools and families. Discuss how your local school could address flexibility, space issues, and diverse roles to make coordination of services work better.
- Integration of community services could be seen on a continuum from
    - Coexistence of services
    - Coordination of services
    - Collaboration among service providers
    - Integration of services

Using these levels of service coordination to suggest models for service provision, identify the issues that you think would need to be addressed at each level to move service provision toward an integrated approach.

ADDITIONAL READING SUGGESTIONS

To learn more about the Rourke Baby Record system for health supervision of children, visit
www.rourkebabyrecord.ca

To learn more about children's play, read

Brown, S. 2009. *Play: How it Shapes the Brain, Opens the Imagination, and Invigorates the Soul.* New York: Penguin Books.

To learn about teaching children who are linguistically diverse, read

Dever, M., and R. Falconer. 2008. "Children who are linguistically diverse" (Ch. 10). *Foundations and Change in Early Childhood Education.* Toronto: John Wiley & Sons.

To learn about key developmental indicators of children's early development, read

Hohmann, M., D. Weikart, and A. Epstein. 2008. *Educating Young Children: Active Learning Practices for Preschool and Child Care Programs.* Ypsilanti, MI: High/Scope Press, 297–532.

To learn more about community-based parenting resources, visit
Parenting 2.0 at http://parent20.wikispaces.com/Literature

5 The Educator Team Comes Together

"It's a plan that will benefit children.... The complementary skills sets of the two professions will enable the teacher and the ECE to create a learning environment that supports the holistic development of young children."

(Littleford and Brand, 2010)

5.1 *Common planning time and goals are key to helping effective teams work in educational settings.*

In this chapter, educator team members will learn about

- the advocacy role of the educator team
- how responsive environments support a child's adaptation process
- sharing a common philosophy and vision
- planning roles within a play-based environment
- sharing strengths
- a curriculum framework for an early learning program

At the end of this chapter, educator team members can reflect on their personal growth through

- CHAPTER SUMMARY
- THINKING AHEAD: Opportunities for Professional Reflection
- ADDITIONAL READING SUGGESTIONS

Teachers and early childhood educators are committed to the growth, development, and well-being of young children. They are committed to providing children with enriching learning experiences mediated by educator team members who have a shared vision of each child's potential and a shared respect for the complementary team member's skills and areas of expertise. Teachers and early childhood educators each bring many skills to an early learning partnership and have many skills to learn from each other. The richness of their program is dependent on their willingness and skill in realizing their combined potential as an educator team.

THE EDUCATOR TEAM: ROLES AND RESPONSIBILITIES

Many of the current challenges with developing early learning kindergarten programs for young children have their roots in the historical background of services in each jurisdiction across Canada. Formal schooling programs are generally the responsibility of school authorities. However, early childhood programs may be the jurisdiction of a wide range of ministries and departments. Many provinces and territories have involvement from several ministries providing variations of early learning supports. Each province and territory has unique jurisdiction for education so the variety of services has evolved in unique ways. These variations (see Table 5.1) can result in confusion for parents and may work against the smooth transition to new services with labour mobility across Canada.

Table 5.1 *Variations on Early Learning Services across Canada by Jurisdiction*

Jurisdiction	Program for Early Learning	Responsibility of:
Federal Government	First Nations and Inuit Child Care Initiative	Human Resources and Skills Development Canada
	First Nations Head Start	Health Canada
	Aboriginal Head Start	Health Canada
	Child Day Care (Ontario, Alberta)	Indian and Northern Affairs Canada
	Aboriginal Head Start New Brunswick	Indian and Northern Affairs Canada
	First Nations Elementary Education (pre-kindergarten and kindergarten)	Indian and Northern Affairs Canada
	Childminding	Citizenship and Immigration Canada
	Military Family Resource Centres	Department of National Defence
	Early Childhood Development Initiative	Human Resources and Skills Development Canada
	Child Care Expenses Deduction	Canada Revenue Agency

(*Continued*)

Table 5.1 *Variations on Early Learning Services across Canada by Jurisdiction, continued*

Jurisdiction	Program for Early Learning	Responsibility of:
Federal Government	Employment Insurance Maternity and Parental Benefits	Human Resources and Skills Development Canada
	Community Action Program for Children	Health Canada
Newfoundland & Labrador	Child Care Services (daycare centres, family childcare, school-age centres)	Department of Health and Community Services
	kindergarten	Ministry of Education
	family resource programs	Department of Health and Community Services
New Brunswick	Child Care (daycare centres, community daycare homes, school-age daycare centres)	Department of Family and Community Services
	kindergarten	Ministry of Education
	nursery schools	regulated only upon complaint or request
Prince Edward Island	Child Care (early childhood centres, school-age childcare centres, family daycare homes, occasional centres)	Ministry of Health and Social Services
	kindergarten (via childcare centres)	Ministry of Health and Social Services Ministry of Education
Nova Scotia	Child Care (childcare centres, preschools, nursery schools, school-age centres, and child development centres)	Ministry of Community Services
	Grade Primary	Ministry of Education
Quebec	Centres de la petite enfance (CPEs including centres and family childcare)	Ministère de la Famille et de l'Enfance
	garderies	Ministère de la Famille et de l'Enfance
	maternelle	Ministère de l'Éducation
	pré-maternelle	Ministère de l'Éducation
	Passe-Partout	Ministère de l'Éducation
	halte-garderies	not regulated
	preschools	not regulated

(*Continued*)

Table 5.1 *Variations on Early Learning Services across Canada by Jurisdiction, continued*

Jurisdiction	Program for Early Learning	Responsibility of:
Ontario	Child Care (centres, nursery schools, supervised private home daycare, home childcare)	Ministry of Community, Family and Children's Services
	kindergarten	Ministry of Education
	junior kindergarten	Ministry of Education
	family resource programs	Ministry of Community, Family and Children's Services
Manitoba	Child Care (centres, nursery schools, family daycare, school age centres, occasional centres)	Manitoba Family Services and Housing
	kindergarten	Manitoba Education
Saskatchewan	Child Day Care (childcare centres, family childcare)	Ministry of Social Services
	kindergarten	Saskatchewan Learning
	preschools	not regulated
Alberta	Child Day Care (daycare centres, nursery schools, approved family day homes, drop-in centres)	Alberta Children and Youth Services
	Early Childhood Services/Kindergarten	Ministry of Education
	out-of-school childcare	not provincially regulated
British Columbia	Child Care (centres, preschool, family child care, school-age childcare, child minding, other centre-based services, Child Care resource and Referral Programs)	Ministry of Community, Aboriginal and Women's Services, Ministry of Health Planning, Ministry of Human Resources
	Supported Child Development for special needs children	Ministry of Children and Family Development
	kindergarten	Ministry of Education
	government integrated early childhood development strategy	Minister of State for Early Childhood Development
Northwest Territories	Child Care (daycare centres, nursery schools, after-school care, family day homes)	Department of Education, Culture and Employment
	kindergarten	Department of Education, Culture and Employment

(Continued)

Table 5.1 *Variations on Early Learning Services across Canada by Jurisdiction, continued*

Jurisdiction	Program for Early Learning	Responsibility of:
Nunavut	Child Care (daycare centres, nursery schools, after-school care, family day homes)	Department of Education
	kindergarten	Department of Education
Yukon	Child Care (centres, school-age childcare, family day homes)	Department of Health and Social Services
	kindergarten	Department of Education
	preschools	not regulated

Used with permission of Nancy Maynes

While there is some evidence of efforts to bring common standards to bear on education at all levels across Canada's provinces and territories, many unique features remain in the service models of different regions of the country. The Council of Ministers of Education, Canada provides an overview of the education system in each province or territory in easily accessible graphic format (see Figure 5.1).

This graphic demonstrates that the education systems in the public domain across provinces and territories include pre-elementary educational services in most areas of Canada. Within these diverse systems of public education, it is the goal of early learning services to establish a strong social and academic starting point for every child.

In the early learning environment, young students benefit when the roles of the members of the educator team are clear and complementary. Educator teams in the early learning environment in some jurisdictions have included a provincially or territorially certified teacher and an early childhood educator. Depending on the makeup of the group of children in a class, there may also be an educational assistant with responsibility for serving the specific learning needs of one or more children under the guidance of the classroom teacher. The dynamics of the relationship among these professionals is crucial to the productive provision of services for the young children in each class.

THE ADVOCACY ROLE OF THE EDUCATOR TEAM

Both teachers and ECE staff are trained as child advocates. However, educator team members are typically trained differently, and their qualifications reflect the variations of standards for their profession as dictated by their governing body. During the last two decades, teachers in many jurisdictions have become members of a college which serves as a governing and disciplinary body. While there are some variations in how these colleges have been introduced and implemented

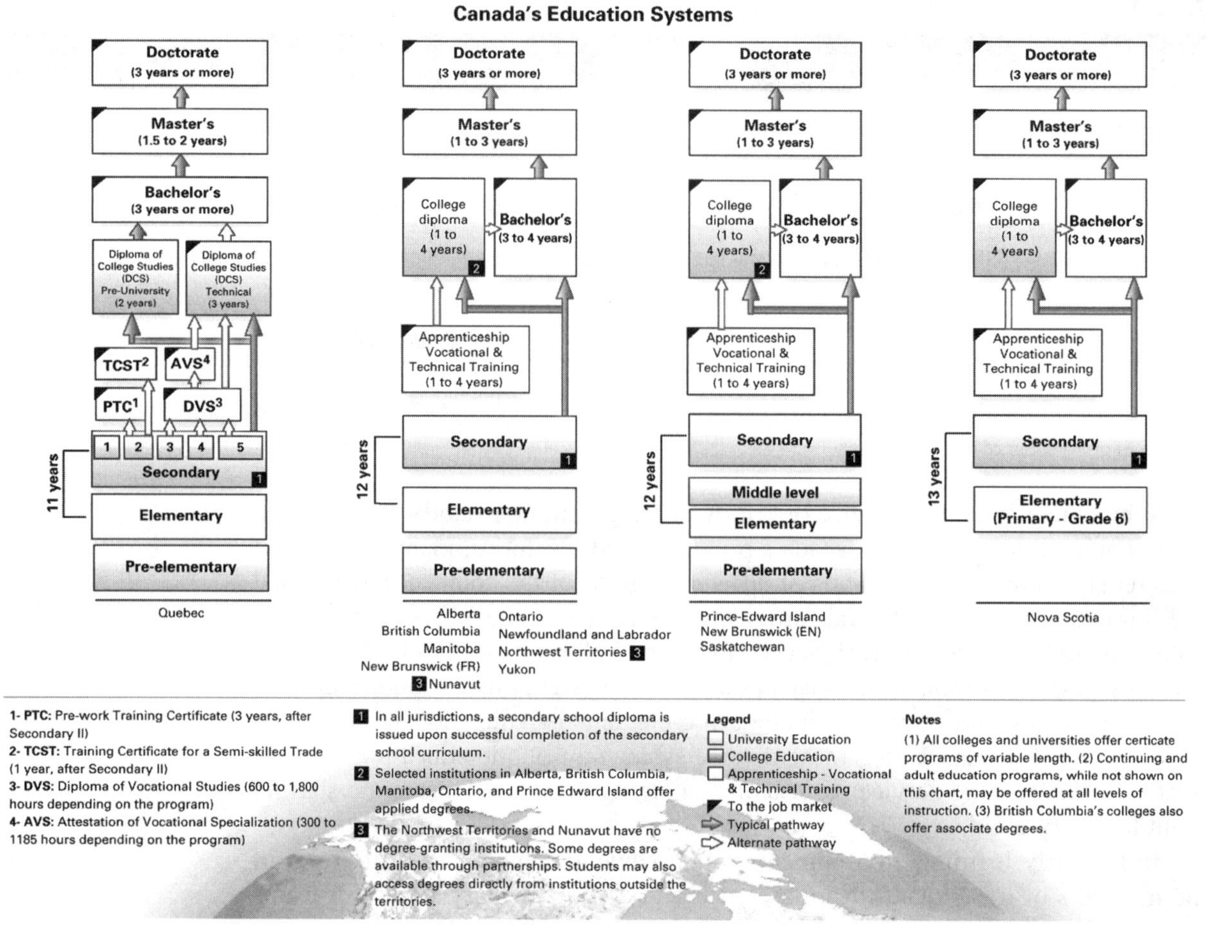

Figure 5.1 *Canada's Education Systems*

Reprinted with the permission of the Canadian Information Centre for International Credentials (CICIC), a unit of the Council of Ministers of Education, Canada (CMEC).

across Canada, in general, the colleges serve to provide a framework of professional standards and a set of professional principles within each jurisdiction. Members of the teaching profession are responsible to their respective colleges for upholding the standards of the teaching profession as defined by these and must submit to the disciplinary actions of their colleges if it is deemed that their actions contravene the colleges' standards.

In recent years, many jurisdictions across Canada have introduced a college membership structure for early childhood educators as well. For example, in Ontario, early childhood educators are guided and governed by the 2007 Early Childhood Educators' Act.

Under the powers of this act, the duties and scope of responsibilities of the early childhood educator are defined in Section 2:

5.2 Early childhood educators may be governed by legislation that supports their professional practices and guides their professional decisions.

Source: Jupiterimages/Thinkstock

Practice of early childhood education

2. The practice of early childhood education is the planning and delivery of inclusive play-based learning and care programs for children in order to promote the well-being and holistic development of children, and includes,

(a) the delivery of programs to preschool children and school-aged children, including children with special needs;

(b) the assessment of the programs and of the progress of children in the programs;

(c) communication with the parents or persons with legal custody of the children in the programs in order to improve the development of the children; and

(d) such other services or activities as may be prescribed by the regulations. 2007, c. 7, Sched. 8, s. 2.

Under such acts, the governing body has broad powers to establish standards of practice for the profession of the early childhood educator.

Similar regulations for teachers across Canada are governed by federation and college structures and governing bodies. It is a challenge both for employers and for members of different governing bodies to work with different standards when they are pulling together educator team members to support learning in JK/SK contexts.

Some jurisdictions used combined educator team approaches in early learning contexts before the use of such teams became more widespread. The experiences of these early teams can guide the development of similar teams in other jurisdictions as funding for full day JK/SK classes becomes more universal.

5.3 The resources provided for children's access during play can help challenge and extend their learning.

One advantage of the team approach in early learning is the play-based training that ECEs have for establishing an early learning environment. Through play-based learning, young children have opportunities to develop self-confidence and to expand their positive attitude toward learning (Littleford and Brand, 2010). While teachers are trained in academic approaches that are based on constructivist theories, many early childhood educators are trained in social pedagogical approaches. **Social pedagogy** views the young child as an independent agent with an active role in shaping his or her learning. The role of the early childhood educator is to extend learning and challenge thinking through learning opportunities that are designed to reflect the team's knowledge of child development, focused observations of learning, and documentation of the child's activities, in cooperation with parents and the broader community supports that may be available.

The academic approaches taught to teachers place more emphasis on planning programs to achieve prespecified learning goals or expectations. Teachers observe children's responses to curriculum input and adjust program opportunities to reflect the best match between children's present learning and the learning as stated in expectations for the program. Academic skills are a focus in teachers' professional preparation programs.

By combining the academic background of both the teacher and the early childhood educator, the educator team can provide a richer program, which builds on the strengths of each team member. Advocacy for young children is enriched by the breadth of training of a diversified educator team. Young children can have a learning experience that is guided by academic goals and respects the children's development, readiness, and orientation towards learning through play. The richness of an effective early learning program is realized by optimizing the strengths of the background training of each member of the educator team.

Various team members may also have different practicum experiences as part of their professional training. Teacher preparation typically includes several weeks of practicum in school settings. In recent years, many teacher preparation programs also include some experience with alternative practicum placements in international, service-learning, or non-traditional school contexts such as outdoor education, Aboriginal reserves, or second-language classrooms. Practical training experiences for early childhood educators can include opportunities to apply course learning in childcare centres, school classrooms, and support-program centres for young children and families. These unique experiences can enrich the understanding and professional perspectives of each of the educator team members.

To realize the full potential of the skills of each member of the educator team, teachers and early childhood educators will need time for common learning experiences within their respective and complementary professions, time and structure for joint planning in the JK/SK context, and employment agreements that support the spirit and intent of team approaches to early learning. Building from different professional backgrounds toward shared responsibility for a vibrant early learning program must be done in a spirit of respect for the skills and training of each member of the new educator team. This will allow each member of the team to develop strong respect for the development and well-being of each child and expand on their commitment to work together in new and respectful ways and to learn from the unique aspects of each team member's professional background.

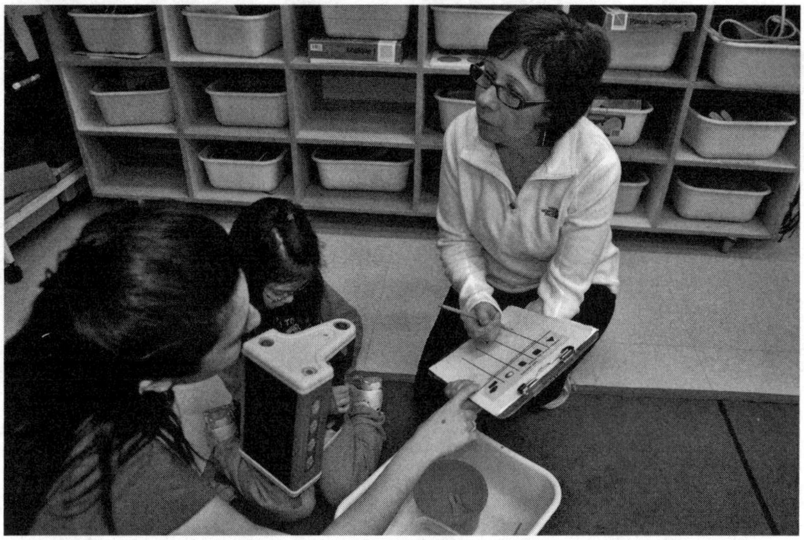

5.4 *Educator team members may have different roles in their team to support learning by building on their professional strengths.*

SHARING A COMMON PHILOSOPHY AND VISION

The development of vibrant and effective early learning classrooms is influenced to some extent by the demographics of the teachers and early childhood educators who will make up the educator team in each classroom. Early childhood education environments are highly feminized. Most early childhood educators and about 95% of JK/SK teachers are women (Brown, 2010). In some jurisdictions, JK/SK teachers are more than twice as likely as other teachers to work part time. This employment picture can create additional challenges for the structure of the JK/SK educator team, as there may be more than two people involved in service provision in the same classroom.

JK/SK educator team members will have the responsibilities governing their profession to consider, the terms of employment within a public institution to consider, and the social aspects implicit in a team endeavour to negotiate. This relationship will present both labour challenges and team membership challenges.

5.5 Educator team members need to work together to plan the best use of space and resources in a play-based environment.

Common time will need to be focused on many program aspects, such as planning, assessment, communication with parents, classroom management, infrastructure dynamics, space usage, and health and safety issues, in addition to the complexities of managing new adult relationships in a close working environment.

In some metropolitan jurisdictions in Canada, almost 70% of early childhood educators hold two-year college diplomas with early childhood specialization (Child Care Human Resources Sector Council, 2007). Immigrants, newcomers to Canada, and visible minorities make up a large proportion of the early childhood educator workforce in many urban areas of Canada (Gestwicki and Bertrand, 2003). Those early childhood educators who are seen by service recipients as the strongest providers may be those who are able to draw on their communication skills both from their professional preparation programs and from their personal background in their cultural world (Bromer, 2001). Educator teams can capitalize on this cultural diversity within the early childhood workforce to provide young children with exposure to visible diversity that is representative of Canada's cultural, linguistic, religious, experiential, and ethnic makeup. This diversity could become one of the strengths of the educator team approach in JK/SK contexts (Gestwicki and Bertrand, 2003), as educator team members not only address their understanding of the role of play in learning but also expand their understanding of the various perspectives on play originating in the diverse cultural backgrounds within both the educator team and the larger community served by the school. As educator team members learn to work together to develop and provide early learning programs, cultural, professional, and individual differences will surface that will need to be negotiated in order to achieve a unified understanding of child development beliefs and practices in the context of each classroom.

When the educator team comes together and the process of establishing an early learning JK/SK program is initiated, conflicts may arise. Managing these

5.6 *The majority of ECE educators in Canada's urban centres are from immigrant backgrounds.*

conflicts productively can lead to positive outcomes for learners. However, educator team members will need opportunities to learn about how to not only manage conflicts but also resolve them in ways that ensure the best interests of children are respected.

Conflict resolution training is critical to team building, because it is difficult to change adult attitudes and behaviours. The most productive relationships will be built around the values and skills of cooperation, communication, tolerance, positive emotional expression, and conflict resolution that are embedded in the culture of the whole school (Girard and Koch, 1996). Entry points for introducing conflict resolution in the educator team development process include developing the curriculum for the JK/SK classroom, determining processes and procedures for classroom management, and initiating new school- or province/territory-wide programs.

Without appropriate training at the outset of an educator team's establishment, team members risk intra-team conflict. Such conflict can undermine the learning of children, who are dependent on the team for learning support. Intra-team conflict exists when a team member, either temporarily or consistently, interferes with or obstructs the behaviours of another member of the team (Deutsch, 1973). In a positively functioning team, educators will come together to determine important issues, create new ideas, release tensions, clarify goals, re-evaluate goals, and strengthen each team member's ability to work collaboratively in the future. Without these positive team functions, educator team members can prolong or even escalate conflicts, or become inflexible, hostile or ineffective (Jehn, 1995; Kuhn and Poole, 2000; Rahim, Manger and Shapiro, 2000).

Educator teams will function best when they share both **task interdependence** and **goal interdependence** (Somech, 2008). Task interdependence is a measure of the extent to which the individual team members need information, materials, and support from other team members to carry out their job. Goal interdependence is a measure of the extent to which team members believe they are assigned group goals or receive group feedback. Creating both task and goal interdependence for the JK/SK educator team should be a top priority for a school's administration when a full-day JK/SK program is first established.

PLANNING ROLES WITHIN A PLAY-BASED ENVIRONMENT

In a classroom where more than one adult has program and care responsibilities for the students, roles need to be clear. When the adults have the advantage of different types of professional training, as is likely to be the case with JK/SK educator teams, the adults can take advantage of their strengths to provide the most vibrant programming possible in the kindergarten context. Team teaching is a classroom approach that has been widely used in some contexts. In traditional team teaching contexts, two teachers share responsibility for a larger-than-average group of students. Team teaching has the advantage of allowing educators to create "flexible learning situations that could more readily accommodate multi-level or differentiated instruction as well as the management of materials and human resources" (Santamaria and Thousand, 2004).

In a typical JK/SK classroom team, the team members are more likely to include one classroom teacher and one early childhood educator. The different types of professional training that the members of this educator team bring to their instructional partnership has the potential to be characterized by rich collaboration, if roles are clearly envisioned as part of the program establishment process. Collaboration in a school context needs to include joint planning, decision making, and problem solving that can occur in a variety of formal and informal configurations to accomplish the common goal of providing a rich learning environment for young children (Friend and Cook, 1992).

5.7 Spontaneous communication throughout the JK/SK day is an important aspect of teamwork.

Successful collaboration is defined by six characteristics (Friend and Cook, 1992):

1. Being voluntary: Educator team members fully understand and accept their various roles in the context of shared responsibility for the students in the class.
2. Requiring parity among participants: Educator team members respect the differences in each member's professional backgrounds and are willing to plan their various responsibilities to take full advantage of the strengths each team member brings to the team.
3. Basing actions on mutual goals: Educator team members share task interdependence.
4. Depending on shared responsibility for participation and decision making: Educator team members have established times to manage program planning as a team and have mutual respect for the input of each member of the team.
5. Consisting of individuals who share their resources: Educator team members share goal interdependence.
6. Consisting of individuals who share accountability for outcomes: In addition to sharing goal and task interdependence, educator team members share responsibility for aligning instruction with play-based learning opportunities, share the tasks related to observation and recording learning, and cooperate in tasks related to reporting learning.

Reflection Point

"Overall, studies on professional collaboration paint a promising picture of success resulting in student needs being met by the most highly qualified people working together toward a common goal" (Howland, 2003: Lam et al., 2002; Singh and Shifflette, 1996; Villa et al., 2004). Discuss how a team approach can ensure that students' needs are being met in a JK/SK context.

Teaching in partnerships is often called **co-teaching**. Co-teaching has many advantages for the students but also provides the advantages of belonging, fun, choice, power, and survival for the co-teaching partners (Villa et al., 2004). Co-teaching is effective for many reasons, including the following:

- It provides opportunities for students to become more capable collaborative learners as they emulate the cooperative and collaborative skills they observe in those who are teaching them (Olsen, 1968).
- Co-teachers have a greater opportunity to capitalize on the unique, diverse and specialized knowledge, skills, and instructional approaches

of other educators (Bauwens, Hourcade, and Friend, 1989; Hourcade and Bauwens, 2002).

- Co-teachers often are able to structure their classes to take advantage of research-proven strategies (Miller et al., 1998).
- Co-teachers tend to be inventive and come up with solutions that traditional school structures often fail to examine (Nevin, Thousand, Paolucci-Whitcomb, and Villa, 1990; Skrtic, 1987).
- Co-teachers feel empowered by having the opportunity to collaboratively make decisions (Duke, Showers and Imber, 1980) and simultaneously increase their own skills (Thousand, Villa, Nevin and Paolucci-Whitcomb, 1995).

The advantages of co-instructional and complementary roles in the classroom are numerous for both the students and the co-teachers.

Reflection Point

Interview a local educator team in a JK/SK context to identify the strategies each team member consciously uses to promote and capitalize on the strengths of the team in their co-teaching responsibilities.

5.8 By planning for task distribution between educator team members, the team can make the best instructional use of their skills.

SHARING STRENGTHS

If the focus of all instruction in the JK/SK classroom is student improvement in all areas of development, the diverse strengths of educator team members are key resources in achieving this focus. To provide the supports needed to maximize the learning opportunities available to the children, educator team members need to share a common vision of beliefs and strategies for differentiating instruction. The purpose of sharing each team member's strengths in the classroom is to provide every possible opportunity and support for each child to succeed with the classroom goals. This is known as **differentiation**. Differentiated instruction is a set of behaviours that involve "instructional practices and teaching strategies that are inclusive in nature, practices that enable all children including those with disabilities to access and succeed in the general education classroom and curriculum" (Santamaria and Thousand, 2004, p.15). Differentiation as a professional concept for instruction involves behaviours that

- initiate instruction where the student's individual current learning is as a starting point,
- utilize the students' different learning modalities to support their learning and growth,
- prompt students to base their achievements and successes on past achievements and successes rather than on competition with others,
- provide specific ways for each student to learn,
- use classroom time flexibly to optimize learning opportunities, and
- engage in diagnosis to identify the best possible instruction for each student. (Tomlinson, 1999)

In the fast-paced context of a JK/SK classroom, educator team members will need to develop faith in each team member's ability to provide **spontaneous differentiation** throughout the day. Spontaneous differentiation (sometimes referred to as *reflection-in-action*) allows educator teams to use their already-learned skills to spontaneously adapt lessons on the spot (Santamaria and Thousand, 2004).

5.9 *Careful observation will help educator team members identify the opportunities for responding to learning, or challenging and extending learning.*

Early childhood educators typically have special training in the strategy of spontaneous differentiation. They are trained in techniques to provide on-the-spot supports to any student in need and to do so in the context of the curriculum leads being provided by the classroom teacher (Gerber, 2000; Stanovich, 1996). By building on the early childhood focus on spontaneous differentiation, the educator team can ensure that the norm of their classroom is the provision of authentic, multi-level instruction and assessment. In this context, educator team members will be able to move seamlessly among a variety of co-teaching configurations to respond to the broad range of the needs of their young students (Villa et al., 2004).

A CURRICULUM FRAMEWORK FOR AN EARLY LEARNING PROGRAM

5.10 *Most provincial and territorial jurisdictions have an early learning framework that guides the work of early years educators*

Source: Jupiterimages/Thinkstock

Many of Canada's provinces and territories either have, or are in the process of developing, a framework for early learning services within their jurisdiction. These frameworks share a common commitment to a philosophy of intentional play-based learning. Intentional play-based learning recognizes the strong link between play and learning in young children. This link is especially strong in relation to problem solving, language acquisition, literacy, numeracy, and social, physical, and emotional growth ("Full-Day Early Learning Kindergarten Program for Four- and Five-Year-Olds: A Reference Guide for Educators" [2010] at www.ontario.ca/earlylearning). A curriculum framework based on intentional play-based learning allows educator team members to embed learning in a play environment where interaction with other learners and the environment is the norm, and children engage in both free play and structured play opportunities. Through intentional play-based learning, young students have many opportunities to explore through many modalities or learning styles, interact with other learners and supportive adults, think creatively and critically, identify and solve problems, inquire in both structured and unstructured ways, and share their learning with others.

A curriculum framework supports the development of the tools and materials needed to support learning and to build learning environments that stimulate the growth of every child.

Play-Based Learning Example

At a water table, young children are challenged to design a boat to float a number of plastic shapes, using a limited set of materials. They learn through experimentation that some materials float better than others, that weight distribution is critical to stability of a floating object, and that some materials are absorbent. Concepts such as *sink, float, absorb, distribute*, and *hull design* can be learned through this play-based activity.

The role of the educator team in such an activity includes

- providing activity materials
- providing a growth-appropriate challenge
- questioning thinking as learners explore
- assessing at different stages of the learning (*before, for, as, of* learning—see Figure 5.2)
- naming ideas as they are discovered by students
- providing opportunities for children to share what they have learned
- recording learning

This play-based learning example provides entry points for educator team members to support the physical, intellectual, emotional, social, and creative abilities of young children.

The early learning framework from British Columbia identifies nine principles that combine to provide a summary of the beliefs about early learning for the province (British Columbia Ministry of Education, 2008). The principles of the British Columbia Early Learning Framework are as follows:

1. Children are born with an innate desire to learn.
2. Families are the primary caregivers of children and have the most important role in promoting their children's well-being, learning, and development in the context of supportive communities.
3. Play is vital to children's healthy development and learning.
4. Consistent, responsive, and nurturing relationships are essential to the health, well-being, and early learning of children.
5. All aspects of children's development and learning—physical, social, emotional, cultural, linguistic, and intellectual—are interrelated and interdependent.
6. Language plays a central role in connecting thought and learning.

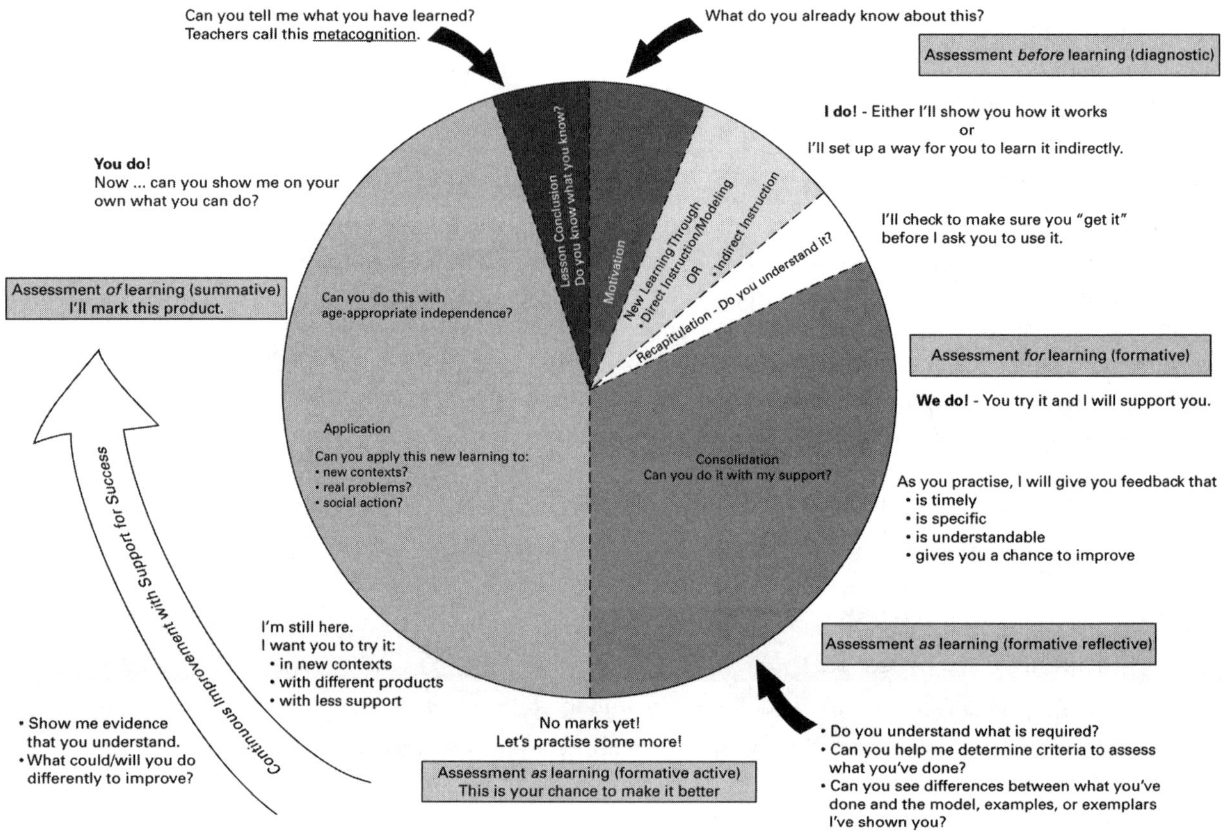

Figure 5.2 *Ways that Early Learning Educators Should Think About the Different Ways of Assessing and Supporting Learning*

Used with permission of Nancy Maynes

7. Children are active participants in their families and communities.
8. The individual, cultural, and linguistic identities of children and families are respected and integrated into early learning settings, programs, and activities.
9. The physical environment shapes children's learning and well-being.

Educator team members use such a framework to guide their planning, implementation, program design, and student assessment. Through **critical reflection**, educator team members apply the framework principles to examine their own beliefs and practices and to help them understand the beliefs and factors that influence their professional behaviours. Critical reflection will help educator team members examine their world views, consider diverse perspectives, understand the operation of power and stability in our culture, and create inclusive understandings that empower all children. Critical reflection will help educator team members think deeply about their shared fundamental beliefs and the factors and forces that have shaped their beliefs, as well as understanding how they can expand their beliefs and practices to create a more culturally inclusive learning context.

Frameworks typically provide identification of the areas of learning within a program. The framework used in the British Columbia document uses a tree analogy to show that learning has its roots in families, the environment, communities, and government, and that, through play (the tree stem), young children can learn skills to support areas of growth (the branches) related to

- well-being and belonging,
- exploration and creativity,
- social responsibility and diversity, and
- language and literacies.

From these framework categories, specific teaching ideas to ensure learning in each area are provided in the resource document "Making Linkages: How the British Columbia Early Learning Framework Links to the Primary Program: A Framework for Teaching" (B.C. Ministry of Education, 2009).

In the Ontario ELECT (Early Learning for Every Child Today, 2007) curriculum framework, the areas that identify essential early learning outcomes include:

- Social: Children are connected with others and contribute to their world.
- Emotional: Children have a strong sense of identity and well-being.
- Language and Literacies: Children are effective communicators.
- Cognition: Children are involved and confident learners.
- Physical: Children make healthy choices and master physical skills.

The ELECT framework is supported by other resource documents that provide program details for early learning. In the resource document "The Full-Day Early Learning–Kindergarten Program" (draft, 2010), the foci presented in the ELECT document are presented as the "big idea" elements of the curriculum framework and used to generate overall learning expectations that in turn are used to generate specific learning expectations. This document also expands on early learning expectations by providing three levels of adult interaction direction for educator team members. Examples of how to interact as children engage in play (see Table 5.2) are provided as ways to respond to, challenge, or extend the learning that children engage in.

For example, for the expectation "Children demonstrate the ability to take turns in activities and discussion," educator team members might challenge students by asking questions such as "How can you share this to make your structure taller?" Educator team members can respond to children's learning by saying, "I see you have worked together to plan and discuss how you could make your structure taller." Similarly, educator team members can work to extend children's learning by providing new materials in the play area that children might choose to incorporate in their structures. Through responding, challenging, and extending interactions as children engage in play-based learning, the educator team can promote individual growth and development in each child.

Table 5.2 *Ways to Respond to, Challenge, and Extend Children's Learning*

Experiences for learning in the early learning JK/SK classroom will include:

- Free exploration
- Independent discovery
- Independent application
- Purposeful literacy instruction (modeled, shared, guided, independent)

Intentional instruction (modeling) is a central strategy for learning in a play-based context.

Educator team members can develop students' learning by responding, challenging, and extending as students explore, discover, and apply.

Examples of responding, challenging, and extending include the following:

RESPONDING includes...	CHALLENGING includes...	EXTENDING includes...
• Modeling	• Showing physical/spatial relationships	• Interpreting
• Rephrasing	• Guessing/estimating	• Assigning/questioning intention in written text
• Questioning	• Making mind–body connections	• Asking for proof
• Showing	• Problem solving	• Making signs
• Labelling	• Shared/partnered writing	• Showing
• Connecting to the home language	• Questioning	• Matching
• Adults joining in play	• Projecting	• Explaining thinking
• Sequencing	• Hypothesizing	• Showing expert learner strategies
• Ordering items	• Making predictions	• Initial reading of pattern texts
• Counting	• Considering options	• Visualization
• Showing movement and change	• Illustrating	• Changing centre materials
• Identifying social issues (e.g., environmental stewardship)	• Asking their own questions	• Inquiry
• Acknowledging	• Analyzing failures	• Exemplifying
• Showing empathy	• Using challenge cards	• Naming
• Making connections to previous experiences	• Using puzzles	• Relating ideas through different styles of presentation
• Comparing	• Naming feelings, emotions, and movements	• Suggesting
• Matching	• Exposing to variations	• Assigning causality
• Blending	• Identifying examples and non-examples	• Charting
• Pairing words and pictures	• Introducing cooperative play	• Graphing
• Demonstrating	• Using symbols	• Sorting by identified criteria
• Drawing	• Connecting colours to feelings	• Connecting

(*Continued*)

Table 5.2 *Ways to Respond to, Challenge, and Extend Children's Learning, continued*

RESPONDING includes…	CHALLENGING includes…	EXTENDING includes…
• Anticipating problems	• Identifying	• Creating
• Retelling	• Explaining	• Considering impacts
• Recognizing personal preferences	• Directing	• Physically demonstrating emotions
• Assigning causality	• Drawing conclusions	• Problem-solving inquiries
• Pretending	• Generalizing across contexts	• Providing opportunities to make choices
• Directing	• Recording ideas	• Sorting
• Sorting	• Posing problems	• Examining examples
• Defining	• Experiencing cultural variations	• Identifying
• Noticing	• Designing	• Making
• Adding detail	• Labelling	• Identifying patterns
• Using tools	• Describing	• Re-creating
• Naming other strategies	• Coordinating	• Considering alternatives
• Grouping	• Changing	• Transferring to new situations to generalize
• Supporting the asking of questions		• Making decisions
• Asking clarifying questions		• Assigning value
• Making things		• Using symbols
		• Changing for a defined purpose
		• Using process vocabulary
		• Sampling
		• Using product vocabulary
		• Considering effects
		• Recognizing in other contexts
		• Testing theories
		• Using props
		• Listening
		• Acting
		• Viewing
		• Reflecting
		• Planning for the future

In addition to these types of overall curriculum and program framework resources, educator team members may have access to resources designed to support specific learning needs. For example, in Ontario, educator teams can access the resource "Supporting English Language Learners in Kindergarten: A Practical Guide for Ontario Educators." This resource provides many practical examples of ways for educator team members to scaffold young students' language learning in a play-based context.

CHAPTER SUMMARY

Educator teams in JK/SK contexts may be many configurations of teacher and support staff, including early childhood educators, educational assistants, community support staff, and volunteers. Whatever the configuration of adults in the JK/SK classroom, they must share a common advocacy role for young learners. Educator teams need time, resources, and structure to work toward developing a common philosophy and vision for their classroom.

While some roles in the JK/SK classroom may be governed by local legislation or individual contracts, many tasks in the classroom will be negotiable among team members. Task and goal interdependence will help educator team members work toward common goals and avoid conflicts. A local curriculum framework can provide the philosophical basis for a common vision within the team. Curriculum frameworks identify commonly held principles that direct program development and decisions.

THINKING AHEAD: Opportunities for Professional Reflection

- Find the document(s) that provide the early learning JK/SK framework for your local jurisdiction. Identify the key principles that are to guide early learning as presented in the framework.
- Create a poster or diagram to demonstrate how the principles as outlined in the local early learning framework relate to each other. (Example: Earlier in this chapter, the B.C. framework was presented as parts of a tree.) Include the guiding principles, curriculum foci, and play-based philosophy in your diagram. Compare your depiction with that of other colleagues and engage in discussing why various people chose certain symbols to represent their framework.
- Work with a group of colleagues to plan how you would build upon several specific examples of children's play to transform the play into play-based learning. Here are some examples you might use for this purpose:

Learning Expectation	Play Context	Play-based Learning
Children should recognize people in their community and talk about what they do.	Have children use costumes at a dress-up centre.	Set up a centre so that children can choose costumes or work clothes, match it to a work implement from a second bin, and, and use the implement to do a play task that simulates a job that could be done by a community member.

(Continued)

Learning Expectation	Play Context	Play-based Learning
Children should develop awareness of ways in which people adapt to the seasons.	Have children work at a centre to show clothing worn and activities that could be done with each Canadian season using a doll or cut-out dress-up activity.	Have children work in season teams and help each other identify materials from a large bin of clothing, play items, heating and cooling supplies, protective materials, and tools, to identify items appropriate for each season and create seasonal tableaus for photographing and/or painting.
Children should explore sounds, rhythms, and language structures, with guidance and on their own.		
Children will listen and respond to others for a variety of purposes.		
Children will use language to talk about their thinking, to reflect, and to solve problems.		
Children will use specialized vocabulary for a variety of purposes.		
Children will demonstrate a willingness to try new activities.		
Children will retell stories (in proper sequence) that have been read by and with the educator team members, using pictures in the book and/or props.		
Children will retell information from non-fiction materials that have been read by and with the educator team members in a variety of contexts.		

ADDITIONAL READING SUGGESTIONS

The following reading suggestions provide a broad list of resources for educators to consider as they study early learning:

For recent research articles about the importance of early childhood education, visit

www.child-encyclopedia.com/en-ca/importance-of-early-childhood-development/according-to-experts.html

For the article "Educational Toys: Learning to play or playing to learn?," visit

www.ccl-cca.ca/CCL/Reports/LessonsInLearning?LinL2010050EducationalToys.html

For more information about the British Columbia Early Learning Framework, visit

www.bced.gov.bc.ca/early_learning/early_learning_framework

For more background about early learning programming, read

Dever, M. and R. Falconer. 2007. *Foundations and Change in Early Childhood Education.* John Wiley & Sons.

Ontario Ministry of Education. 2010. *Growing Success: Assessment, Evaluation, and Reporting in Ontario Schools.* Toronto: Queen's Printer for Ontario (also available at www.edu.gov.on.ca).

Brown, S. 2009. *Play: How it Shapes the Brain, Opens the Imagination, and Invigorates the Soul.* New York: Penguin Books.

6 Communication

"An effective JK/SK early learning educator team will have courageous conversations about their professional practice as a regular way of interacting for the benefit of children. Team members' personal and interpersonal capacity is 'deeply affected by the kinds of organizations within which the individuals work.'"

(Mitchell and Sackney, 2001)

6.1 *Communication among learners is an important aspect of the JK/SK learning environment.*

In this chapter, educator team members will learn about	At the end of this chapter, educator team members can reflect on their personal growth through
• communication within the educator team • communication with parents and guardians • communication with young children • the ELL kindergartner	• CHAPTER SUMMARY • THINKING AHEAD: Opportunities for Professional Reflection • ADDITIONAL READING SUGGESTIONS

The way that the educator team functions together on a day-to-day basis will have a direct impact on the successful learning of the young children in the classroom. Conflict is expected in a team effort; how the conflict is managed is crucial to its outcomes. Teachers have typically been isolated, trained for their profession through individual paths of preparation and development, and may have focused on specialization. The need to work out a team approach in the full-day JK/SK classroom can threaten the sense of autonomy that the teacher has developed and may present many occasions for conflict as team roles are engaged. Successful management of these potential conflicts is critical for creating the positive learning climate so necessary for young children to thrive.

COMMUNICATION WITHIN THE EDUCATOR TEAM

The educator team in a JK/SK context is first and foremost a team. As a team, the teacher and early childhood educator must share **task and goal interdependence** (see Chapter 5). Task and goal interdependence are critical for the team members to pull together and work toward the common good of the team. Team-effectiveness models (Campion, Papper, and Medsker, 1996; Kirkman and Rosen, 1999) use three guiding principles to ensure the effectiveness of team efforts. The three principles are as follows:

- Leaders take various actions to structure teamwork.
- These leadership actions have a direct effect on the way team members interact.
- The interaction of the team members creates important outcomes.

6.2 Strong school leadership is needed to structure effective teamwork with clear goals for the early learning JK/SK educator team.

In the case of educator team members building a team approach, the leader is likely to be the school administration (principal, vice-principal, or primary division coordinator); the team members will include the teacher and ECE (early childhood educator) and may also include other support staff, such as an educational assistant, nurse, community liaison, or child speech pathologist. The team will benefit if all members of the team not only know their roles in ensuring positive learning for all children but also have strong conflict-management skills. Group theories (McGrath, 1991) indicate that conflict can be predicted as part of team formation and as an aspect of the team's developing productive relationships as it works toward a shared outcome.

Typical conflicts in a school context can revolve around some predictable situations, such as

- vague assignments and lack of clarity about roles,
- refusal to accept feedback,
- unfair distribution of work,
- incompatible goals, and
- incompatible personalities.

(Ayoko, Hartel and Callan, 2004: Zornoza, Ripoll and Pieró, 2002)

When the JK/SK educator team is formed, many of these sources of potential conflict can be addressed at the same time as program goals and relationships are being defined. This is time well spent, as it will establish goal and task interdependence within the educator team.

Conflicts that do arise in the normal course of teamwork can be either constructive or destructive in nature. Positive team functions will help to maintain focus on the shared team goals by addressing issues professionally, re-establishing short- and long-term goals for the team, and nurturing working relationships to ensure positive interactions in the future. Trust and respect are cultivated in a team when there are opportunities to discuss different perspectives and experiences. Simply being faced with the requirement to engage in team work can lead to conflict and tension among professionals and can affect their sense of solidarity and teamwork in a school (Weiss, Cambone, and Wyeth, 1992).

Over time members of a team will begin to use similar conflict management styles to resolve issues. Up to 82% of teams can be expected to adopt similar styles of conflict management (Kuhn and Poole, 2000). Team members can have powerful effects on each other's behaviour, influencing their information levels, their affective states, and even their behaviours (Hackman, 1976). It may be also that similar people are attracted to, selected by, and retained in work settings that require high levels of interaction (Schneider, 1987). This may have some implications for the way that educator teams are formed. Teachers may find it most comfortable and affirming of their values and approaches to have a role in the hiring or assignment of the early childhood educators who are to be part of the JK/SK classroom team—thus creating relatively homogenous behaviours in the educator team from the outset.

Regardless of how the educator team is formed, when conflicts arise, team members will benefit from having some productive conflict-management strategies to help resolve differences. The degree to which each party in the conflict attempts to satisfy his or her concerns or satisfy the concerns of the other party in the conflict will influence the style of conflict management that is used by the parties. Blake and Mouton (1964) identify the following five styles of conflict management:

- integrating
- obliging
- dominating
- avoiding
- compromising

Each of these types of conflict management is explained further in Table 6.1.

Table 6.1 *Styles of Handling Interpersonal Conflict*

Conflict-Management Style	Explanation
Integrating	This is a problem-solving approach whereby the parties show high concern for both self and other; it is oriented toward finding a solution, cooperating, and maintaining positive interactions.
Obliging	This is a less straightforward problem-solving approach whereby one party concedes a position to avoid further tension immediately; it may result in longer-term problems of resentment and distrust.
Dominating	This approach relies on one party asserting their interests and disregarding the interests of the other party. It creates a win–lose relationship among team members.
Avoiding	This approach relies on the tacit agreement of both parties to pretend that no conflict exists. It can lead to a lack of cooperation and can undermine future goal and task interdependence.
Compromising	This approach relies on both parties conceding some aspects of an issue and finding a middle ground they can agree upon, at least temporarily. It may be a form of avoidance of the immediate or underlying issue and in the long run may undermine task and goal interdependence.

It is important for educator team members to understand and have skills in using more cooperative conflict-management approaches, which are more likely to result in positive team and organizational outcomes (Kuhn and Poole, 2000; Tjosvold, 1999; Tjosvold et al., 2005). Competing styles of conflict management, in which the needs of others are not considered, are more likely to produce escalating behaviours and negative results (Korabik, Baril and Watson, 1993). Ultimately, if the educator team members consistently consider the best interests of the children, they are most likely to select cooperating strategies to manage conflict situations. It will be important for educator team members to have time during the instructional day to address and resolve conflict situations.

In learning to handle team conflict, it is valuable to remember that conflict can have an aftermath (Somech, 2008). Team effectiveness is promoted by the use of integrating conflict-management styles. Dominating styles of conflict management may reduce and even hamper team performance because team members who were dominated in the ultimate decision may continue to try to find better solutions, thus prolonging the conflict state. By ensuring that educator teams are aware of how their goals and tasks are interdependent, teams can become more aware of their specific contributions and the importance of these contributions to the team (Morris and Steers, 1980).

6.3 Educator team members need time and goal interdependence to arrive at key decisions by integrating ideas.

Team members can anticipate that they will experience four phases of conflict phenomena when they are faced with various new classroom situations requiring their knowledge, values, and experience to find productive solutions, but may not agree with other team members. The conflict stage is often referred to as *storming* (Zenger, 1994) and is the second stage of the usual evolution of conflicts (see Figure 6.1)

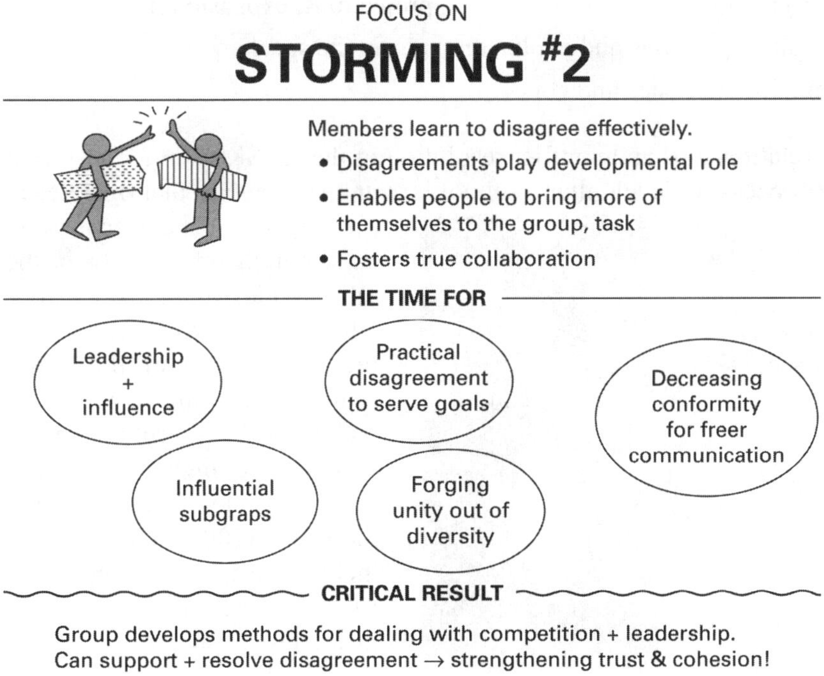

Figure 6.1 *Storming Stage of Conflicts*

Source: Sharon Mulgrew. Reprinted with permission.

Reflection Point

The four stages of conflict evolution (Zenger, 1994) are

- forming,
- storming,
- norming, and
- reforming.

Consider a specific conflict that could take place within a JK/SK educator team. In a small group, discuss the appearance of each of these stages of a conflict as you might expect them to evolve in this professional context.

Active listening strategies can help team members work through conflicts productively and respectfully while maintaining focus on team goals and tasks. Active listening strategies (Ivarie, 1995) include

- acknowledging the speaker,
- paraphrasing,
- reflecting the emotions of the speaker,
- clarifying ideas (through examples, projections, expansions),
- seeking expansions and explanations from the speaker, and
- summarizing issues and concerns.

Positive relationships and conflict resolution in the JK/SK team are also part of the larger process of developing a school learning community that operates at full capacity. The teacher and early childhood educator in the JK/ SK classroom are partners who need to work together in the mini-culture of the classroom community but also within the larger culture of the school community where, according to Mitchell and Sackney (2001), their tasks include "identifying and confronting the problems and mysteries of professional practices." These researchers contend that open communication to build interpersonal capacity allows individuals to "engage collective inquiry" (p. 6, online

6.4 Active listening helps each member of the educator team understand their contribution to the team efforts.

document), which will lead to "shared understandings about the purposes, values, and commitments and to generate new directions for professional practice within the school." These shared understandings must be central parts of forming an educator team that can work together productively. Mitchell and Sackney identify three phases in developing shared understanding (see Figure 6.2).

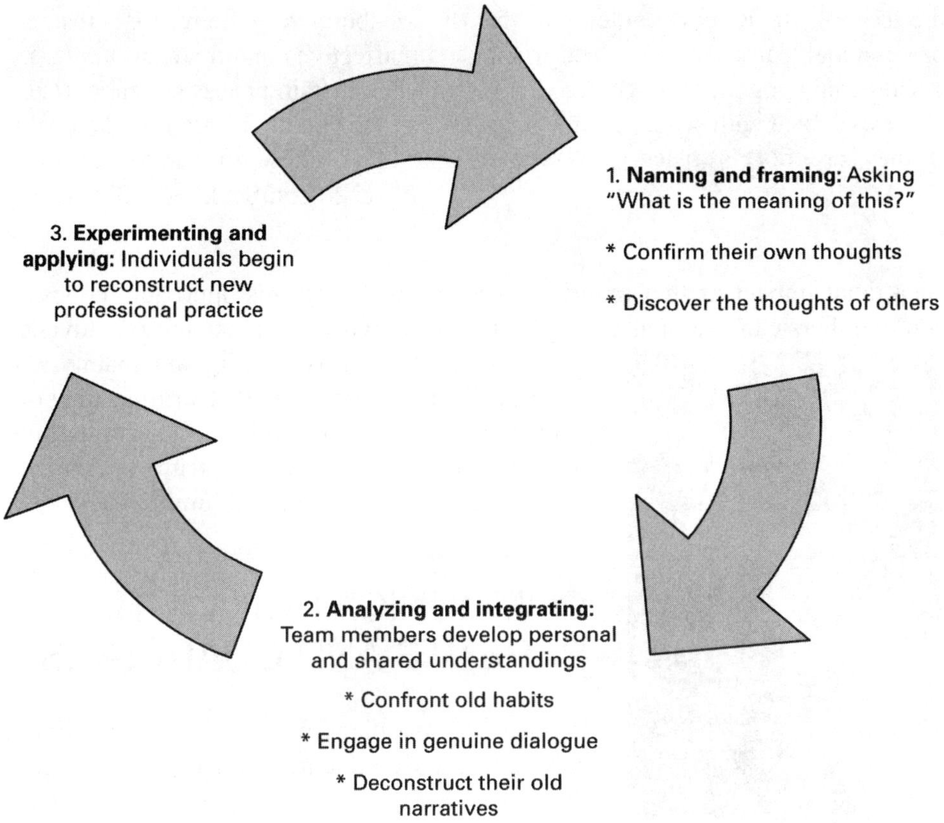

Figure 6.2 *Shared understandings emerge through three recursive phases of team development.*

Used with permission of Nancy Maynes

One advantage of working in an educator team structure in the early learning environment is the ability to sustain learning while collecting data about learning. As one member of the team observes the learning and records observations for later conversations, the other team member can support ongoing learning. The data provided through careful observation will provide information and a solid foundation for reflection about team professional practice and the

Reflection Point

Discuss the following paragraph with colleagues:

"All of this implies that a learning community asks individuals to build the capacity to work well with one another. Interpersonal capacity is as much about how people relate to one another as it is about the dominant normative culture of the school. It is our contention that a collaborative culture that fosters professional learning is enhanced when certain affective conditions are in place, when certain cognitive processes occur, and when certain phases are supported. Our experience with school people suggests that the conditions are foundational; if they are not in place, the processes are less likely to be successful."

~ Mitchell and Sackney, 2001, p. 7

educational impact of that practice on learning. Using this approach, educator team members can use their strengths as a team, working to capacity to advance learning. A team that is working at capacity will commit to the professional learning of both team members and to building and maintaining the relationship between team members (Haskins, Liedtka, and Rosenblum, 1998).

6.5 By using the strengths of each team member, educator teams can maximize learning for children and achieve professional goals for the team.

COMMUNICATION WITH PARENTS AND GUARDIANS

Parents and guardians who have young children enrolled in a JK/SK classroom may be bringing them from a preschool setting into a school for the first time. In the preschool setting, parents and guardians are accustomed to easy access to the adults who have cared for their child all day. At contact points during the day, especially at drop-off and pick-up times, daycare staff may have been available to discuss plans for the day or to discuss progress and learning throughout the day with the other adults in the child's life. Many parents and guardians will expect similar access to educator team members at the beginning and end of the day in JK/SK classrooms. Educator team members will need to consider how they will manage the interest of parents and guardians to have this one-on-one daily contact with the competing demands of their school roles.

Communication will be particularly challenging if one team member is employed on an hourly basis, as is often the case with early childhood educators, while the other team member is employed on a professional contract and determines the length of their day beyond the instructional requirements.

"Involving parents is the bridge that allows educators to better understand children's prior and current experiences."
~ Ontario Ministry of Education, 2010b

Strong communication is essential to building strong relationships with the families of early learners. Communication that is flexible and meets the needs of all adults involved with the child will build trust and respect. The educator team will need to establish two tiers of communication (Bridgemohan, van Wyk, and van Staden, 2005). The first tier is organizationally directed communication, in which the focus is on communicating about the child and related problems. The second tier is communication that is unique and individually directed toward parents, focusing on their problems, issues, and concerns. These parental communications may not always be school related, but they create the context for the child's in-school development and should be a concern for the educator team. Educator team members will need to remember that the needs of young children cannot be seen outside of the context of the needs of their families (Dinnebeil, 1999; Kaiser et al., 1999; Mahoney et al., 1999; Miller, Replogle, and Weiss, 1995; Shores, 1998; Turnbull and Turnbull, 2001). By addressing the communication needs of parents on these two tiers, educator team members demonstrate respect for the roles of families as partners in the child's education.

6.6 *Frequent communication with parents about each child's progress should include input from all members of the educator team.*

Reedy and McGrath (2008) suggest thinking of communication from three perspectives and provide direction about how to overcome the challenges of communication from each perspective (see Table 6.2).

Table 6.2 *Overcoming the Challenges of Communicating with Families to Support Partnering in the Child's Education*

Characteristic of the Communication with Families	Overcoming the Challenges of this Communication
Communication must be ongoing and continuous.	Educator team members must • communicate regularly, • provide multiple opportunities to gain information, and • be able to communicate in ways that are responsive to the parents' or guardians' schedules.
Communication must be open and bi-directional; both educators and parents can initiate any discussion. Honesty must be a characteristic of the communication.	Educator team members must • communicate regularly, • document learning and be able to show examples, and • use active listening.
Support parents through education.	Educator team members must • demonstrate their professional competence, • use outside supports and expertise to assist the team in providing optimal service for every child, and • involve parents and guardians in consultations and workshops about their child's learning.

Strong and effective communication with parents will have several features. These include the following:

- Recognize parents' and guardians' schedules and competing demands on their time: Parents often prefer end-of-the-day communications.
- Communicate as soon as possible: If an issue arises, waiting for scheduled conferences to speak about it can be counterproductive (McGrath, 2003).
- Provide full disclosure, so that parents can understand the scope and impact of the issues: Honest and clear communication should be expected by all partners in the communication.
- Be purposeful in the communication: Educator team members must maintain an unwavering commitment to ensuring that the best interests of the child are the focus of every communication.
- Be available: Plan for accessibility to respond to parents' and guardians' concerns and questions at contact points at the beginning and end of the school day, and ensure unhurried attention to the speaker.
- Use various styles of communication: Understand that no one style of communication will meet every parent's or guardian's needs, so establish several ways to communicate. Understand that multiple opportunities for timely dialogue create greater understanding.

Reflection Point

Discuss ways you would ensure consistent, timely, and respectful communication with JK/SK students' families.

Consider how the communication approach described in the following quotation might work in a local JK/SK context:

"We schedule our workshops and our meetings between the hours of 3 and 7 p.m., which makes it more convenient for parents, because at 6 p.m. they are going home to prepare dinner and we understand that. We set up information in the front office and as parents come in, we grab them for a moment, briefly discuss a topic, give them some handouts, and let them know on their way out if they want to stop they can return and talk more about the topic. We have sessions on nutrition, kindergarten transition, health issues, mental health and other topics. It is kind of a one-on-one. Because it is educational, non-threatening and convenient, parents take the time to stop" (Reedy and McGrath, 2010).

By making communication with parents and guardians clear, timely, useable, and closely linked to improving learning success for the child, educator teams can ensure that parents and guardians will engage in reciprocal communication.

While a daily conversation between parents and the educator team is optimum, a wide range of written materials can also be provided to support regular, timely, and open communication with children's families. These can include:

- a daily message board at the classroom door: The morning message can outline the planned activities for the day; the afternoon message can report on the successes of the day and provide opportunities for announcements and reminders about upcoming events. A board at eye level is most likely to be seen by parents and guardians as they come and go at contact times.
- cubby messages and letters
- newsletters
- web pages
- parent contracts
- parent handbooks
- developmental benchmark information
- curriculum nights (Pajama nights, where children also come and listen to bedtime stories while parents and educators talk, are effective for optimizing participation.)
- questionnaires and surveys (paper copies or online)
- photographs and learning logs, portfolios

- resource libraries, including videos
- home-school journals or agendas
- phone trees

Open communication with parents and guardians can be achieved if the educator team ensures that all efforts to communicate are culturally respectful, accommodate community language diversity, are a regular part of the interaction with parents and guardians, provide full and timely disclosure, and include opportunities for parents and guardians to be involved in the school program. When information is both useful and comprehensible, families will appreciate and read it. Strong communication with families will allow the educator team to know families and to know how they support the child's needs within the family. This knowledge will allow the educator team to plan for either complementing or compensating for family dynamics to provide the best possible support for the child in the JK/SK program.

6.7 Parents prefer end-of-day messages because they are convenient. Message boards outside the classroom allow easy communication about key ideas at natural contact points during the day.

Educator teams must remember that interactions will motivate learning. To ensure that children feel comfortable interacting in the classroom, educator teams will need to negotiate respectful connections with parents and extended families. By engaging families in the planned and strategic communications with the school, educators can create a culture of high expectations and a common vision for student success that is shared by all school community participants.

Joyce Epstein, a researcher at Johns Hopkins University, has identified six levels of parental engagement with schools in a typology introduced in Chapter 4 (see Table 6.3). This typology can be used to assess a school's current level of communication with children's families and to plan for strengthened communication.

Table 6.3 Epstein's Typology of Family Engagement with Schools

Typology Level	Explanation	Samples of How to Do This with JK/SK Families
Parenting	Help all families establish home environments to support children as students.	• Provide parent education and other courses or training for parents (e.g., college credit, family literacy, school-based workshops for parents, such as literacy or numeracy nights). • Provide family support programs to assist families with health, nutrition, and other services. • Create easily accessed school displays and brochures about community support resources. • Establish and advertise school website links to community services and resources. • Make home visits at transition points from preschool.
Communicating	Design effective forms of school-to-home and home-to-school communications about school programs and children's progress.	• Schedule formal conferences with every parent at least once a year. • Use student-led parent-teacher conferencing for reporting students' progress. • Use language translators to assist families as needed. • Schedule useful notices, memos, phone calls, newsletters, and other communications. • Provide portfolio samples of students' work. • Teach parents about assessment criteria and standards. • Plan for an inclusive registration to JK/SK, so that parents have easy access to information in their own language and in formats and environments that respect their cultural backgrounds. • Include daily message boards in many languages to reflect the makeup of the classroom. • Remember that families will also be undergoing their own acculturation and will move through the process of acculturation from first impressions, to culture shock, to recovery and optimism, and finally to acculturation; each family will do this in its own way and at its own rate. • Consider culturally manageable ways to collect background information for each child. • Have strategies for pre-assessing preschool experiences children may have in other cultures.

(Continued)

Table 6.3 Epstein's Typology of Family Engagement with Schools, continued

Typology Level	Explanation	Samples of How to Do This with JK/SK Families
Volunteering	Recruit and organize parent help and support.	• Establish a school and classroom volunteer program to help teachers, administrators, students, and other parents. • Provide financial support to parent volunteers to facilitate acquisition of criminal reference checks as needed. • Provide a parent room or family centre for volunteer work, meetings, and resources for families. • Support access to school facilities for special community events. • Engage parents in an annual postcard survey to identify all available talents, times, and locations of volunteers. • Make early phone calls home to introduce the educator team early in the school year. • Use daily message boards at the classroom door at parent contact times. • Provide babysitting services when parent–teacher conferences are scheduled.
Learning at Home	Provide information and ideas to families about how to help students at home with homework and other curriculum-related activities, decisions, and planning.	• Provide information for families on skills required for students in all subjects at each grade. • Develop and provide information on homework policies and how to monitor and discuss schoolwork at home. • Organize family participation in setting student goals each year. • Provide book bags and rotating classroom mascots as reading buddies to support family reading with the children.
Decision Making	Include parents in school decisions, developing parent leaders and representatives.	• Maintain active parent organizations, advisory councils, or committees for parent leadership and participation. • Establish independent advocacy groups to lobby and work for school reform and improvements. • Create networks to link all families with parent representatives. • Provide a forum for parent-to-parent communications.

(*Continued*)

Table 6.3 Epstein's Typology of Family Engagement with Schools, continued

Typology Level	Explanation	Samples of How to Do This with JK/SK Families
Collaborating with the Community	Identify and integrate resources and services from the community to strengthen school programs, family practices, and student learning and development.	• Provide information for families on community health, cultural, recreational, social support, and other programs or services. • Promote coterminous location of community supports, with the school as the hub of service. • Provide information on community activities that link to learning skills and talents, including summer programs for students. • Organize service to the community by students, families, and schools (e.g., recycling, art, music, drama, and other activities). • Provide a buddy safe-walk system for younger children in the school.

Used with permission of Nancy Maynes

Some jurisdictions across Canada are developing policies to guide the communications undertaken by the school. Educator teams can use such policies as reminders of the range of ways communications can happen and the considerations to which they must be sensitive in designing a communication plan for their JK/SK classroom. Communication should not be accidental; rather, it should be planned carefully to focus the attention of all adults in the child's life on the task of supporting the child's success at school. Both the individual child and the whole school can improve if parents and educators work together toward that end. The cooperation that children witness between their families and the school adults they work with shows children that caring adults are coming together to support them and that all of the adults value their education and are there to support their learning success.

COMMUNICATION WITH YOUNG CHILDREN

Both members of the educator team must have expertise in and understanding of effective communication with young children. In the JK/SK classroom, play-based learning will provide much of the communication structure of the learning. Through positive communication in the classroom, young children will learn to build, maintain, and protect their identity as learners (Toohey and Day, 1998).

When young children are observed trying to learn new words and concepts, it is evident that opportunities to play in the words and with the language are critical to using and understanding new ideas. The small group is often used in supporting early learning because of its many advantages. Small groups in the JK/SK context facilitate children's easy access to the learning of their peers and provide each student with more turns to talk. According to Tooney and Day (1998), young children, even those who seemed competent in regard to the intellectual demands, become more tentative and less confident in teacher-led lesson contexts. These authors conclude that discourse in which one person has some authority over another, whether that person is an educator team member or another child, creates situations that give children no opportunity to play in words and to test concepts. Play-based learning, in contrast, provides opportunities for experimentation with words and contexts, and learners can engage in **interanimation** (open discussions not limited by a position of authority) to explore ideas and make meaning. A play-based approach allows the educator team to become more aware of children's competencies, identify the skills needed by each child to negotiate the school day, and then target the teaching of those competencies through play (Lazarus, 1983).

In the early learning context, there are some specific practices that educator team members can use regularly to support conceptual and linguistic growth in young children. Choral speech, through poems, charts, or practice with series concepts such as number sequences, names of days of the week or months, or reading the morning message chorally, aided by the teacher's verbal modeling, support language growth and participation over time (Tooney and Day, 1998). Such choral practice is often repeated spontaneously and openly by young children as they go about other tasks, providing evidence of their practice of playing in words. Students appear to find the rhythm of choral work pleasurable, and their participation increases their sense of community within the classroom.

6.8 Choral communication supports children's understanding of ideas, classroom culture, language rhythm, and print concepts. Team members can each have a role in choral work.

Similarly, songs and rhymes provide strong invitational contexts for participation among young children. Songs and rhymes give reluctant speakers or English language learners (ELLs) not only words to appropriate and test in other contexts but also safe opportunities to connect with the culture of the classroom and the broader community.

For young learners, oral skills are their first set of literacy skills. Strong oral skills provide the basis for phonological skills and print awareness that also support literacy. Communication with young children needs to be based on supporting growing skills in the three areas of oral communication, phonological awareness, and print awareness (see Figure 6.3).

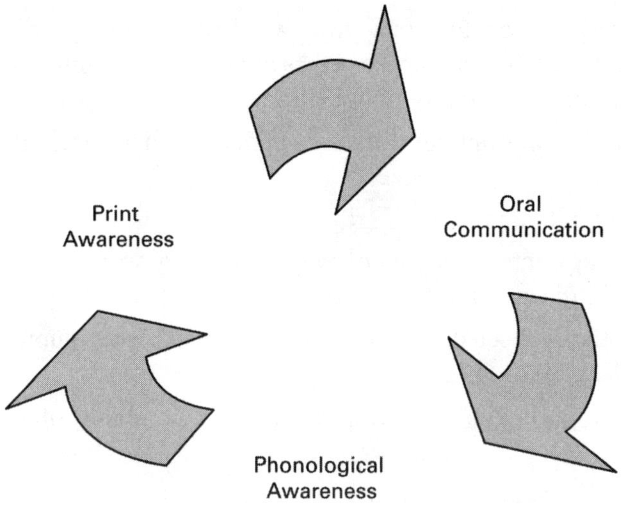

Figure 6.3 *The Three Elements of Literacy Development in Young Children*

Communication in the JK/SK classroom needs to focus on helping young learners to see themselves as capable communicators in the areas of speaking, listening, understanding contexts for messages, understanding print concepts, printing, understanding words, and seeing themselves as emerging readers and writers.

As educator team members develop communications with young learners, it will be important to consider the various forms of literacy. In addition, the early learning framework for the jurisdiction is likely to provide information about other areas of the curriculum that will also be the focus of development for ongoing communication and conceptual acquisition. Frameworks will present specific learning goals around curriculum areas such as exploration and creativity, aesthetic and artistic development, developing a personal sense of well-being and belonging, physical development, emotional and social development, languages and other forms of literacy, intellectual development, understanding of diversity, and social responsibility.

The rules and routines used in the early learning classroom will help to develop young children's sense that the classroom is a special place with special ways of interacting respectfully and inclusively to create a safe and nurturing learning environment. In a play-based environment, there are many routines that can be used to help young children understand expectations and operate with considerable independence even before they are able to read. In such an active learning environment, children will engage with many resources in the classroom. Routines for their use will help to communicate the educator team expectations and preserve learning time. These resource-use routines could include the following:

- organizing materials so that they are physically accessible to all children,
- labelling bins, shelves, and containers with a word or picture symbol and, as practical, labels in other languages representative of the common first language cultures of the classroom population,
- providing material and opportunities for open-ended inquiry that will encourage exploration,
- promoting small group interaction,
- modeling and providing picture models of ways for using some of the key centre resources in the classroom,
- providing resources that reflect the various cultures of the community and the students in the classroom, and
- providing materials and books that respect and teach about other cultures.

6.9 Classroom resources should be organized to help students transition from symbols to print and should support English language learning in communities with language diversity.

Using these routines will also support young children's developing comfort with the classroom environment.

When classroom interactions are designed to motivate learning, the educator team will

- understand each child's unique way of learning;
- show respect for the culture of the child and the family;
- include parent and guardian involvement in the classroom's undertakings by inviting parental expertise and culture into the classroom to enrich the learning;
- nurture relationships between children and supportive adults and nurture positive child-to-child relationships;
- develop a nurturing and rich early learning environment to provide many opportunities for children's growth;

- extend children's learning by responding, challenging, and expanding from their current learning by introducing new concepts, connecting home and school ideas, and making links to new learning opportunities;
- assess learning using a variety of techniques that support assessment *before, for, as*, and *of* learning.

THE ELL KINDERGARTNER

In some areas, and particularly in large urban centres across Canada, many JK/SK classrooms will include learners for whom English is the second, or even third, language. As they enter the early learning environment, these children and their families will need special support to create a family path toward effective interaction with the school. English language learners (ELLs) will also bring a wide and diverse set of experiences, backgrounds, and skills to the classroom. They will have diversity in their strengths and in their educational needs.

English language learners may continue to need support for the development of their first language as they develop understanding of their new home and learning environments. If new academic skills can first be learned in the child's native language, the transfer of the skills to academic use will be facilitated. Literacy processes such as story reading and storytelling can be done in the child's first language to help them develop confidence and learn to take risks with English learning. Families and children should see English as an addition to their native language and should continue to value and use their first language rather than substituting it. Opportunities to use both languages in learning contexts will help children see language as a way to represent meaning and support flexibility in language acquisition. Educators can provide conversation partners for young children, grouping children from the same language background to provide peer support for each other in developing English language skills.

Young children will transition to English language use through some predictable stages, including:

- using their first language,
- going through a silent period when they do not speak in the second language context,
- using a few key phrases or titles for interactions, and
- producing more complex structures and vocabulary in the English language (Tabors, 2004).

As English language learners go through these phases of incorporating the English language into their skills, educators can provide support by affirming attempts to speak in English, providing opportunities for children to explore sounds, **scaffolding** developing strategies (e.g., use all modalities when teaching concepts, provide manipulatives, structure explorations, use pictures and symbols, allow pointing and gesturing as a form of language transition, modeling, repeating, extending, labelling in two languages, and introducing new vocabulary in timely ways).

It will be important for educator team members to remember that each child will transition to competence with a second language in a unique way. Different instructional supports will be needed for each child, and they will mix terms from each language as they develop the rhythm and cadence of English. Music will be an important resource in classrooms with second language learners. The children will often make their initial attempts at speaking a new language through the music they are exposed to in their classroom.

Early English learning strategies and those that may be more effective as English language learners develop more familiarity with English can vary (see Table 6.4).

Table 6.4 *Early and Later Strategies for the English Language Learner (ELL) in a JK/SK Context*

Stage of English Language Acquisition as a Second Language	Strategies for Supporting English Language Acquisition as a Second Language
Early English language acquisition	• use key phrases from both languages • ask simple questions to promote engagement • use music, poetry, rhymes, pictures, and symbols to allow language experimentation • provide a conversation buddy • respond to key English phrases by repeating and expanding • repeat key ideas in simple sentences as work is progressing • model use of text (e.g., to demonstrate page layout in English text)
Later English language acquisition	• use patterns in language • retell in simple oral text • support text with pictures, drawings, and symbols • challenge students to describe and explain their thinking • use familiar routines • give directions simply; check for understanding • provide opportunities for peer-group learning and interaction during learning • expose students to letters, their symbols, and their sounds • provide frequent individual and small group support • engage students in shared reading and print opportunities • provide a letter centre where students can use concrete materials to make letters (e.g., beans, sand, magnets) • provide a listening centre where students can listen to words and stories in their second language • provide "speak and write" software • speak more slowly and carefully to allow English language learners (ELLs) to hear proper enunciation of words • invite parents and other family members to the classroom so that they can also learn key phrases in English

It is important that early learning educators observe often and carefully as children begin to acquire the English language. Through careful observation, opportunities for intervention and extension will become evident. Educator teams can learn about each child's threshold for learning each day to help them avoid the exhaustion and comprehension overload demands of learning a new language. Careful observation will also help educator team members determine what needs may be attributed to language differences and whether any other needs related to learning may be surfacing that will require other forms of support for learning success. The play-based learning environment of the JK/SK classroom will provide interaction and support opportunities for young learners to develop English language skills as they master new concepts. The learning environment of the JK/SK classroom will help students retain respect for their first language and culture, as well as their personal identity, as they negotiate a new community environment.

Just as English language learners may bring different preschool experiences to their early learning in JK/SK, so too may the parents and families bring different backgrounds. Parents will need to have understandable information from the educator team about routines for communication; school closures; the yearly schedule and calendar; the curriculum; play-based learning; clothing requirements for indoors, gym time, and outdoors; and behavioural expectations with adults and other learners.

Parents and families of English language learners should also be encouraged to continue their first language discussions at home with their children about what they are learning at school. Reflecting on learning in the first language will help young children acquire more **conceptual language** and relate ideas so that they can apply these in the English language when they are in school.

Frequent contact with parents and family members may be even more important for English language learners than for other families as they try to navigate the new culture of Canada and support their child's ongoing learning at home. The educator team should model respectful inclusion of the child's culture and family background in the classroom context. This will ensure that the child will feel safe and more able to take learning and social risks in their new learning environment.

CHAPTER SUMMARY

Positive and productive communication is essential within an educator team and among people who interact with the team, including young children, English language learners, parents, and guardians. Educator teams need to be formed carefully to optimize the nature and success of communication and to ensure compatibility. Training educator team members in conflict resolution strategies and the recognition of stages of conflict evolution can help the team work productively through conflicts.

Educator teams should develop sustainable, persistent, timely, and frequent communications with parents and guardians in ways that respect the culture of each child's family. Communications with young children as they engage in learning should be interanimated, with children having control of the majority of conversational leads. The English early learner will need communications that support the child's first language while advancing facility with the language of instruction in the school.

THINKING AHEAD: Opportunities for Professional Reflection

- In this chapter, you learned about five styles of conflict management:
  - integrating
  - obliging
  - dominating
  - avoiding
  - compromising
- The statements below describe various possible responses to conflicts. Sort these statements into the five styles of conflict management listed above:
  - is unconcerned with the team goal
  - physically withdraws from the site of the conflict
  - does not seem to be concerned about addressing and preserving a positive relationship with the other team member
  - uses physical response to try to coerce cooperation
  - changes the subject away from the conflict topic
  - is assertive about ensuring that a personal perspective is heard
  - will discard personal needs in favour of a quick solution to a conflict
  - gives in to the opinion of others very readily
  - uses verbal means to coerce the other team member to adopt their view
  - is strongly committed to the team goal at any cost
  - is not committed to a common goal
  - withdraws engagement in the conflict by being inattentive, not making eye contact, multi-tasking during discussion, etc.
  - shows impatience with the time needed to reach a broadly agreeable solution
  - seems unconcerned about the feelings or views of other team members
  - seems willing to abandon the goal readily and wants the other party to the conflict to abandon it too
  - is deferential to other team member's views and desires
  - is strongly committed to the goal
  - believes finding a solution is paramount to the goal or relationship
  - always wants a win-win situation from conflict

- sees conflict as natural, predictable, and workable
- will put the time and effort into reaching a solution
- can appreciate the perspective of other team members
- uses active listening strategies during conflict
- is aggressive in discussing issues (demeaning, dismissive, unresponsive to others' views, challenging, disrespectful, intimidating)
- is strongly committed to ensuring that a positive team relationship is a priority outcome of the conflict
- puts the team relationships ahead of goals and tasks

- Create a conflict role-playing scenario. Have the audience examine the role-playing scenario by finding examples of the conflict-management styles identified in the list above.

ADDITIONAL READING SUGGESTIONS

To find out more about home-school communication, read

Trehearne, M, et al. 2000. *Kindergarten Teacher's Resource Book.* Scarborough, ON: Nelson Education. p. 409–414.

To find out more about play-based learning, read

Rybczynski, M. and A. Troy. 1995. "Literacy-Enriched Play Centers: Trying them out in 'The Real World'." *Childhood Education* 72 (1): 7–12.

Saracho, O. and B. Spodek. 1995. "Children's Play and Early Childhood Education: Insights from History and Theory." *Journal of Education* 177 (3): 129–148.

To find out more about using print with young children to communicate, read

Hannon, J. 1999. "Talking Back: Kindergarten Dialogue Journals." *The Reading Teacher* 53 (3): 200–203.

To find out more about different cultures and family values, visit

Settlement Workers in Schools at www.settlement.org.

To find out more about ways to differentiate reading instruction for young learners, visit

www.eworkshop.on.ca.

7 The Early Learning Classroom Environment

"A preschool classroom environment must provide welcoming, safe, warm, and stimulating areas to promote the development of the whole child, especially to strengthen, expand and deepen learning."

(Librera et al., 2004)

7.1 *A classroom that is bright and well organized, and has dedicated work areas, will interest and engage students. This classroom is the Early Learning and Kindergarten Teaching room at the Brantford-Laurier Concurrent Education Program, Nipissing Schulich School of Education, Brantford, Ontario (designed by Professor Jennifer Guibert).*

In this chapter, educator team members will learn about

- establishing tone
- cultural integration and respect
- using space wisely
- safety and children's health in a group environment
- equipment storage and maintenance
- washroom spaces
- outdoor spaces
- transitions

At the end of this chapter, educator team members can reflect on their personal growth through

- CHAPTER SUMMARY
- THINKING AHEAD: Opportunities for Professional Reflection
- ADDITIONAL READING SUGGESTIONS

The JK/SK classroom is a purpose-built and purpose-maintained space. It is a learning space where form and function need to be in perfect harmony in order to provide optimal learning conditions for every child. It is a space where the planning and implementation skills of each educator team member must find a way to interrelate harmoniously to provide a positive, safe, and caring learning environment for every child and a welcoming space for every family. JK/SK classrooms that are situated as community service hubs can also provide a meeting place for parents, where they can access services conveniently and in an integrated manner to optimize access.

ESTABLISHING TONE

To establish the type of early learning JK/SK environment that has been described in earlier chapters, educator teams must determine some of the main principles that will be used to design and maintain the classroom space and the outdoor environment. Among these principles, educator teams should consider

- the role of the children in planning the space within the classroom,
- the level of literacy of the children and how that literacy impacts both displays and routines in the classroom,
- planning for social interaction and conversations about learning that are supported by a classroom that promotes talk,
- safety,
- support access, and
- a mixture of active and quiet spaces.

7.2 Classroom rules in a JK/SK classroom should be simple, few, and accompanied by pictures that show main ideas.

Decisions made about each of these issues provide some insight into the values and principles that will guide the tone of instruction in the classroom.

When educators talk about tone in the classroom, they are referring to the **rapport** between the adults and the children in their care. Classroom management practices establish the rapport that is needed. Classroom management includes both *proactive* and *reactive* approaches. Proactive approaches to classroom management include those things that the educators might do before children arrive in the classroom to help ensure that the learning day runs smoothly. Proactive approaches include such things as setting an agenda for the day, planning lessons, providing resources for centres, photocopying, planning observation tasks and roles, determining snack and break details, organizing supervision, and arranging space for various activities. Reactive approaches to classroom management are those that are responses to specific incidents that may disrupt learning. Reactive approaches vary greatly with the age of the students, the type of behaviour, the students' learning needs, the nature of the group, the time of day, the support of parents or guardians, and the best interests of the children.

Many educators have specific reactive classroom management strategies that they use routinely when the need for such management is evident. Generally, these strategies include steps that escalate if the initial step is not effective and form a type of progressive management system.

> **Example:** Two children are working together in the outdoor garden area. They have been asked to pick five ripe tomatoes each from the vines and return them to the classroom in the baskets. One basket is red and one is yellow. One student is upset because the other one was given the red basket that she wanted.

Steps in a progressive reactive management system might include

- Decide whether the behaviour is interfering with the child's learning or the learning of others. If it is not causing interference in the learning, it can be ignored. This is sometimes referred to as *planned ignoring*.
- If the behaviour is interfering with the child's learning or the learning of others in the classroom group, educators must act to change the behaviour to more positive behaviour. With young children, this action can often be a distraction from the issue that is causing the behaviour, a break from a certain type of activity, or a quiet discussion in which the child has an opportunity to voice their concern and explain why they are showing the unacceptable behaviour.
- If the behaviour persists after the educators have acted to change the behaviour, the child needs to understand the acceptable choices that are possible to resolve the situation. The educators can present the choices and the desired outcome and follow this with a clear statement indicating that the educators hope the child will make the best choice. This sequence of actions creates a supportive intervention for the child while also assuring everyone in the class that a certain tone is going to be re-established to promote learning.

  > **Example:** "You can either choose to use this other basket, or you can share this basket. I hope you choose to…"

- If the behaviour still continues after the choices have been given to the child and they have indicated that their choices were understood, the educator must follow through with reasonable consequences. Punishment is not a consequence and is not productive in establishing the learning tone in the classroom that young children will need to feel safe and secure. Consequences should be logical and closely related to the actions that are exhibited. In the educator team context, the team approach may allow educators to spend more time addressing individual behaviour concerns than may be typical in other school contexts. A reasonable consequence for negative behaviours about using a particular basket might include such things as quiet apologies to the other student who was treated badly, making plans for other options the next time baskets are needed, moving to another activity, having the basket removed, or making only one colour of basket available.

7.3 Designated quiet areas in the classroom can allow children to find a rest space as they become fatigued during the day.

When educators work with minor behaviour situations among young children, they need to determine the degree to which fatigue may be a contributor to the behaviour and then take the time to teach young children alternative and more productive ways to manage conflicts. These steps will help to ensure the most positive outcome: the re-establishment of a calm and respectful tone in the classroom. Many potential conflicts in the classroom can be prevented through good planning, so educators should ensure that the routines and procedures they use in their classroom are carefully designed to promote the tone they want.

Some quick management reminders that the educator team can use to structure interaction for the first few days of school will set a positive tone for the classroom and allow for the gradual introduction of curriculum as routines become established. Here are some management reminders:

- Use soft voices indoors and teach children to do this (e.g., "Indoor voices," "table voices," or "30-centimetre voices").
- Use positive statements, and teach children to compliment others.
- Make the classroom feel welcoming and personalized by designing it to be child friendly.
- Provide many early opportunities for success.
- Develop rules and routines that children understand and buy into.
- Promote generosity of spirit in all interactions to maintain a focus on learning and a productive classroom environment.
- Promote social skill development in every lesson, and provide opportunities for children to develop leadership skills.
- Be clear and consistent in your expectations.

Using these management approaches will help children develop a sense of security in the classroom and promote confidence in the leadership of the educator team.

Reflection Point

What materials would you want to include in a quiet rest area of a JK/SK classroom? Why?

CULTURAL INTEGRATION AND RESPECT

When young children are new to a culture, classroom expectations may be confusing to them. Language barriers may cause them to misunderstand or even withdraw, as they try to figure out what is expected of them in this new environment. Even children from the community's culture may experience a period of disorientation in a school environment, where the JK/SK context is very different from their preschool or home learning environments. In such cases, children would benefit from efforts to provide transition planning, so that the integration into the full-day JK/SK classroom goes smoothly. Several ideas for providing integration opportunities for English language learners (ELLs) were provided in Chapter 6.

The organization of and activities in the classroom have a powerful impact on children's ability to integrate into the culture of the classroom and into the opportunities to interact with others as they learn. Educator teams should ensure that several actions have been taken to make their classroom a culturally respectful place to learn. The following list provides some ideas for doing this:

- Make home visits to each family as an educator team prior to school opening.
- Create a learning profile for each student by recording what the parents, the child's first teachers, tell you about their interests, learning styles, and sensory preferences (see Figure 7.1).

Sensory Preferences of Learners

Visual learners learn best through seeing. They prefer to have ideas and concepts demonstrated for them. They like to see how something will work. Charts, pictures, examples, diagrams, and visual displays help the visual learner.

Auditory learners learn best by listening and talking through ideas with others. They enjoy working in a group or with a learning buddy. They may prefer to have information read aloud or to have opportunities to discuss it with others. They may ask many "how to" questions.

Tactile/Kinesthetic learners prefer to be physically active as they learn. They enjoy hands-on activities using concrete materials and the opportunity to move about and engage in physical activity. They may spend a considerable amount of time touching and exploring with objects

Figure 7.1 *Main Sensory Preferences of Learners*

- Provide message boards in the child's native language as well as English.
- Provide a learning buddy from the same culture if possible to help the child learn key phrases in English.
- Show respect for the child's first culture by creating classroom displays that teach about the culture; create activities that will help other children learn about the new culture.
- Use translations of key communications.

Strong educator teams will ensure that every lesson and learning opportunity provided for JK/SK learners includes many options that reflect their sensory preferences. In addition, the development of learning profiles will help educator teams to use strategies for learning that include attention to each child's learning style strengths. Gardiner's multiple intelligences are often used to identify learning styles in school children. Gardiner identifies peoples' intelligences as any combination of the following: linguistic, logical/mathematical, musical, spatial, body/kinesthetic, intrapersonal, interpersonal, spiritualistic, and naturalistic. Many children will show a tendency to demonstrate their learning most effectively if they have opportunities to learn through their most dominant intelligence. Educator teams should note that many children will show strength in more than one type of intelligence. Using a multiple-intelligence approach to understanding children's preferences for learning can enable educator team members to support their learning most effectively, by providing opportunities to learn through dominant styles. If this approach is explained to students, they will quickly learn to think in terms of their strengths for learning.

Educator team members can create a class profile of learning styles (see Figure 7.2) by observing children's approaches to open-ended tasks. How they approach the task will provide clear indications of what learning styles they prefer.

Dominant learning style approaches may relate to the child's background in their first culture. It is important for the educator team to show respect for these culturally based learning styles and to support each child's learning through their preferred style; at the same time, it is important to promote activities that will help the child strengthen other styles of learning.

Educator team members may also find it helpful to understand their own cultural and natural learning style preferences, since these may influence the opportunities they offer to children. Personal learning style inventories are available online at **www.Idpride.net/learningstyles.MI.htm**.

Reflection Point

What is your most dominant learning style? How do you know?

What professional practices would you use to ensure that you are providing children with opportunities to learn through their own learning styles and not only through your styles?

Name	Multiple Intelligences									Sensory Preference
	Linguistic	Logical	Musical	Spatial	Body/Kinesthetic	Intrapersonal	Interpersonal	Naturalist	Spiritualist	Auditory/Visual/ Tactile

Figure 7.2 *A Class Profile of Learning Styles*

USING SPACE WISELY

The physical space in the classroom is the most flexible learning resource available to educators. The physical space should be used carefully to create the rich learning environment that should characterize every JK/SK classroom. Plans for the physical space in the JK/SK classroom should be made with several ideas in mind about the use of the space to promote learning.

The learning space comprises a combination of the indoor and outdoor space and the transitions between the two. This space should be planned to

- ensure opportunities for the children to contribute to the design of the space,
- provide extensive storage,
- provide easy access,
- promote interaction among learners, and
- ensure safety.

Table 7.1 provides ideas for the educator team to consider when planning the JK/SK space to meet these space requirements. By attending to the physical environment, educator teams can create a safe and nurturing place that provides a foundation for an effective play-based curriculum.

Table 7.1 *Considerations for Making Wise Use of the Learning Space*

Planning Requirement	Steps Educator Teams Can Take
Ensure opportunities for the children to contribute to the design of the space	• Provide spaces where children's work can be displayed. • Provide display areas for personal items children bring to share. • Have open and closed storage areas. • Label storage areas with words and pictures; add languages from other represented cultures, if appropriate. • Teach children strategies for maintaining order in the learning space. • Create transition routines (e.g., with music) for the times during the day when cleanup is needed before children move on to other activities or areas. • Provide a personal storage space (e.g., cubby or basket) for each child and demonstrate regularly how this space is to be maintained.
Provide extensive storage	• Store things that children will use regularly at an accessible height. • Have the children work directly with educator team members to retrieve and store learning items, so they know their location. • Use child-friendly storage bins, so they will not be damaged if they are tipped or banged. • Provide lids for storage bins for occasionally used items. This will reduce the need for dusting. • Use designated areas in the classroom for certain types of activities, and keep related supplies close to those areas. • Use low-profile shelving to designate and separate areas of the classroom. • Use colours for storage bins, to indicate access regulations (e.g., green = anyone can use this at any time; yellow = anyone can use this, but must have an educator team member's permission first; red = educator team members only).
Provide easy access	• Be clear among educator team members which storage areas children will have access to and which they will not. • Put frequently used items on low shelves in open bins. • Buy bins that are portable, so they can be moved if they are needed in another area of the classroom. • Teach children what is recyclable and what is disposable. • Provide recycling bins in the classroom, and engage children in sorting into the proper bins.
Promote interaction among learners	• Place work areas that accommodate more than one child (e.g., paint easels) side by side, so they can discuss their work. • Use moveable carpet squares or interlocking rubber mat squares, to allow children to create their own work and conversation areas as needed. • Limit the amount of covered floor space in the classroom, so that there are flexible learning spaces available throughout the day. • Allow children to move lightweight furniture as needed. • Provide tables with larger surfaces for some tasks.
Ensure safety	• Create a line-of-sight layout in the classroom, so the educator team members can always see every child at a glance. • Be aware of fencing as a potential hazard in the outdoors space; place larger pieces of equipment well away from fences. • Ensure that all outdoor equipment meets local safety standards. • Inspect the playground area every day before children arrive (i.e., look for sharp objects, trash, glass, and deterioration of equipment). • Maintain an outdoor play area inspection log. • Never store heavy items in open cupboards above a child's head height. • Avoid the use of glass. • Survey the entire classroom for potential hazards every morning before children arrive. • Clean equipment regularly. • Designate an eating area in the room that is either not used for other purposes or is cleaned thoroughly before and after eating. • Teach bathroom hygiene.

7.4 JK/SK classrooms can be laid out in many ways, if the principles of designing this learning space are considered.

Planning classroom space is a major team consideration before children arrive for the school year. Many of the elements in the classroom space will be stationary because of their size and location. However, other equipment in the classroom may change location, as learning needs require different learning spaces. The sketches (see Figure 7.3) show some options for the layout of classroom space in a JK/SK classroom.

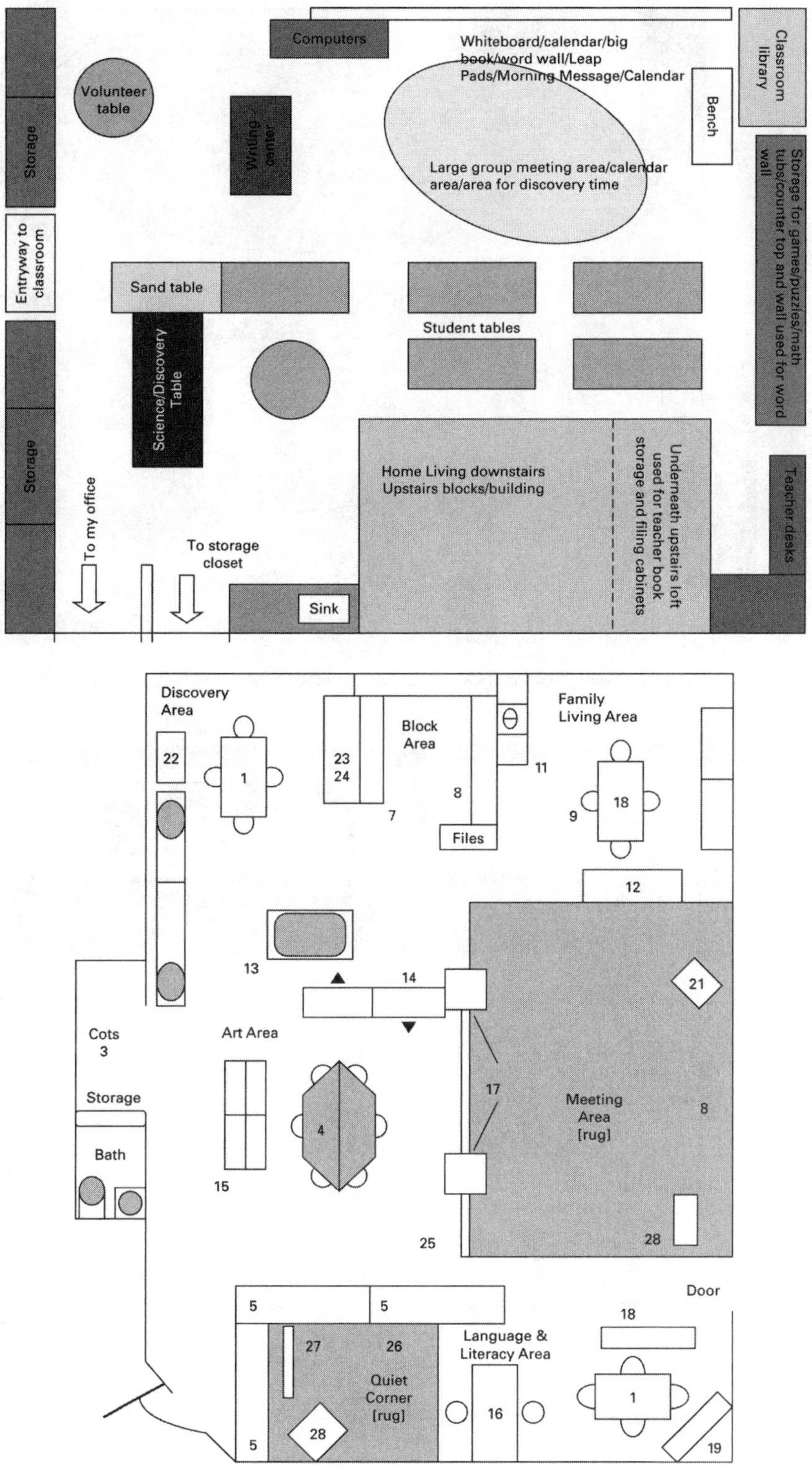

Figure 7.3 *There are many options for the physical layout of space and equipment in a JK/SK classroom. The sketches above show four possibilities. (continued)*

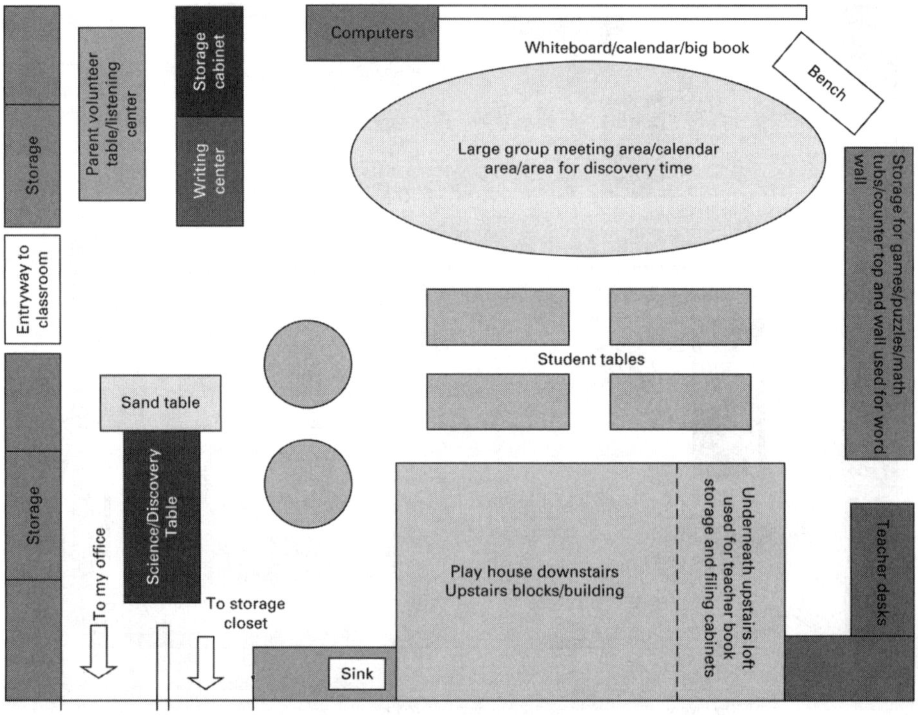

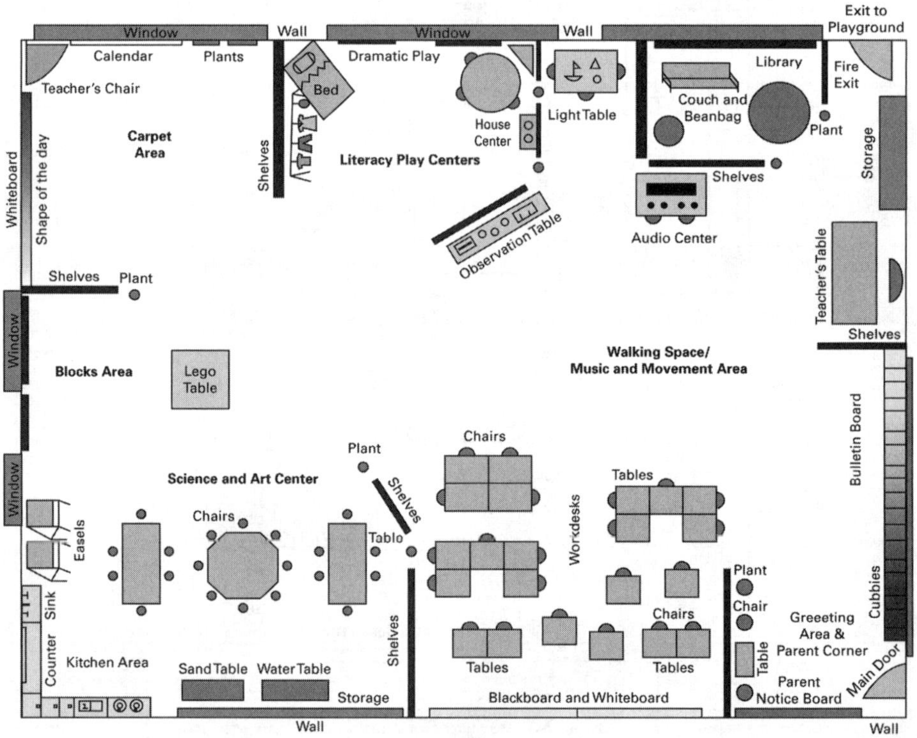

Figure 7.3 *There are many options for the physical layout of space and equipment in a JK/SK classroom. The sketches above show four possibilities.*

Reflection Point

In a small group, plan the ideal layout for a JK/SK classroom from your perspective. Include features that would allow easy use of the room for extended day programs if they were offered in your school. After your plan is complete, compare your thinking about organizational issues (e.g., safety, traffic flow, ease of access, etc.) to the samples provided in Figure 7.3.

SAFETY AND CHILDREN'S HEALTH IN A GROUP ENVIRONMENT

Most school environments have institutional health and safety inspection teams. In many jurisdictions, these teams report directly to the building administration and may also file reports for the local school boards or authorities. Educator team members may have opportunities to serve on these teams. This is a good way to become aware of health and safety standards.

Educator team members' training in relation to health and safety issues in the classroom may vary. Regulated daycare facilities have strict guidelines, and early childhood educators may bring different guideline backgrounds to the classroom. It is important that part of the educator team's early planning include a discussion of both standards and the duties of each member of the team in relation to health and safety in the classroom.

Liability for inattention to unsafe conditions is an issue that requires careful attention by educators. A person is liable if they fail to meet standards that might normally be expected by a reasonable person operating in similar circumstances. Educators have a **duty of care**. They also must meet the **standards of care** expected in their local context. Both duty and standards of care should be defined in the employment conditions of each educator team member and should be part of the team building process, so that members of the team can support each other in meeting their duty and standards of care. Both of these may be defined in provincial or territorial legislation for each profession and should be well known to team members.

7.5 Safety is a prime consideration in the design of a JK/SK kindergarten. The perspectives of many people should be considered.

Fire regulations govern the layout of classrooms. These regulations will affect the use of floor space, egress areas, some types of materials allowed in the classroom, displays on fire doors, and the percentage of materials that may be posted on classroom walls. Fire regulations typically do not allow any materials to be hung from classroom light fixtures or to be attached to the classroom ceiling. These regulations need to be known to educator team members and must be followed explicitly when establishing the classroom layout. Local fire personnel are generally available on request to visit classrooms and examine the area for potential hazards or infractions.

EQUIPMENT STORAGE AND MAINTENANCE

The educator team will need to determine the best matches in equipment and storage for the children who will use the classroom and outdoor space. A rich learning environment in JK/SK will have several classroom learning centres. Centres may be established for many purposes and may be either rotating or permanent centres in the classroom. The nature and location of centres will have an effect on the storage of equipment that may be needed for some aspect of each centre. When considering storage and maintenance of equipment, educator team members will need to consider the time requirements for setup of a learning centre, the safety issues related to access of some equipment, and the flow of people around centres as children work on activities.

The rich learning environment in the classroom can be supported by ensuring that the classroom area has several characteristics, including the following:

- The learning centres in the classroom are designed to promote curiosity, creativity, and exploration.
- Activities allow for curriculum integration.
- Activities are designed to foster inquiry.
- Materials are easily accessible; they are within reading level, within reach, encourage independence, and welcome use.
- Activities are established in different play areas to encourage children to learn to make choices, mingle with other learners, and pursue their personal interests with engaging tasks.
- Activities and areas of the classroom are colourful, inviting, and encourage active participation.
- All types of play (see Chapter 3) are encouraged throughout the day, both indoors and outdoors.

Reflection Point

In a small group, design a centre for an activity of your choice. Identify it as a permanent or a rotating centre. In your design, show or explain how you have planned storage and maintenance of equipment needed in the centre.

Some equipment that will be used in the classroom will need regular cleaning or washing. The potential for the spread of communicable diseases such as cold and flu viruses, and pests such as head lice, will require that educators plan for the careful use and regular maintenance of equipment that is used by children. Diseases may spread very quickly among young children, because germs generally spread more quickly in group settings, especially where children make frequent physical contact with their young friends many times throughout the school day. Young children have not yet developed their own natural resistance to many germs. As well, many communicable diseases are contagious for a long period of time before symptoms appear, a fact which complicates efforts to prevent their spread.

Diseases in the classroom space can be spread through many sources of contact, such as saliva, mucus, stool, body discharges, and blood. To prevent infection from these sources, educator teams will need to develop a rigorous plan to prevent infections and teach about germ control. Young children should be taught to

- avoid sharing drinking glasses and food utensils;
- use tissues for sneezes;
- cough into their sleeves;
- wash their hands thoroughly and regularly throughout the day (e.g., after using the washroom, before eating, after sharing toys, after coming in from outside); and
- avoid touching open sores or having contact with sores or blood from another person.

In terms of disease control and equipment maintenance and to promote safety in the classroom, educator team members will need to set up a schedule and identify responsibilities for checking the cleanliness and condition of equipment regularly (see Figure 7.4). Many accidents can be avoided if equipment is stored and maintained properly.

Reflection Point

During a grounds check on Monday morning the teacher noted on the day's equipment log that there were several burn marks through the edges of the plastic slide on the playground equipment. In a small group discuss:

a) Are these holes an immediate safety concern for young children?

b) What should the educator team do to address this damage?

Inclusive classroom resources need to be managed faithfully to ensure that they are available when needed. They can be made readily accessible to children as their independence increases by ensuring that they are labelled, stored within reach of children, easily returned to the correct spot after use, durable, easily cleaned, and can be represented to children through both symbols and translations as needed.

Date: ______________________ Checked by: ___________________________

Outdoor Area

Equipment Condition	Equipment Location	Grounds Check for Trash	Grounds Check for Sharp Objects	Grounds Check for Glass

Classroom Learning Areas

Area	Inspection Notes	Action Needed	Action Completed On
Music/listening centre			
Gathering/carpet area			
Bulletin boards			
Tables			
Book shelves			
Chart paper stand			
Computer centre			
Drama/home/community store area			
Sand/water table			
Building centre			
Food area			
Math centre			
Measurement centre			
Painting centre			
Art centre			
Working with words centre			
Writing centre			
Coat/boot/shoe storage area			
Other: Outdoor equipment bins			
Other:			

Figure 7.4 *Sample Schedule for Checking the Cleanliness and Maintenance of Equipment*

WASHROOM SPACES

Purpose-built JK/SK classrooms will have child-accessible washrooms and may even have spaces for laundry. These spaces should be checked regularly throughout the school day and each morning before the children arrive to ensure that they are ready for use throughout the day.

It will be important to make certain that children are taught a system for letting adults know that they are going into the washroom area, so that their time out of the line of sight of an adult is monitored. If the washroom is outside of the actual classroom, many educators will want to establish a buddy system for using the washroom, so that children are never leaving the classroom alone.

Requests for washroom maintenance throughout the school day can be made of caretaking staff to match the rhythm of the classroom program. These areas can be cleaned while young children are in the yard area or in a gathering place in the classroom for whole-group instruction.

It is important to remember that young children are very curious. Cleaning fluids and powders should never be stored in these washroom areas and should be safely out of the reach of children.

7.6 *Young children can be reminded of washroom routines by the inclusion of signs and pictures at accessible levels and in strategic locations.*

OUTDOOR SPACES

The design and use of outdoor space is critical for young children's play-based kindergarten programs. Many schools have outdoor equipment dedicated to use by the youngest members of the school population. Some schools have dedicated play areas for the JK/SK classes, and others have separate times of the day for JK/SK students to play in the yard when older students are not using the facilities. Many schools introduce specially supervised common school recess times to SK children in May or June to acclimatize them to a busy school yard.

When the school has the option to design a dedicated outdoor space specifically for the JK/SK students, many design criteria need to be considered for the space. It should also be noted that children's choice of equipment for outdoor play typically differs along gender lines (Kuo, 2009). Outdoor play equipment may serve one of three play purposes (Chen, 1990):

- creative play (e.g., assembling activities with sand, wood, clay, water)
- challenging play (e.g., motion equipment such as slides, swings, and tilting equipment such as seesaws)
- social play (e.g., equipment that requires social interaction or that might be constrained in play by usual use, such as with cooking utensils, clothes, dolls, or models)

Typically, outdoor fixed play equipment consists of many attached and transitional pieces, forming a maze of elements that children can engage and move among fluidly (see Table 7.2).

Table 7.2 *Elements in Typical Outdoor Fixed Play Equipment for Young Children*

Element	Developmental Needs Addressed by this Play Element	Creative Play	Challenging Play	Social Play
slides	play enjoyment; satisfaction	☆		
climbing shelves and apparatus	muscle development; sense of height; goal setting; achieving goals		☆	
swings	motor control; balance; hand-eye coordination; muscle development; confidence building		☆	
boat shapes (with motion)	improving sense of rhythm and sense of balance		☆	
bridges (with motion)	improving sense of rhythm and sense of balance		☆	
tilts (chair-shaped or hanging)	promoting balance; developing sense of height		☆	
rotating chair (chair-shaped, stand-on, or hanging)	promoting sense of balance; developing arm strength		☆	
platforms	developing planning skills; developing social interaction skills		☆	☆
slides	play enjoyment; satisfaction	☆		

Researchers recommend that, in the process of selecting fixed outdoor play equipment for young children, several design principles be considered to ensure that health and safety, as well as children's engagement in the equipment, are investigated before equipment is installed (Lu, 2006):

- health considerations: ventilation and temperature, shade
- safety considerations: design and maintenance
- meeting developmental needs: physical ability, gender, current muscle development
- interest levels: ability to stimulate interest, attractiveness
- economic limitations: meeting developmental needs that cannot be met with other kindergarten materials
- multiple functions: for economic, practical, and spatial considerations

- pleasing to the eye: motivating to children, so they want to use it
- convenient: allowing for adaptation over time and place, flexible uses

7.7 Outdoor play equipment should be carefully designed to promote creative, challenging, and social play.

Most jurisdictions will also have standards for outdoor equipment design, installation, and maintenance. Educator teams should work with local experts in playground equipment and consult local school jurisdiction policies before installing outdoor equipment for JK/SK classes. With thorough planning, educator teams can ensure that outdoor play equipment has multiple functions, is stimulating for children, promotes interest and curiosity, develops physical skills, promotes social interaction and cooperation, and challenges problem-solving abilities.

Portable outdoor equipment can also provide many opportunities for creative, challenging, and social play. Sand, water, and adapted construction elements such as cardboard boxes, can provide many opportunities for engaging inquiry in the school yard.

Regardless of whether play equipment in the school yard is stationary or portable, it should include elements that promote play-based learning; it should be safe and well designed, easily accessible, practical to the needs of young children, adaptable to the range of ages and skills of the children, low maintenance, bright and colourful, variable and flexible in use, and fun (Kuo, 2009).

TRANSITIONS

Transitions during the school day in any classroom require careful planning. This is particularly true in classrooms for very young children. Transitions

7.8 Transition times can be planned to become community-building aspects of the JK/SK day. Music sets the pace and tone for transitions.

occur whenever one learning activity must be stopped to engage in another type of activity, for instance, when it is time to begin group work, move to activity centres, have snacks or meals, change from indoors to outdoors, or when visitors come to the classroom. Carefully designed transitions will maintain a focus on preserving learning time while simultaneously teaching students to be self-reliant, responsible, responsive, and thoughtful toward others.

Many teachers find that well-planned transitions do not need to stop the learning; instead, they can foster further social learning because they use procedures for that purpose. For example, many teachers of young children introduce transitions with a rhyme and use the transition time to interweave music and stretching with cleanup activities and movement to another location. There are many types of rhymes and many strategies that can initiate a transition. Educator team members may find it helpful to have several rhymes that they use interchangeably for this purpose, so that children are always challenged to consider what is being required of them. An example of a transition rhyme that requires a choral response from students is:

Adult says:	"One, two, three, Look at me."
Children say:	"One, two, Looking at you."

Once new directions are given, the adult starts a music selection from a recording, and the children and adults sing along or complete required actions as they clean up and move to the new spot in the room. The volume and pace of the music should be chosen very deliberately; it should set the tone for the transition and perhaps be changed at the end to soothing and soft music, to help children start the new activity attentively.

By managing transitions through this type of strategy, educators can ensure that the positive tone of the classroom is maintained, since the transition is being accomplished in the least intrusive way and learning time is preserved.

CHAPTER SUMMARY

The way that educators plan interactions with children in the classroom influences the tone of the classroom. Effective rules and routines ensure that the JK/SK classroom remains positive, productive, and focused on supporting young learners. Educators should develop practices that focus on respect. Knowing each child's culture, learning style, and preferences can help educators to plan for a respectful learning environment. Class profiles can be maintained to monitor changes in children's strengths, interests, and areas for growth.

The JK/SK classroom space should be purposefully designed to optimize safety, ensure easy access to equipment, provide space for dynamic learning centres, and allow for the inclusion of creative, challenging, and social play in the program. Transitions during the JK/SK day should be managed to preserve learning time and minimize disruptions to the flow of the day.

THINKING AHEAD: Opportunities for Professional Reflection

- Examine and listen to many examples of the commercially available transition music for classroom use. Consider ways you might use or adapt these music sets for your classroom. Create a resource booklet of transition rhymes that educators may use in the classroom.
- Participate in a classroom inspection led by the school's Health and Safety Committee to become more aware of the range of criteria they consider when looking for health and safety issues in public buildings.
- Take a focused look at the outdoor equipment available at your school. Consider what likely safety issues the equipment might present for the JK/SK children in the school.
- Examine the website **www.metapatterns.wikidot.com/members:jeffbloom** to find out more about The Innovative Kids Project. Consider how you might use such project ideas in the JK/SK context.
- A revised version of the Comparative Family Policy Database is now available and covers the period 1960 to 2008. It was assembled under the direction of Anne H. Gauthier. It is the most comprehensive data collection on historical trends in family policies in developed welfare states, making it highly valuable for comparative studies on the development and effects of family policies. Examine this data online at: **www.demogr.mpg.de/cgi-bin/databases/FamPolDB/index.plx**.

ADDITIONAL READING SUGGESTIONS

A designated reading and quiet area should be part of the JK/SK classroom space. Shelves and book bins should be close to the ground, easily accessible, and easily maintained. This library should include picture books, rhyme books, electronic books, magazines on children's topics, big books, and books that can be read to children by adults. Some of these books may become **touchstone books** that have several messages about values and social behaviour to teach young children (for a list of these, see Chapter 4). These books may be read over and over during the course of the year and will provide the context for students to engage in discussions about how they relate to each other, other adults, and the environment around them.

Many of the books that are to be part of the learning in the JK/SK classroom will need to be acquired or renewed over time. These are some of the excellent books available for this age group of students:

- *A Rookie Reader, Cowboy Up* (Sharon Gordon) — This book shows students how to solve problems and work out concepts on their own.
- *The Legend Of Lightning Larry* (Aaron Shepard) — This is a humorous story about a cowboy who shoots lightning bolts of kindness into the hearts of outlaws.
- *Armadillo Rodeo* (Jan Brett) — Bo, an adventurous armadillo, thinks he has found a new friend in a red armadillo. He finds out that his new best friend is really a shiny cowboy boot.
- *The Three Little Javelinas* (Susan Lowel) — This book is a fractured fairy tale story based on "The Three Little Pigs."
- *The Three Pigs/Los Tres Cerdos Nacho, Tito and Miguel* (Bobbi Salinas) — This is a very creative story based on "The Three Little Pigs."
- *Cyrano The Bear* (Nicole Rubel) — This story is about a sheriff who is very brave, except when it comes to the affections of the lovely Roxanne.
- *A Campfire For Cowboy Billy* (Wendy K. Ulmer) — This story is about a little boy who pretends that the big city he lives in is really the Old West.
- *How I Spent My Summer Vacation* (Mark Teague) — This story is about a young boy who shares his incredible summer adventures with his teacher and his classmates.
- *Once There Was A Bull…frog* (Rick Walton) — This story is about a bullfrog that has lost its hop.
- *Jack and the Giant: A Story Full of Beans* (Jim Harris) — This fairy tale takes a twisted spin on the well-known story, "Jack and the Beanstalk" told through words and illustrations.
- *Drawing With Children* (Mona Brookes) — The book shows teachers how to draw using the five elements of shape.
- *Pumpkins, Pumpkins Everywhere* (Tara Bardeen) — This resource shows teachers many ways to use pumpkins in their teaching across subject areas.

Educator teams may wish to organize classroom books by theme (e.g., interpersonal awareness) as was done with the list provided above. Using pictures and symbols to help young children recognize themes in books makes it easier for them to navigate the classroom library. Children should also be taught to respect and care for the books they use, because they are a shared resource. Modeling the care and storage of books will help them acquire the habits and attitudes needed to make books a valued part of their daily learning. An extensive list of books suitable for a JK/SK classroom library is provided in the Instructor's Manual that accompanies this course text.

To find music that can be used in teaching young children and to manage classroom transition times visit the site "Songs for Teaching: Using Music to Promote Learning" at **www.songsforteaching.com/drjean/tidyup.htm**.

8 Early Learning: The Kindergarten Curriculum across Canada

"Young children begin their personal and social development by learning about themselves, about themselves in relationship to others, and about themselves in relationship to the world. Social, personal, and emotional growth and learning develop through interactions, and are interconnected with other areas of development, such as cognitive and motor skills."

(Ontario Ministry of Education, 2010a)

8.1 *Children learn academic skills as they develop social skills and personal strengths.*

In this chapter, educator team members will learn about

- curriculum strands
- planned and seamless integration
- planning templates
- learning and activity centres
- educator team member roles in the curriculum planning and implementation of curriculum
- developing effective classroom learning centres

At the end of this chapter, educator team members can reflect on their personal growth through

- CHAPTER SUMMARY
- THINKING AHEAD: Opportunities for Professional Reflection
- ADDITIONAL READING SUGGESTIONS

When educator teams approach the task of developing a curriculum for their JK/SK classroom, they have many decisions to make. They must decide what they will teach, how they will teach it, and how they will assess what students are learning as they teach. They must decide what resources are needed, how these resources will be made accessible to the children, how resources will be replenished and maintained, and how parents and guardians will know about the curriculum and the ways they can support it. All of these decisions must be made within the framework of guidelines that govern the nature and content of the curriculum for local schools. In Canada, these guidelines are developed at the provincial or territorial level and may provide some latitude for local topics of study within a broader framework.

CURRICULUM STRANDS

It is important for educator teams to understand the various elements that are part of local curriculum guidelines, so that they can be successful in implementing the type of learning experiences that are envisioned by the guidelines and understand the extent of the latitude they may have in adapting the guidelines to local contexts. Guidelines in education typically have the status of a legal document, and educators are held accountable for ensuring that the spirit and specifics of guidelines are implemented as expected. School administrators are responsible for ensuring that guidelines are implemented in the schools as expected by the local educational authorities and that the integrity of the approach as outlined within guidelines is respected in the implementation process.

Curriculum guidelines in all jurisdictions are reviewed regularly to ensure that they continue to be responsive to the needs of learners, the needs of society, the mandate of the schools, and recent research and practices in education. Guidelines are regularly examined by a process that includes *review* of the guideline in evolving contexts, *development* of new and more progressive content and sometimes strategies or philosophies, and renewed phases of *implementation* if significant changes result in a revised guideline. This three-phase process is often referred to as the CRDI cycle: **c**urriculum **r**eview, **d**evelopment and **i**mplementation (see Figure 8.1). CRDI cycles may be addressed on a regular schedule, such as five years, whereby one year is spent gathering data to review the existing guideline, one year is spent writing the new guideline, and three years are spent addressing full implementation of a guideline. The length of a CRDI cycle is locally mandated; it may vary across jurisdictions and for individual guidelines, with guidelines that are radically different in approach taking longer to develop and implement. Local jurisdictions usually support the development process by seconding experienced educators to contribute to the writing of new guidelines. Provincial or territorial authorities may also provide in-service professional development for educators within a local context, so that much of the in-service can take place during the working day.

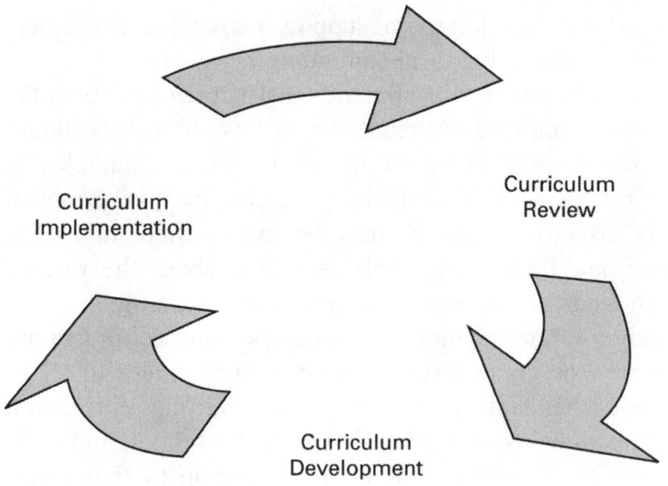

Figure 8.1 *The CRDI Cycle*

Guidelines may include preambles that address the many local considerations that educators are asked to examine when using these documents to plan the details of classroom experiences. Provincial or territorial guidelines may include introductory comments to position the specific guideline in the context of the overarching approach to teaching and learning that is promoted in education within a jurisdiction. Such an introduction may include a vision of the learner who is to benefit from this guideline and may provide some insights into why this approach is preferred. Envisioning the learner is often the first development activity undertaken when a new guideline is being written. Developers may identify all of the learning outcomes they envision for students and then base the development of the remainder of the guideline on this vision of the learner. As educator team members examine guidelines that guide their programs, they should ensure that they have a clear understanding of the vision the guideline is designed to achieve. Visions of the learner are often embedded in a guideline's preamble and may require some skill in interpretation to ensure a common understanding among members of the educator team.

Reflection Point

In a small group, consider the question, "What skills and attributes should a child have acquired after two years in a JK/SK program?"

The answers to this question form the vision of the learner that should be used to design the JK/SK program.

Introductions within guidelines may also include directives to all of the adults who have some responsibility for ensuring that the spirit and specifics of a guideline are properly understood. They may include consideration of the roles of teachers, early childhood educators, classroom support personnel, principals, parents and guardians, and members of the local community.

It is also typical of guideline introductions that they instruct readers about the overall structure of the guideline and provide examples of how educators should interpret the structure of and specific terms within the guideline. Examples of assessment and evaluation methods for a particular guideline may be provided and the role of a uniquely effective approach may be exemplified. In JK/SK guidelines, educator teams may find considerable guidance about the role of observation as an assessment and evaluation approach for early learning.

Educators may also find direction in guidelines about the approaches that are favoured within a subject area or grade level. Current guidelines are likely to provide direction about approaches suitable for play-based learning, curriculum integration, curriculum connections to activities outside of the school, and literacy and numeracy goals within the program. It is also common to find topics such as the use of educational technology, support for English language learners (ELLs), classroom design and resource advice, and strategies for supporting children with special needs. Additionally, health and safety considerations related to implementation may be addressed, and local issues such as culturally responsive teaching and cross-cultural communication may be included.

It is important that educator team members have a full understanding of these introductory aspects of local guidelines, because they will provide both context and tone for classroom-based implementation. Many guideline introductions also provide support by identifying other resource materials that educators should access and understand before they begin the task of planning for learning in their classroom.

Reflection Point

Make a list of all of the resources that you think should be available in a JK/SK classroom. Compare your list with those of other course participants and generate a master list to share among you. Now, examine photographs of JK/SK classrooms and revise your resource list based on your observations.

Some local jurisdictions may also provide a graphic metaphor (e.g., a tree, a building, an apple) to represent the structure of the program described within their local guideline. Such metaphors are usually intended to educate users about the foundations and underlying assumptions of the guideline, its embedded principles to inform approaches, and the various strands addressed for specific types of learning within the auspices of the guideline.

Finally, many locally developed curriculum guidelines provide specific overall direction about how children of this age level might be expected to approach learning opportunities. These examples reflect and exemplify the principles and mandates described throughout the curriculum document and are intended to support educators by expanding understanding of the tone and direction of the

8.2 *A wide variety of resources is needed in the JK/SK classroom to support a variety of learning approaches.*

document. Table 8.1 provides an example of such references and shows how guidelines may include examples to support the professional understanding of the educator team.

In this table, the JK/SK strands of curriculum may include different wording than that used in some locations, but virtually all kindergarten guidelines provide direction for growth strands related to a child's physical growth, health and well-being, sense of belonging, social skill development, knowledge acquisition strategies (including eagerness to learn, exploration, and inquiry skills, and creativity), emotional growth and development (including independence), multiple literacy growth (including literacy with first and second languages, numerical concepts, media and technological literacy), social literacy skills (including respect for diversity, consideration, cooperation, and appreciation of cultural differences, social justice values, social responsibility), and general knowledge expansion.

Guideline strands reflect our current understand of how young children develop, learn, seek support, and grow. They typically reflect our understanding of young learners from the perspective of developmental psychology, cognitive psychology, and constructivist beliefs and practices (see Chapter 3). These strands may be provided in a holistic way to show the interconnectedness of the child's growth and development regardless of the traditional school subject area that may be addressed.

Table 8.1 Planning Responsive Play-Based Programs for Four- and Five-Year-Olds

Program Curriculum Strand	Characteristics of Early Learners	Instructional Actions to Support Growth in This Area
Physical growth	• Need and enjoy activity • Need opportunities for both large and small muscle development • Need opportunities to develop hand–eye coordination • Vision is still developing (acuity)	• Provide active learning opportunities. • Offer a combination of inside and outside play throughout the day. • Provide frequent changes of activity as learning is engaged. • Provide open spaces in the classroom. • Offer a combination of structured and unstructured play throughout the day. • Provide many opportunities to work with large and small equipment during play and **work play**. • Provide matching opportunities that strengthen visual acuity and hand–eye coordination.
Health and well-being	• Need nutritious foods • Need small snacks throughout the day • Need to be taught the difference between healthy and unhealthy food choices • May have allergies and strong food preferences • Some foods may have cultural significance	• Provide open opportunities for snacks as needed. • Provide access to nutritious snacks. • Provide instruction about "daily foods," "sometimes foods," and "never foods." • Use cultural events and food options to support knowledge and respect for other cultures. • Offer a choice of snacks that are healthy, but allow children to choose among preferences.
Sense of belonging	• Need routines and predictable schedules • Need a sense of safety in their immediate environment	• Establish the daily routine of outlining the schedule for the day. • Use reassurances and repetition to support growing independence. • Implement a buddy system for new experiences.
Social skill development	• Need to use talk to help them make sense of experiences • Need a variety of group interaction experiences and open opportunities to engage in different types of play (see Chapter 3)	• Be consistent in expectations. • Strongly model respectful interactions. • Offer many group tasks. • Encourage interchangeable group memberships. • Provide many play and work play opportunities throughout the day. • Create an invitational environment.
Knowledge acquisition strategies (including eagerness to learn, exploration, inquiry skills, and creativity)	• Need to play • Need to understand free play and work play parameters • Need to revisit new skills in many new learning contexts before they become internalized • Need to have many opportunities to learn by doing • Need options to learn through different modalities that respond to their learning styles	• Maintain well-developed learning profiles for each child. • Advance learning through educator team members who are well trained in the use of **pedagogical narrative** techniques. • Provide active learning environments. • Provide activity centres. • Offer choices. • Provide a bright, well-maintained, and stimulating learning environment.

(Continued)

Table 8.1 *Planning Responsive Play-Based Programs for Four- and Five-Year-Olds, continued*

Program Curriculum Strand	Characteristics of Early Learners	Instructional Actions to Support Growth in This Area
Emotional growth and development (including independence)	• Need to feel safe to take risks • Need to feel a sense of ownership of the learning environment • Are supported when they understand reasons • Need cultural validation • Need to develop their vocabulary to express feelings, needs, and wants • Need modeling of social problem-solving approaches • Need friends and a sense of acceptance within groups	• Maintain a readiness approach to new tasks. • Provide instruction for students in how to clean up after tasks, so they become invested in the classroom space. • Give advance warning about significant changes in the learning environment. • Discuss events of influence. • Provide instruction in ways to generate and consider options in complex situations. • Teach group work skills. • Model cultural acceptance frequently.
Multiple literacy growth (including literacy with first and second languages, numerical concepts, media, and technological literacy)	• Growth may not proceed in a straightforward and predictable way • Need to develop print concepts and number recognition and correspondence	• Provide repetition. • Maintain a well-stocked classroom library. • Have **touchstone books** that are read repeatedly and address the values and behaviours that are desirable in the group. • Maintain a print-rich classroom. • Promote access to age-appropriate computer software. • Use media for instruction as appropriate.
Social literacy skills (including respect for diversity, consideration, cooperation, and appreciation of cultural differences, social justice values, and social responsibility)	• Need rules and routines • Need predictable schedules • Need to see and hear how respect and acceptance look and sound in group contexts • Need to understand fairness • Need opportunities to hear about, talk about, and experience empathy for others • Need to begin to develop an understanding of social norms and expectations • Need to learn social **self-regulation** skills • Need to be able to express ideas in acceptable ways	• Engage children in establishing a few key rules for their classroom. • Post the daily schedule in picture form and in representative languages. • Recognize and reinforce the use of respectful interactions. • Discuss events that are potential sites of learning. • Teach social skills; practise them. • Use role playing frequently. • Debrief social conflict situations to identify options that might have reduced conflict. • Maintain a positive tone in the classroom. • Preserve learning time.
General knowledge expansion	• Need to learn cognitive self-regulation (metacognition) skills	• Review learning frequently. • Engage students in discussions about what they learned frequently throughout the day. • Use and promote the development of metacognitive language (i.e., "Today I learned…"). • Post samples of children's work in the classroom. • Look for ordinary learning moments that may be sites for expanding learning by saying, doing, representing, responding, challenging, or extending.

8.3 A wide variety of resources is needed in the JK/SK classroom to support a variety of learning approaches.

In other areas and jurisdictions, program strands may be more aligned with traditional subject areas, and they may reflect learning skills and development as well as knowledge and skills within a subject area context. For example, some jurisdictions may identify curriculum strands such as personal development, social development, language and literacy, mathematics and number recognition, science and technology, health, physical activity and development, and the arts.

8.4 A wide variety of resources is needed in the JK/SK classroom to support a variety of learning approaches.

Regardless of the approach taken to identify the strands for the program, educator team members will need to be knowledgeable about the strands in local guidelines and match program strategies to address these strands.

PLANNED AND SEAMLESS INTEGRATION

The kindergarten day should have a seamless flow that minimizes transitions and interruptions to learning. When children understand how the day is structured and can anticipate changes throughout the day, these changes are less likely to be disruptive or to cause anxiety and confusion. Well-established routines can minimize stresses as the day progresses.

Educator teams should plan the flow of the kindergarten day carefully to minimize transitions. By thinking of the flow of the day rather than timetabling, arrangements for activities throughout the day can be planned to be reflexive and responsive to needs and changes that may not have been anticipated. A flow-of-the-day chart can be sketched out, posted where the children can see it, and reviewed early in the day. This creates an anticipatory mindset for the children, and they can look forward to the things that are planned for the remainder of the day.

To plan flow-of-the-day schedules, educator teams should consider a number of criteria that will address evolving needs and the need for some structure. This planning must reflect

- the children's needs,
- community needs,
- the school schedule,
- the professional priorities of the kindergarten program,
- opportunities for communication with parents and other colleagues,
- educator team input, and
- the need for flexibility to respond to evolving events and interests throughout the day.

When planning a flow-of-the-day schedule for JK/SK classrooms, the educator team should consider the many characteristics that are desirable in early learning environments. These characteristics are outlined in Table 8.2, along with some ideas for how each characteristic might be achieved.

Table 8.2 *Characteristics of an Early Learning Flow-of-the-Day Schedule*

Characteristics of an Early Learning Flow-of-the-Day Schedule	How This Might Be Achieved
Transition times during the day should be minimized.	• Plan the day in quarters. • Institute flexible snack and rest times. • Teach and model cleanup routines. • Use music to make transitions fun and maintain a pace that preserves learning time.
Transitions are well managed to minimize loss of instructional time.	• Sing along with music as transitions progress, to support literacy development. • Start new activities as children recongregate, and allow others to join the group as they become ready. • Use key phases that children come to know as signals for time limits and routines.

(Continued)

Table 8.2 Characteristics of an Early Learning Flow-of-the-Day Schedule, continued

Characteristics of an Early Learning Flow-of-the-Day Schedule	How This Might Be Achieved
Literacies are integrated throughout the day.	• Create a print-rich environment. • Provide many tools for writing and speaking to reflect different levels of fine-motor control. • Read to students many times throughout the day. • Have an easily accessible classroom library, so students always have access to reading materials and picture books. • Develop a library of big books that are used for whole-group read-aloud and choral reading times. • Establish and maintain challenging literacy centres throughout the classroom (e.g., reading spots, listening centres, computer centre, print centre, book-making centre).
Mathematical and numeracy concepts are integrated throughout the day.	• Use numbers throughout the day. • Repeat instructions to build children's one-to-one correspondence skills throughout the day. • Provide math and numeracy centres and challenges through **pedagogical narrative** throughout the day.
Opportunities to engage in all strands of learning are available every day.	• Design integrated activities that draw skills and expectations for learning from many areas of the curriculum strands. • Design centres to integrate curriculum strands when possible. • Update centres regularly to maintain their ability to challenge learners. • Plan classroom space carefully. • Use classroom volunteers to observe and extend learning conversations with children.
Opportunities for all types of play (see Chapter 3) are provided many times throughout the day.	• Plan for large blocks of play time. • Use all types of play purposefully. • Observe carefully during play. • Respond, challenge, and extend thinking during play. • Plan the day so that educator team members can engage in purposeful interventions in play with various students throughout the day.
There is balance throughout the day for times that involve investigation and inquiry, exploration, free play and work play, guided instruction, explicit instruction, observation, and engagement in a pedagogical narrative with educator team members to respond to, challenge, and extend learning.	• Use educator team strengths strategically to optimize learning throughout the day. • Teach children the difference between free play and work play. • Regroup children freely to optimize instructional needs.

(Continued)

Table 8.2 Characteristics of an Early Learning Flow-of-the-Day Schedule, continued

Characteristics of an Early Learning Flow-of-the-Day Schedule	How This Might Be Achieved
The physical environment supports various forms of play and is maintained and adapted throughout the day.	• Maintain physical order in the classroom. • Teach children to be responsible for maintaining parts of the classroom. • Schedule for generous use of yard and gym time. • Maintain a schedule for checking classroom and yard equipment for safety and security.
Large blocks of time are available throughout the day for play-based learning.	• Plan learning around play needs. • Plan interventions on an individual basis. • Clarify educator team member roles during play to optimize opportunities for intervention, individual teaching, and observation.
Planning reflects the curriculum strands of the local jurisdiction but also is reflective of children's interests and ideas.	• Offer choices throughout the day. • Support children's interests and ideas by adding to and adapting centres and play challenges. • Maintain current learning profiles for every child; add to them regularly.
Groupings vary by purpose throughout the day and include many opportunities for individual, small-group, and large-group instruction.	• Adopt team roles that support both individual and small-group supervision and intervention. • Plan a flow-of-the-day schedule.

Parents favour JK/SK learning programs that reduce the number of transitions among caregivers that children may experience during the day (Houdsen and Kam, 1992; Johnson, 1993). Because full-day kindergartens can also reduce the in-day transitions through effective planning, children in full-day kindergarten situations also benefit more socially and academically than children who experience half-day programs (Cryan et al., 1992; Karweit, 1992; Gullo, 2000; Rothenberg, 1995). Full-day experiences with well-placed and well-managed transitions make it possible for educator teams to provide learning that allows children to explore topics in depth, reduce the transition-to-learning time ratio, provide continuity in the child's day, and allow for blocking of the day to include developmentally appropriate learning and play.

Flow-of-the-day schedules may vary widely depending on circumstances. An example of a flow-of-the-day template is found in Figure 8.2.

Some educator team members may use a breathing analogy to help young children understand how they group and re-group during the flow of the JK/SK day. For example, coming together in a whole group meeting time may be referred to as a "breathing in" time while separating into other configurations for individual, small group, or partner activities may be referred to as "breathing out" time. However the flow-of-the-day schedule is organized, it should provide flexibility, include smooth transitions that respect the value of learning time, and maximize the skills of each member of the educator team.

	Outdoor Time/Arrival	
	Entry Transitions	
	Large group time Individual time	
	Outdoor learning time	
Learning centres	Individual instruction and observation	Small group instruction
	Transition/Lunch or Nutrition Break	
	Outdoor time	
	Transition	
	Large group time	
Learning centres	Individual instruction and observation	Small group instruction
Outdoor Time	Individual instruction and observation	Small group instruction
	Dismissal	
	Extended day program	

Figure 8.2 *Flow-of-the-Day Sample Schedule*

In any of the indoor or outdoor individual, small-group, or large-group contexts, educator team members can engage children in a wide range of learning and assessment approaches. These may include

- sign-in routines
- choosing or assigning learning centres
- read-alouds, buddy reading, or independent reading
- working in small groups
- working individually
- working with an educator team member
- engaging in teacher guided activities
- observing a demonstration
- documenting and recording learning episodes or examples of pedagogical narratives
- intentionally interacting to question, respond, challenge, or extend
- providing targeted support
- differentiating instruction to meet developmental needs or interests
- initiating reading strategies
- participating in writing strategies
- participating in math strategies
- learning inquiry skills

8.5 *A wide variety of resources is needed in the JK/SK classroom to support a variety of learning approaches.*

- engaging in arts activities
- observing modeling
- engaging in physical activities
- playing games
- engaging in imaginary play
- participating in teacher-guided activities

Through the different types of play that are part of the scheduled learning in a JK/SK classroom, children have many opportunities to develop skills, and educator team members have many opportunities to observe and record learning and to use these observations to plan extended learning (see Table 8.3).

Table 8.3 *Scheduled Play Opportunities Support Learning Throughout the JK/SK Day*

Form of Play	What the Educator Team Might Be Doing
Pretend or pretense play	• Monitoring for safety • Ensuring that all children are included as they wish • Providing resources to enrich the play • Providing space
Socio-dramatic play	• Providing costumes and props • Providing space • Reinforcing group cooperation skills • Reinforcing understanding of symbols and actions • Placing new materials in accessible places
Constructive play/Problem-solving work play	• Designing materials to support learning • Recording observations and pedagogical narratives • Asking questions to challenge and extend thinking • Interpreting observations • Planning for new learning episodes based on observations • Limiting work materials, to force children to find ways to work together and cooperate • Modeling skills for learning and for successful social interaction • Encouraging exploration and risk taking • Managing centre rotations • Celebrating learning • Managing artefacts that testify to each child's learning (e.g., photos or anecdotes for a portfolio)

8.6 Observations can be made in ordinary moments; recording sheets should be readily available in learning areas, so that both educator team members can make notesas they observe children. Care must be taken to ensure the confidentiality of assessment records.

PLANNING TEMPLATES

Planning templates can support the organization of the JK/SK classroom by providing two important and commonly understood aspects of good instruction. One aspect is the establishment of workable routines that are understood by the children and the adults who work in the classroom. The other aspect is the curriculum planning that must go into managing the mandated curriculum of the jurisdiction. In this section, each of these purposes for using planning templates will be addressed.

Routines are used in classrooms to preserve learning time. They have the added advantage of helping to reduce anxiety for some children, because routines allow them to relax when they know what is expected. When children are relaxed, they are inclined to risk more overt efforts as they explore and learn. A well-run JK/SK day starts with a routinized entry. In the JK/SK context, children may be dropped off at the school at different times or they may arrive by school bus. They will take different amounts of time to organize their belongings, remove coats and boots, scarves, and mittens, store snacks and lunch pails, provide notes from parents, and get ready for the first tasks of the day. Educator teams can fill this transition time with meaningful tasks by having an active entry routine in which each student has a job to complete.

Example: As children enter the classroom, they go to a carpeted area where metal discs, each with a child's name printed on it, have been placed in the centre of the carpeted area. The child takes his or her name tag and places it in the basket at the front of the carpet area. This allows the educator team to take attendance instantly. From beside the basket, each child takes a small tray filled with white sand back to their sitting area on the carpet. The children use their index fingers to print the morning message in their sand trays. The message is on a piece of chart paper at the edge of the carpet, and the message varies from day to day (e.g., "It is sunny today."). If budgets allow, more high-tech approaches can serve the same purpose (e.g., slate boards, Etch A Sketch pads, or iPads).

This sample routine serves many purposes with young learners. It can

- allow children to enter the classroom in a relaxed and purposeful way,
- provide educator team members with time to speak to parents and guardians as they drop children off at the classroom,
- allow educator team members time to help some children prepare their belongings to enter the classroom,
- remove the burden of time related to taking classroom attendance,
- provide students with opportunities to take ownership of their classroom,
- support independence,
- expose students to print concepts, and
- support development of hand–eye coordination skills.

Well-developed classroom routines will serve multiple purposes as this example does. Early in their classroom experiences, young children may need symbols to prompt their actions. As they start to develop print concepts, words can support symbols in the areas of the classroom where routines are needed. See Figure 8.3 for symbols that can be photocopied and cut out for this purpose.

Reflection Point

What other multiple-purpose routines might you use in the JK/SK classroom? Share your ideas with colleagues.

Educator team members should try to ensure that all the print below symbols is shown in the languages represented by the various first-language cultures of the students in the classroom. Parents and guardians can be very helpful in determining what words should be used from their language to match the symbols.

8.7 *Thematic units can be planned on a year-at-glance chart to help the educator team arrange resources and supports effectively.*

Other templates that may be helpful to educator teams in the JK/SK context relate to curriculum planning and assessment in a play-based program. Many of the provincial and territorial curriculum guidelines for JK/SK early learning provide specific statements of what young children are typically expected to learn during the two-year program. Expectations are often sorted and grouped according to traditional subject areas, such as language and mathematics, but may be grouped more broadly into skill and attribute categories, such as

Figure 8.3 *Symbols that Will Remind Young Children of Classroom Routines*

exploration and creativity. Regardless of how learning expectations are categorized within mandated guidelines, educator team members may want to collect expectations into themes that can guide the types of learning activities they will plan during a short time period. Themes can be broad enough to expand across all areas of learning in the program and can provide many contexts for integrating curriculum in the early years.

Program Area	Learning Expectations	Sept.	Oct.	Nov.	Dec.	Jan.	Feb.	Mar.	Apr.	May	June	Notes
Personal development												
Social development												
Language/Literacies												
Mathematics/Numeracy												
Science/Technology												
Health/Physical Activity												
Arts												

Figure 8.4 *Year-at-a-Glance Integrated Curriculum Planning Template*

To plan integrated activities for the JK/SK curriculum, educators can use a template such as Figure 8.4 as the first step in identifying appropriate themes for the children's learning experiences. This type of planning is often called *year-at-a-glance* planning and is the most general form of long-range planning that encompasses plans for the whole school year. Year-at-a-glance planning has the added benefit of allowing educators to plan for and secure resources well in advance of anticipated needs.

Reflection Point

Learning expectations may also be called *objectives, goals*, or *aims*. For use at the classroom planning level, it is helpful for educators to write expectations in the form of "Today students will learn to…".

Examine a local curriculum guideline for JK/SK. Practise wording any sample expectations from that guideline into expectation statements in the form of "Today students will learn to …".

After checking thoroughly in the local JK/SK curriculum guideline, educators found that one expectation for learning at this level required that students demonstrate respect and consideration for individual differences and alternative points of view. The educator team then developed several specific learning expectations to be the focus of centres and activities over the next week in order

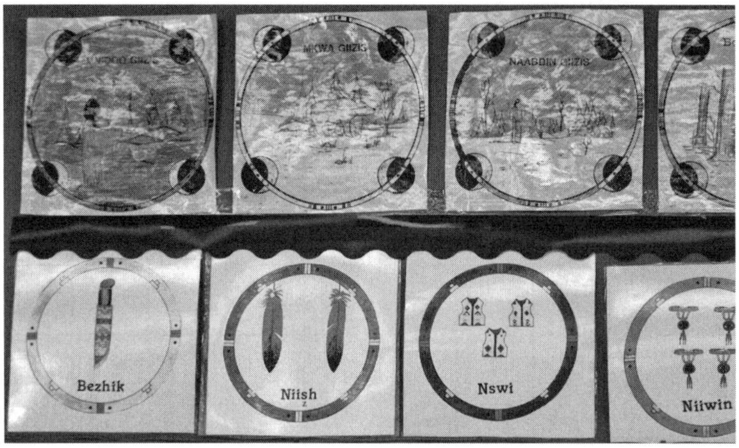

8.8 Thematic units can be used throughout the year to support curriculum integration.

to help students achieve the stated expectation. Their list of learning expectations included the following:

- Today students will learn to share and serve others by considering their needs first.
- Today students will learn about celebrations and traditions in three of the cultures represented by the makeup of our classroom.
- Today students will show that they can listen to other points of view and express their point of view in a respectful way.

By wording expectations in this way, educator team members can be certain of focused opportunities to learn in the classroom.

LEARNING AND ACTIVITY CENTRES

There are many themes appropriate for an early learning context and curriculum integration where learning expectations are drawn from many areas of the curriculum to provide guidance for the development of learning centres and activities. Care must be taken to ensure that activities lead to learning and that learning is tied to guideline directions. Time spent doing things at centres or completing activities is not necessarily time spent learning.

If, for example, educators chose to develop a thematic unit about friendship, they might design learning centres and activities such as the following:

- Personal Development: A family living centre would allow children to explore ways of sharing and serving others.
- Exploring and Creativity: An arts centre would provide craft and viewing opportunities, so that children could make traditional crafts and watch video clips showing how they might be used in ceremonies and local cultures.
- Literacy Centre: A reading centre would provide picture books and audio-tapes that teach about different cultures.
- Oral Literacy Centre: A "My Turn" focus would provide children with opportunities to try to speak phrases in other languages; these phrases could be built into classroom routines throughout the day (e.g., children could learn to greet each other in four or five languages represented in the class makeup, and these greetings could be used to match children with new elbow partners throughout the day).

- Math Centre: Children would be challenged to address one-to-one correspondence skills by planning a snack for a small group and using symbolic food cut-outs to serve those foods that various participants chose from the selections.

Careful and purposeful observation of children as they work at learning centres will ensure that time spent at them is advancing learning and that opportunities to extend learning are used to maximum advantage. Both educator team members can contribute to observation records of learners if observation charts are located at each centre. Since there may be many visitors in the classroom, efforts must be made to protect the confidential nature of recorded observations while also making them easily accessible. A sample template for observation records might be organized to allow many entries in an efficient way that focuses on the specific learning expectation for the centre (see Figure 8.5).

Centre: Learning Expectation(s): Today children will learn to:				
Date	Child's Name	Educator Team Initials	Observation	Intervention Notes (questioning, responding, challenging, extending)

Figure 8.5 *A Sample Template for Centre Observations*

DEVELOPING EFFECTIVE CLASSROOM LEARNING CENTRES

Effective learning centres will have several characteristics that can be planned by educator teams. Each centre should

- have a distinct and clear learning purpose;
- be intuitive, so that young children do not need much direction about how to use the centre;

- be easily accessible and use materials that are safe, sturdy, and easily cleaned;
- provide easy storage for centre components;
- allow for a broad range of levels of engagement, so that children can learn, practise, consolidate, and apply learning;
- allow for individual, partner, and small-group accessibility of materials;
- provide some open-ended elements that promote unhindered exploration;
- allow choice and promote risk taking;
- promote talk and shared problem solving;
- provide enough resources so that collaboration is possible; and
- promote embedded opportunities for assessment by self, peers, and educator team members in non-intrusive ways.

Learning centres may be of three general types. They can be permanent centres that remain in place all year to provide learning opportunities for generic activities; these may include a listening centre, a literacy spot, a wet area for arts and crafts, a technology centre, a building and construction centre, and a mathematics centre where manipulative materials are available to advance number concepts. Other learning centres may be more focused on opportunities for children to enrich general learning skills and may include a computer centre, a print centre, and an arts and crafts centre. The third type of centre may be thematic, with content that rotates with the various themes of study; these may include a writing centre, a word or literacy centre, an art centre, a painting centre,

8.9 *Children can rotate among a variety of centres during "breathing out" times of the day.*

a discovery centre, a problem-solving centre, a water centre, a puppet centre, a drama centre, a dress-up centre, and a sand centre. At each thematic centre, the complementary materials that are added to the basic centre materials (e.g., a sand table) can be varied to address the current theme.

As centres are being planned for the JK/SK classroom, educator team members will need to develop an overall scheme for ensuring the proper set-up of each centre (see Figure 8.6) and a workable method of tracking students' rotation (see Figure 8.7) to various centres.

Centre Name	Learning Expectations for this Centre	Focused Learning Interventions for this Centre	Centre Materials and Strategic Resources	Assessment Approaches for this Centre

Figure 8.6 *Planning Template for Classroom Centres*

A centre planning framework can complement the year-at-a-glance that an educator team uses to manage space, resources, and functions within the JK/SK classroom. Team members will need to decide how to introduce centres to the children. They might begin by allowing a small group to access one centre, using this novel experience to teach the routines and expectations for centre use to small groups before other centres are introduced. Alternatively, educator teams could establish and open several centres that all relate to a common curriculum area. For example, to support literacy expectations, they might have a library centre, a listening centre, an alphabet centre, and a computer centre that all relate to print concepts. A more common approach is to have several centres that relate to the full breadth of the JK/SK curriculum, with specific activities at each centre that vary across the school year to reflect changing program themes.

With young children, a rotation system is needed that is lightly dependent on words (see Figure 8.7) and uses intuitively recognized symbols. This approach works well to show students which centre they should work at during centre rotation times in the flow-of-the-day schedule. Learning centre rotations can be set up in various ways: students can move on to new centres when specific tasks are finished, when an allotted period of time has elapsed, through a regular daily rotation schedule whereby they are at different centres each day of the week or at each centre time during the day, or by personal choice that reflects interests. If centres are set up with multiple tasks at each centre and provide many ways for students to demonstrate their learning, the option to set up rotations by choice is more viable.

Figure 8.7 *A Centre Rotation System that Uses Intuitively Recognizable Symbols to Help Children Communicate Choices*

Using this approach, educator team members can be sure that children are addressing the mandated curriculum expectations while still having some measure of **autonomy** in their learning. Rotations into centres will often be needed because of the size of the centre area or the number of materials available at the centre.

Educator team members can also set up individual centre profile sheets that help them track each child's centre choices, so that they can monitor breadth and diversity of choices. A centre profile sheet would include the names of all possible centres and a list of dates or days of the week when the child has worked at each centre.

Regardless of how educator teams monitor or rotate children among classroom centres, it is important to keep the focus on what children have learned from each centre, not merely how much time they have spent at each centre. Educator teams will also need to determine the role of each team member in planning, establishing, maintaining, engaging, and monitoring each centre as it is used.

EDUCATOR TEAM MEMBER ROLES IN THE CURRICULUM PLANNING AND IMPLEMENTATION OF CURRICULUM

Some educator team roles will be defined by the contracts of each member of the team. In most situations, the teachers will be accountable for knowing and implementing curriculum guideline requirements, preparing progress reports, and interpreting evidence of learning. They may also have sole responsibility for reporting to parents.

However, as educator team approaches evolve and become more common to manage learning in the JK/SK context, members of the team will benefit from sharing common professional development experiences. While teachers may retain the same responsibilities for planning, assessing, and reporting, creating common understandings among team members will strengthen their team approach in the classroom and allow the team to take full advantage of the strengths and talents of each team member. Early childhood educators have irreplaceable roles to fill in setting up, maintaining, and observing learning in the classroom, as well as engaging in interactions that support each child's learning. This approach will optimize the opportunities that can be made available to children. When educator team members support each other's strengths, they will be most fulfilled and satisfied in their complementary roles.

CHAPTER SUMMARY

The JK/SK curriculum is designed to identify what young children should learn, how they learn it, and how their learning can be assessed. JK/SK curriculum guidelines are developed at the provincial or territorial level and provide guidance about many areas of a child's development. These include physical development, health and well-being, a sense of belonging, social skill development, knowledge acquisition strategies, emotional growth, multiple literacy growth, and general knowledge development. A wide range of learning and assessment strategies is used in the JK/SK classroom to support many forms of learning and learning styles.

The JK/SK curriculum is planned to be deliverable in a day that flows and incorporates many opportunities for play. These characteristics of the learning environment help young children make connections in their learning. Educator teams can support the curriculum by planning for the long-range integration of learning through activity centres and play-based learning.

THINKING AHEAD: Opportunities for Professional Reflection

- Use a local guideline to plan a series of centres for a set of learning expectations. Use a planning template (as per Figure 8.6) to develop details for each centre.

- Collect several examples of flow-of-the-day schedules for JK/SK. Discuss the advantages and disadvantages of each sample with colleagues.
- Identify a variety of ways to use symbols to support language use at several standard classroom centres. Use several common languages that are typical in your area to provide language translations to support English language learners.
- Brainstorm ways to manage transitions in the classroom and to use these times effectively for additional learning.
- Select ten books that are suitable for a JK/SK classroom. For each book you have chosen, suggest several themes that it might support in the JK/SK curriculum in your area.

ADDITIONAL READING SUGGESTIONS

The classroom library or reading area is an aspect of the learning environment that requires careful planning by the educator team. Books will support learning in much of the JK/SK curriculum. The library area(s) of the classroom need to provide books at many reading levels and that can be used for many purposes throughout the JK/SK program. Books should be chosen for use in read-alouds, shared reading, and independent reading. While many JK/SK children will be developing initial print concepts during their kindergarten years, some children enter junior kindergarten already able to read with some independence. The classroom library must be designed to support all of these purposes and literacy levels.

Earlier chapters have included some suggestions for books that relate to specific ideas, such as the first day of school. This and subsequent chapters will provide suggestions for additional books to include in classroom libraries.

Suggested books for a JK/SK classroom library include the following:

1 One-Year Old: Counting Children 1 to 10 – Juliet Bawden and Helen Pask
10 Bears in My Bed: A Goodnight Countdown – Stan Mack
10 for Dinner – Jo Ellen Bogart
12 Ways to Get to 11 – Eve Merriam
26 Letters and 99 Cents – Tana Hoban
A Dozen Dogs – Harriet Ziefert
A Quarter from the Tooth Fairy – Caren Holtzman
Across the Stream – Mirra Ginsburg
All in One Hour – Susan Stevens Crummel
All Year Long – Nancy Tafuri
Always Room for One More – Sourche Nic Leodhas
Animal Numbers – Bert Kitchen
Annie's One to Ten – Annie Owen
Anno's Counting Book – Mitsumasa Anno
Aunt Lulu – Daniel Pinkwater
The Balloon Tree – Phoebe Gilman
The Baseball Counting Book – Barbara McGrath
Bears at the Beach: Counting 10 to 20 – Niki Yektai
Bears on Wheels – Stan and Jan Berenstain
The Best of Times – Greg Tang
Big or Little – Kathy Stinson
Brian Wildsmith 123 – Brian Wildsmith
Bunches and Bunches of Bunnies – Louise Matthews
Canadian Garbage Collectors – Paulette Bourgeois and Kim LaFave
Chalk – Bill Thomson (wordless picture book)
Claude the Dog – Dick Gackenbach
Clocks and More Clocks – Pat Hutchins
The Completed Hickory Dickory Dock – Jim Aylesworth
Count to a Million – Jerry Pallotta
Counting on Calico – Phyllis Tildes
The Curious Garden – Peter Brown
Elephant and Piggie (book series) – Mo Willems
Even Steven and Odd Todd – Kathryn Cristaldi
Flat Stanley (series) – Jeff Brown
Frog Counts to Ten – John Liebler
From One to One Hundred – Teri Sloat

Go Away Big Green Monster – Ed Emberly
Going to Grandma's – John Tarlton
The Grapes of Math – Greg Tang
The Grouchy Ladybug – Eric Carle
Hello School!: A Classroom Full of Poems – Dee Lillegard
Here Are My Hands – Bill Marin Jr. and John Archambault
How Many Bears – Cooper Edens
How Many Feet in the Bed – Diane Johnston Hamm
How Many Snails – Paul Giganti
How Many, How Many, How Many – Rick Walton
How Much is a Million? – David M. Schwartz
I Spy Two Eyes: Numbers in Art – Lucy Micklethwait
I Went to the Zoo – Rita Golden Gelman
If I Were a Cat I Would Sit in a Tree – Ebbitt Cutler
The Important Book – Margaret Wise Brown
In the Woods: Who's Been Here? – Lindsay Barrett George
Ish – Peter H. Reynolds
It's too Noisy! – Joanna Cole
The Last Puppy – Frank Asch
Lemonade Parade – Ben Brooks
Little Pea – Amy Krouse Rosenthal
The Magic Hat – Mem Fox
Math Appeal – Greg Tang
Math for All Seasons – Greg Tang
Math-terpieces – Greg Tang
The Mitten – Jan Brett
Moira's Birthday – Robert Munsch
Monster Math – Anne Miranda
More Bugs? Less Bugs? – Don. L. Curry
More Than One – Miriam Schlein
Mr. Brown's Magnificent Apple Tree – Yvonne Winer
Much Bigger Than Martin – Steven Kellogg
Nine Ducks Nine – Sarah Hayes
One – Kathryn Otoshi
One Bear in the Picture – Caroline Bucknall
One Hundred Ways to Get to 100 – Jerry Pallotta
One Step, Two – Charlotte Zolotow
The One That Got Away – Percival Everett
One Zillion Valentines – Frank Modell
One, Two, One Pair! – Bruce McMillan
Pancakes for Breakfast – Tomie De Paola
Penelope Gets Wheels – Esther Peterson
Pezzettino – Leo Lionni
Pigs Aplenty, Pigs Galore! – David McPhail
Quack and Count – Keith Baker
Raven: A Trickster Tale from the Pacific Northwest – Gerald McDermott
Reading Makes You Feel Good – Todd Parr
Red Light, Green Light, Mama and Me – Cari Best
Rhinos for Lunch and Elephants for Supper – Tololwa Mollel
Rooster's Off to See the World – Eric Carle
Rosie's Walk – Pat Hutchins
Round Trip – Ann Jonas
Seven Stars More! – Kathy Mallat
The Shapes Game – Paul Rogers
Simon and the Snowflakes – Gilles Tibo
Slower Than a Snail – Anne Schreiber
So Many Cats! – Beatrice Schenk de Regniers
Something from Nothing – Phoebe Gilman
Spoon – Amy Krouse Rosenthal
Spots, Feathers, Curly Tails – Nancy Tafuri
Statistics – Jane Jonas Srivastava
Stay in Line – Teddy Slater
Surprise Shapes (series) – by Patricia and Victor Smeltzer
Ten Black Dots – Donald Crews
Ten Little Rabbits – Virginia Grossman
Ten Sly Piranhas – William Wise
Ten, Nine, Eight – Molly Bang
This is Our House – Michael Rosen
This is the Farmer – Nancy Tafuri
Too Much Noise – Ann McGovern
The Tortoise and the Hare: An Aesop Fable – adapted by Janet Stevens
Under the Sun, Over the Moon – Kevin Crossley-Holland
Wednesday is Spaghetti Day – Maryann Cocca-Leffler
What Am I?: Looking Through Shapes at Apples and Grapes – N. N. Charles
What Comes in 2s, 3s & 4s? – Suzanne Aker
Who's Counting? – Nancy Tafuri

Educator team members may also reference the following book about early learning as they choose books for the JK/SK classroom library. Each chapter has a book list at the end, and many will be suitable for the JK/SK classroom:

Miller, D. 2002. Reading with Meaning. Portland, ME: Stenhouse Publishers.

9 Curriculum in Action

"Play is a state of mind, rather than an activity."

(S. Brown, 2009)

8.1 *Outdoor play opportunities should be provided daily, except in the most inclement conditions, to give children an opportunity for all types of play.*

In this chapter, educator team members will learn about

- active, play-based learning
- creativity and imagination in a play-based context
- when learning can be structured
- learning centres: planning, extending, maintaining, and changing centres for optimal learning

At the end of this chapter, educator team members can reflect on their personal growth through

- CHAPTER SUMMARY
- THINKING AHEAD: Opportunities for Professional Reflection
- ADDITIONAL READING SUGGESTIONS

This chapter will address many concepts related to the development of plans for classroom instruction set within a play-based learning environment. When play is a central component of program design, educator team members will approach the tasks of designing instruction in ways that are markedly different from instruction in other classrooms. Careful assessment of a child's play history prior to school and during the JK/SK years can provide valuable insights into the child's learning style and preferences, which will in turn support the informed development of their learning profile.

ACTIVE, PLAY-BASED LEARNING

Curriculum directives for programming for young children include information to guide educators about the nature of play-based learning. Employers have found that those who did not have opportunities to play and work with their hands as they grew up lacked necessary problem-solving skills as adults in a work environment (Brown, 2009). The correlation between youthful play and adult problem solving alone is a compelling argument for including play in the JK/SK classroom context.

> "Play is the vital essence of life. It is what makes life lively.... Play is the stick that stirs the drink."
> Brown, 2009

Play has the potential to promote healthy neural pathway development and rejuvenation, spark curiosity, and promote alert observation. Ideas can be revisited through play in which new connections are made and new levels of energy are brought to tasks. The mind at play can provide solutions to problems and new perspectives on issues. Work and play share the common characteristic of opening us up to creativity. Play is a form of re-creation in that it opens ideas to expansive input, allows for practice in safe contexts, and extends our creativity. Play incorporated into work can promote a sense of personal satisfaction. In JK/SK classrooms, this incorporated play might be called **work play**.

9.2 Work play may happen at classroom centres but can also be engaged in less structured ways both indoors and outdoors.

Play also provides opportunities for cooperative socialization with peers and adults in the classroom context. This provides a sense of trust, sharing, caring, and empathy among the children and those who support their learning. Cooperative socialization helps to develop children's sense of fairness and their comprehension of social justice concepts.

Play also increases communication and understanding and has the elements essential for

9.3 Imaginative play allows children to consider perspectives as they adopt various roles.

reducing conflict and violence as children work toward sharing and solving problems. Through play, children can find common ground and mutually acceptable solutions and options.

Play is also a vehicle for teaching our culture to young children. In a play-based learning environment, children can explore the local environment through activities that expand their vocabulary, widen their exposure to the ways others might see a situation or address a problem, and demonstrate instances when differing perspectives might be relevant. Through literature, personal stories, music, choral speaking, rhyming, celebrations, and exposure to people from other cultures, play-based experiences can broaden each child's world. Through play comes innovation, and through innovation comes increased self-confidence.

In a play-based learning environment, imaginative play is essential. Through imaginative play, children learn to step back from problems and consider both the emotional and the intellectual aspects that need to be part of finding the most viable solutions. Centres in the classroom can be designed to provide opportunities to engage and step back for reflective examination. At centres and through free play times, young children can step outside of the boundaries in their thinking that may be present in other learning situations; they can stretch the rules of thought, consider options for action, and behave in ways that allow exploration and redefinition of their understandings.

9.4 Rough-and-tumble play helps children learn to control impulses and manage appropriate interactions.

Dr. Stuart Brown believes that a person's dominant mode of play falls into one of eight categories (see Table 9.1). Most young children will not have any solidified play type and may have limited exposure to people whose play type differs from their own. This may become a source of conflict in play circumstances and may require some adult support for children negotiating the play types of other children.

In JK/SK, children will engage in many forms of social play throughout the day. Chapter 3 introduced types of play by looking at play configurations. Here we will examine types of play by looking at the goals of each type.

Table 9.1 *Play Types*

Play Types	The Person Will Often Use This Approach to Play:
The Joker	Talks nonsense and enjoys practical jokes
The Kinesthete	Needs to move to think; not necessarily competitive but likes sports and exercise
The Explorer	Emotionally or physically delves into new ideas and areas
The Competitor	Plays to win; enjoys specific rules
The Director	Organizes; enjoys power and instigation
The Collector	Enjoys having items and collecting them; includes collecting experiences
The Artist/Creator	Enjoys making things; may be mechanical
The Storyteller	Enjoys imaginative interactions with stories, movies, and conversations; enjoys performing

In parallel play, children share resources without sharing goals or cooperating through talk; they can observe their peers and increase their ability to empathize with others' views. In cooperative mutual play, children who share resources also begin to discuss what they are doing with others, giving them further opportunities to develop empathetic interaction.

Rough-and-tumble play is a form of play that is difficult in a classroom context. Safety issues and school rules may legislate against this form of play, even though it has been demonstrated to be a necessary form of play in developing and maintaining cooperation skills and furthering one's sense of social roles, boundaries, fairness, and altruism. When children lack opportunities for some rough-and-tumble play, they may develop poor impulse control and violence control in later life (Brown, 2009). Rough-and-tumble play varies with the child's age. In the JK/SK context, games such as tag and chases of various forms can support children's need for this form of play. Rough-and-tumble play will be friendly and engaged in a spirit of play and with smiling faces. Children will be familiar with examples of rough-and-tumble play they have witnessed among young animals. Rough-and-tumble play experiences in

9.5 *Celebratory play helps children understand social norms and values and supports happy memories.*

the school setting require some faith that the children can differentiate between friendly and real aggression and that in some instances individual children will become self-appointed leaders of a group.

Celebratory and ritual play is a form of social play. This play is a reenactment of social events that children equate with positive feelings. Celebratory and ritual play could include children acting out experiences such as birthdays, weddings, Thanksgiving dinner, and other events that have included them with family and friends.

Reflection Point

Observe some young children at play. Can you tell from your observations which form of play these children are exploring?

Discuss in a small group how educator team members could support each type of play without interfering or imposing adult structure on it.

Storytelling and narrative play is an important form of play to help children understand their world. Through making up, telling, and listening to stories, children develop their **schema** (i.e., their mental frameworks) for how things fit together and how things are supposed to function. Through storytelling, children learn that reading and speaking to others can be pleasurable, that some issues are timeless, and that they can imagine events and places if they are described in interesting ways.

9.6 *Many forms of play reflect children's fantasy story backgrounds.*

Through some forms of play, children can change patterns of behaviour and explore new realities. Forms of play that allow children to engage in fantasy help them see new possibilities for reality and develop perspective. New ideas are introduced and new visions created. Through fantasy play forms, children get exposure to history, the future, adult roles, and problem-solving contexts that may challenge their thinking. When asked about what led them to teaching as a career, many teacher candidates talk about their love of "playing school" as young children. Transformative, integrative, and creative play gives children the opportunity to try on new ideas and explore their parameters. By limiting adult intervention in fantasy or transformative play, we can ensure that children get opportunities to mould and design the elements of this play form to suit the range of possibilities they can imagine.

The JK/SK classroom space should be designed to optimize space for play while providing for ease of movement and supervision (see Chapter 7). By considering the four main variables in types of play that may be available indoors in JK/SK classrooms, educator teams can be sure to make the most of available space. The four spatial variables that should be considered are

- wet areas,
- dry areas,
- quiet areas, and
- noisy areas.

To support active, play-based indoor learning, educator teams can divide the classroom into four zones so that activity centres can be as separate as possible to form compatible locations during active periods of the day. Play-based zoning (see Figure 9.1) will also optimize safety and reduce cleanup tasks throughout the day.

New Brunswick, Quebec, Ontario, Manitoba, Saskatchewan, and British Columbia have each developed early learning frameworks to guide work with children who are under 5 years of age, and these frameworks are applicable to both early learning and care systems in each province.
~ Canadian Network for Leadership in Education and Early Learning and Care

DRY	QUIET
NOISY	WET

Figure 9.1 *Play-Based Zoning of the Classroom Space to Support Various Forms of Play*

This organization of the space can help to create the management and tonal qualities that will make the classroom most productive when it is busiest.

CREATIVITY AND IMAGINATION IN A PLAY-BASED CONTEXT

It is not difficult to think of young children and imagination and creativity in the same sentence. As we watch children play, we can see their imaginations at work and their sense of freedom to express what they can imagine is often wondrous to watch. Children's inventive play is creative and imaginative. In the JK/SK context, the question to consider becomes "Are there some types of creative and imaginative play that should be discouraged in the classroom?"

Various researchers (Parten, 1933; Rubin, Fein, and Vandenberg, 1983) have found that children's play at a young age tends to be solitary. As they become older, children's engagement in social forms of play increases. Solitary play is not an indicator of anti-social behaviour or a lack of social skills. It is simply a choice that children may exercise from time to time. During solitary play, young children can be deeply involved in imaginative and creative aspects of play. They may even talk aloud and use a variety of voices and postures to indicate changes in characters and perspectives. Children are most likely to engage in complex play when the adults around them participate rather than merely observe, and when they play in pairs rather than alone or in small groups (Sylva, Roy, and Painter, 1980). In the JK/SK context, children are most likely to engage in complex exploratory play, constructive play, pretend play, and games in dyads. Often the choice of whom to play with will influence how the play is engaged. By providing choices, educators can ensure that children have options and opportunities to play in a wide range of formats.

To create opportunities for creative and imaginative play, educator teams must be particularly vigilant about providing diversity in the resources that are openly available for play periods. Resources must be those that engage children through many senses. Items that can be used in representative ways will allow a variety of applications. The buttons that are counters one day may be lily pads in the frog's magic kingdom the next. Educator teams should seek the support of parents in acquiring sensory materials. Newsletters that request "beautiful garbage" from home, with examples, will help build up the resources in the classroom. By planning ahead, educator teams can ensure that the resources are suitable and can be stored in areas of the classroom that are easily accessible during play times.

Learning Style Preference	Indoor Play	Outdoor Play
Visual/spatial – Learns through pictures		
Logical/mathematical – Learns through numbers		
Naturalist – Learns through associations with plants and animals		
Intrapersonal – Learns through imagining and reflecting		
Verbal/linguistic – Learns through speaking and discussing or reading		
Interpersonal – Learns through interaction with others		
Kinesthetic/bodily – Learns through movement		
Musical/rhythmic – Learns through music, rhyme and rhythm		
Spiritual – Learns through thoughtful contemplation and insight		

Figure 9.2 *A Planning Framework for Gathering Resources for Creative and Imaginative Play*

Educator teams can plan play resources by deliberately thinking about play from the perspective of learning styles. A range of play choices will support growth if children's options for learning through play are easily available and they can not only use many learning style preferences but also engage with play partners who may help to extend their play style preferences. A planning framework (see Figure 9.2) for gathering play resources may help educator team members brainstorm the possibilities.

WHEN LEARNING CAN BE STRUCTURED

Work is not the opposite of play. Various forms of play may prepare young children to engage in work play or may prepare them for interaction when short periods of more structured teaching may be suitable. When children know that they will be able to play with the ideas they are being taught, they can put the more structured periods of input into balance. They can differentiate between open play and work play. Through play-based learning, children can be assured of the emotional distance and supportive interaction that will allow them to learn through their interests and reflect their readiness to learn, while providing approaches that optimize their learning styles. Play allows children to react to situations in contexts that are safe and nurturing while they explore other possibilities for reaction.

> "As with many things in life, the problem is not the problem; the problem is how you react to the problem."
> ~ Brown, 2009 (p. 130)

When structured teaching is desired, as is often the case when new concepts are introduced and new vocabulary is needed, educator team members will need to share a common vision of the steps that should be used to ensure successful learning for all children (see Figure 9.3). When introducing new learning, teachers will be responsible for the teaching or input part of the lesson. This part of a lesson is often called the *new learning phase*. Modeling, through telling and showing, is often used to address new learning. Teachers learn to start new learning by motivating children to want to learn the new idea, modeling what it is, then following the modeling with closely supervised practice. Closely supervised practice is called *consolidation*. During consolidation, educator teams will observe, make observation notes, and engage children in questioning, responding, challenging thinking, and extending ideas. After students have had success with closely supervised practice, they can start to use the new learning in new contexts. This is called *application*.

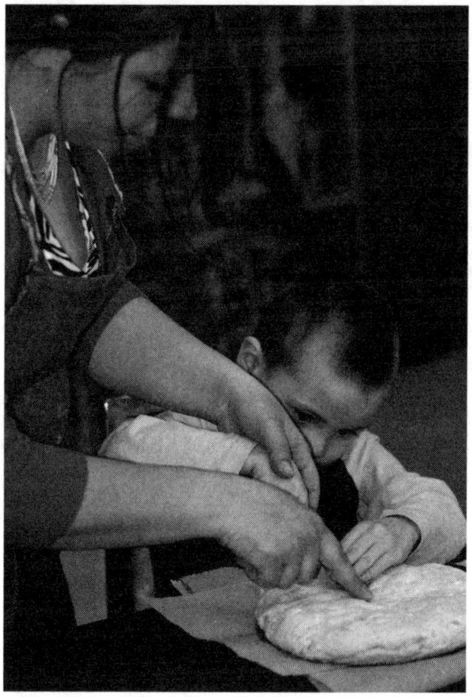

9.7 New learning can be shown and explained to young children through teacher modeling.

During application, JK/SK educator teams introduce new materials and scenarios to make the learning more engaging and to extend children's understanding. This is often when educator teams will open new activity centres

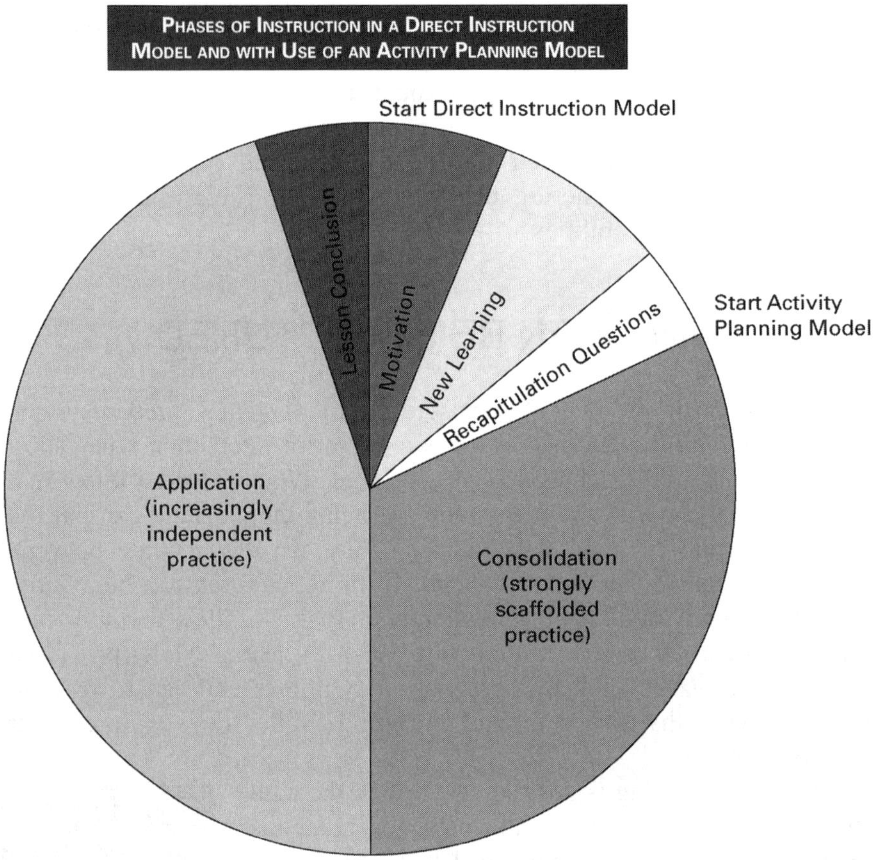

Figure 9.3 *The Phases of Instruction model will help the educator team determine when to use direct instruction and when to use activity centres to support learning.*

related to the new learning and provide children with many choices for how they can apply new ideas. After children have had many opportunities to apply new ideas in a variety of contexts, the educator team may bring the children to the carpet area of the room and discuss what they have learned. This provides a lesson conclusion and allows children to acquire and confirm the correct language to describe what they have learned. When children have vocabulary to describe their learning and can say what they know about a topic, this is called **metacognition**. Metacognition means knowing what you know.

In a JK/SK classroom, addressing all of the phases of instruction for a new concept may take several days or even weeks. For example, if the educator team introduces the concept of one-to-one correspondence, children may be asked to make "finger pencil" marks in the air to show the number of items on a tray. During modeling, the teacher may demonstrate counting the objects by moving them one at a time to count them, saying the numbers *one, two, three, four, five, six* as each item is removed from the tray. Then each pair of students may be asked to use a smaller tray with several objects, and while one child counts them as the teacher did, their learning partner says each word to count the objects. During this practice, educator team members observe the children carefully and note which students are successful with practice and which students require further demonstration. Those students who have practised successfully are then assigned to, or choose, activity centres where the concept of one-to-one correspondence can be practised with more independence. Those who were not successful with initial practice work with either of the educator team members to experience more modeling and get more strongly supported practice before joining the other children at centres. Supported practice is called **scaffolding**. Scaffolding refers to the range of supportive practices that educators can use to help children be successful with practice. The combination of these actions is referred to as **direct instruction**.

Children's exposure to some concepts may require an extended period of introduction to create a common background among students and to allow children to develop related vocabulary before more complex ideas are introduced. Figure 9.4 shows that activities (i.e., such as might be undertaken in activity centres) are used to best effect after new learning has been modeled and introduced. If activity centres are used too early in the learning sequence, children may come away from experiences at centres that allow for misconceptions and actually block learning, because the learning purposes of the practice opportunities at centres are unclear.

Using this model allows educator team members to differentiate instruction for children. As each child moves through the phases of instruction, educators can provide different examples (content), show different ways to understand each new idea (process), and support children as they attempt to use the new learning and show what they understand (product). By changing the content, process, and product for any learning situation, educators can appeal to different interests and learning styles and increase each child's chances of early success with the learning. The supports that can be provided for children are identified in Figure 9.5.

The educator team will also engage children in different forms of assessment as they acquire information about the children's learning. As educators engage children in a **pedagogical narrative** to discuss what they understand and what they are discovering, educators will match how they challenge and extend learning to the phase that best represents each child's current understanding and the solidification of their new learning. The reflective process that educator team members will go through as they support children at different phases in their learning is represented in Figure 9.5. By ensuring that each child is supported as their needs are identified, educators can ensure that they provide **focused teaching**. Focused teaching is teaching that ensures that each student receives the instruction best suited to their current understanding.

Assessment has many different purposes. It can be used to identify what children already know about a topic or the skills they already have developed before opportunities to learn are provided. This is often called *diagnostic assessment* and sometimes may be referred to as *surfacing prior knowledge* if it is used as a strategy to motivate learners. This type of assessment is also referred to as *assessment for learning*. As learning starts, educators use formative assessment to

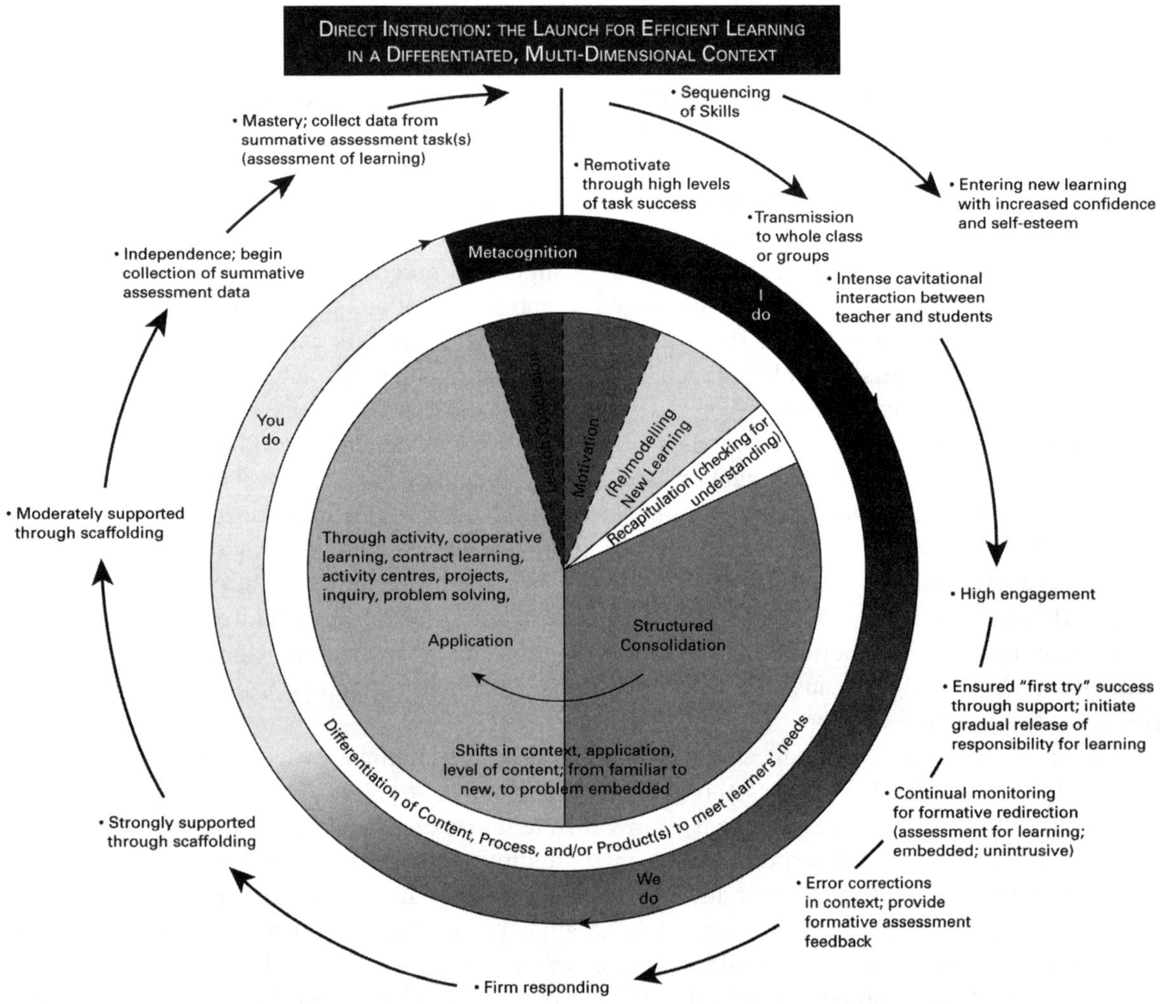

Figure 9.4 *Planning for Activity Centres that Follow New Learning that has been Modeled*

Used with permission of Nancy Maynes

ensure that they are addressing the learning needs of children and can be responsive by adjusting their strategies if they are not. This form of assessment is sometimes also called *assessment as learning*. Assessment *as* learning can be of two types. The first is assessment that requires the learner to be reflective and to understand the criteria and standards for a learning task. In Figure 9.5 this is referred to as *formative reflective assessment*. The second form of assessment *as* learning is referred to as *formative active assessment* in Figure 9.5. Formative active assessment supports the learner as improvement is undertaken in relation to the criteria and standards for a task. The final form of assessment is *summative assessment*. This is sometimes also referred to as *assessment of learning*. Using summative assessment, educators examine products that children create to demonstrate their learning, compare each product to the required standards and

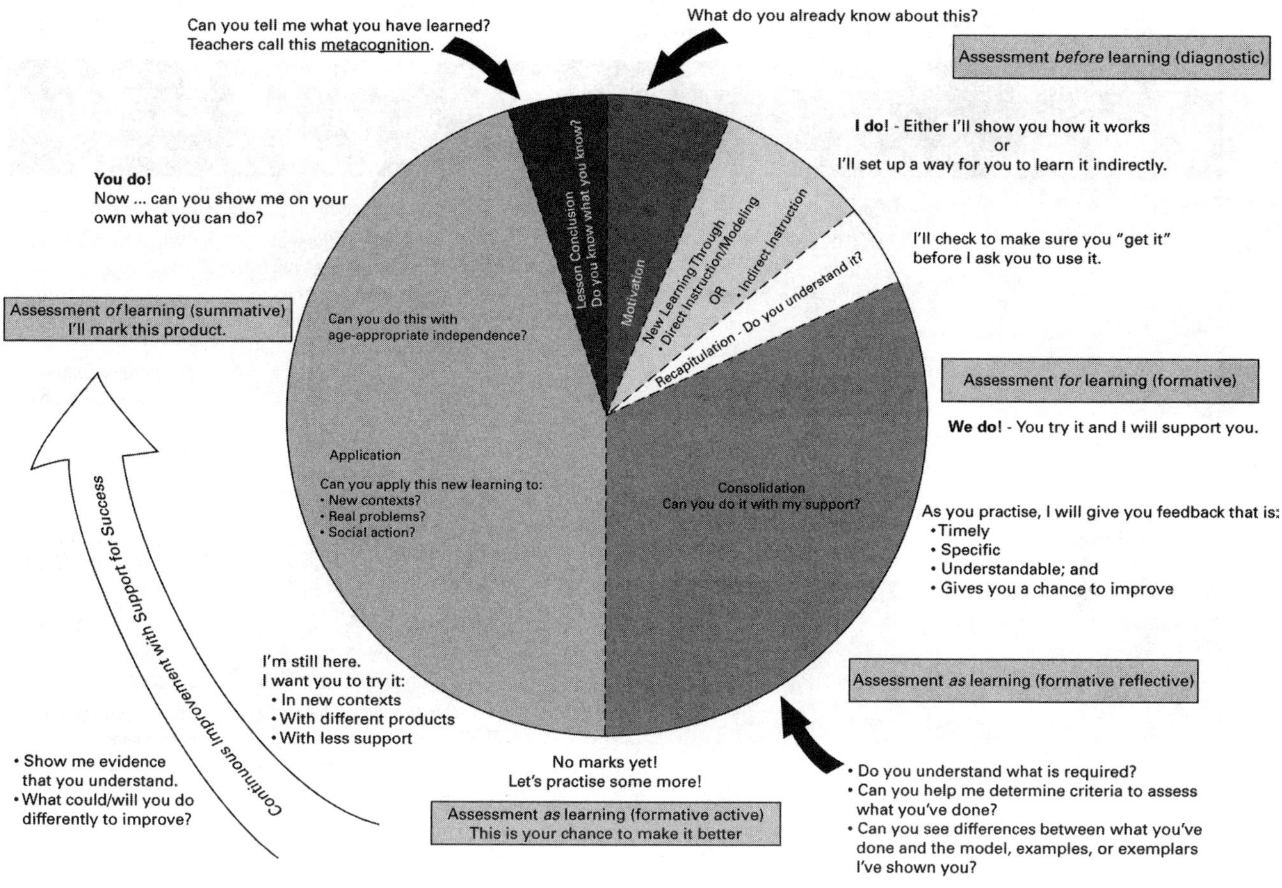

Figure 9.5 *A Framework for the Pedagogical Narrative between Educators and Children*

criteria, and assign an evaluation based on their professional judgment. Evaluations can then be used to plan the next learning opportunities for the children.

Table 9.2 provides further details about each form of assessment and details about how each form of assessment should be used. It includes some strategies that educators can use for each form of assessment as well. While some of these strategies are readily applicable with JK/SK students, many will apply to older children when reading skills are strong. However, this overview should help educators understand the full range of possibilities for assessment and some strategies that may apply to individuals in the JK/SK classroom.

9.8 *As educator team members observe children at play they should make notes of the learning episode to help them plan play extensions for the future.*

Table 9.2 *Understanding Assessment within Instruction*

Phases of Instruction	Gradual Release of Responsibility	Forms of Assessment	Roles of Each Form of Assessment	Uses of Each Form of Assessment	Strategies for Assessment
Motivation	*I do*	Diagnostic • To determine students' prior knowledge and skill levels • To identify misconceptions • To identify interests • To reveal learning preferences	Assessment *before* learning	• Not graded • Should be done in such a way as not to diminish students in the eyes of their peers	• Concept/ mind maps • KWL or KWML charts • T/F quizzes • Drawings • Surveys • Brain drains (e.g., four corners, scribble writing, flip cards, sticky notes, etc.)
New Learning			Assessment *for* learning	• Ongoing and continuous • Provides information about learning progress • Provides information to guide scaffolding • Provides information to determine accommodations or modifications that may be needed • Will often be ungraded	• Eye contact • Awareness of the body language of the learner • Q & A to determine individual understanding • Practice embedded in modeling • Rubrics used as growth schemes (i.e., to show the required criteria and standards)
Consolidation	*We do*	Formative • Formal and/or informal approaches can be used • Usually non-graded • Does not interrupt the flow of the learning • Criterion based • Students understand the criteria and the standards of expected performance • Focus is on the improvement of work • Teaches students to self- and peer-assess		• Helps students see their progress and focus on improvements • Includes teaching self- and peer-assessment techniques in age-appropriate ways	• Quizzes • Skills checklists • Individual response techniques (e.g., slates, clickers, etc.) • Personal communication (e.g., learning log, conference, hand signals, etc.) • Q & A • Observation • Exit cards/tickets • Graphic organizers • Rubrics

(*Continued*)

Table 9.2 Understanding Assessment within Instruction, continued

Phases of Instruction	Gradual Release of Responsibility	Forms of Assessment	Roles of Each Form of Assessment	Uses of Each Form of Assessment	Strategies for Assessment
Application	*You do*	Summative • Seeks to make the learner aware of their own new learning (metacognition); attaches language to new concepts • Aligned with learning goals (backwards design) • Authentic; the knowledge and skills can be transferred to real contexts • Provides choice to be responsive to each learner's learning style and preferences, interests, and learning profile	Assessment *as* learning • All tasks respect learners' time and effort by being worthwhile • All products are evaluated against clear and understood criteria; no surprises	• Focus on metacognitive awareness • Self- and peer-assessment • Use of self-assessment prompts • Examples: - What part of your work was most effective? - What is the evidence? - What part of your work is least effective? Why? - What actions will improve the process you used? - What actions will improve the product(s) you created? - What actions will strengthen your knowledge of this topic? - What will you do differently next time?	• Quizzes • Skills checklists • Individual response techniques (e.g., slates, clickers, etc.) • Personal communication (e.g., learning log, conference, hand signals, etc.) • Q & A • Observation • Exit cards/tickets • Graphic organizers • Rubrics
Lesson Conclusion			Assessment *of* learning	Feedback informs the next round of new learning	• Performance tasks • Portfolios • Learning logs • Tests that include higher level thinking skills • Evidence of increasing independence with learning

In Table 9.2, the terms *I do, we do*, and *you do* are used to identify the changing relationship between the child and the educator as the child gains more confidence and independence with new learning. The term *I do* refers to the modeling role of the educator team member. The term *we do* refers to the supportive role of the educator team as children practise new learning. The term *you do* celebrates the increased understanding that the children are demonstrating and recognizes their readiness to internalize that learning into their overall schema.

If educator team members share a common understanding of these instructional concepts, they are able to adjust their practice on the spot to support learning as children demonstrate different needs throughout the day.

LEARNING CENTRES: PLANNING, EXTENDING, MAINTAINING, AND CHANGING CENTRES FOR OPTIMAL LEARNING

Learning centres are an important feature of JK/SK learning climates for many reasons. By using centres, educator teams can ensure that children have many opportunities to explore, consolidate, and apply new ideas to help them make personal meaning of them. This type of exploration is necessary to provide children with the right balance of structure and freedom to engage in work play. Work play is important for supporting the learning of young children, because it allows children to carry out their intentions, play with purpose, engage in social interaction with peers and adults, solve problems, and seek support as needed. Work play times in the classroom may provide experiences where children are caught "between surprise and familiarity, partial resemblance and partial difference, what they expect and what they find" (Fromberg, 1987).

Activity centres in the classroom should be established to optimize learning possibilities from each area of the curriculum that is mandated within the local jurisdiction. Many educator teams choose to develop centres that are organized to integrate curriculum areas. Through integration, children can experience curriculum that meets their needs and see connections rather than artificial separations among ideas. Table 9.3 shows possibilities for the planned integration of curriculum areas to reflect the foci of a variety of centres that might be developed. Educator teams can adapt the integration framework to other centres they might design for their classroom.

When children are working at centres, educator team members play many roles that will shift fluidly as various needs become apparent during centre time. Educator team members may have a regular rotation schedule of observation and interaction planned for centre times, or they may choose to observe and determine areas where either observation or intervention is required, based on observations in different contexts. Behaviours such as soliciting help, inactivity, stalling, avoiding, hesitating, withdrawing, or becoming upset or frustrated will be easy to see in centre contexts. Also, positive behaviours such as following personal goals and plans, showing enjoyment, carefully observing others, making suggestions to peers, cooperating, exploring, welcoming others, and building or creating, will be signals for the educator team to challenge, question, or extend learning opportunities.

Table 9.3 Planning Centres for Rich Integration

Centre Type	To Integrate Literacy Activities	To Integrate Math Activities	To Integrate Science, Environmental, and Technology Activities	To Integrate Personal and Social Development Activities	To Integrate Physical Skills and Well-Being Activities	To Integrate Creativity Activities
Literacy	• connects to new concept learned from classroom books by retelling, relating, extending, or responding • examines books • explores print concepts • rehearses alphabet songs and rhymes • begins to self-correct letter reversals	• makes cardinal numbers in various media • uses various print and paint instruments to make tally tables and form numbers • begins to show awareness of one-to-one correspondence	• uses science terms for size, shape, and location accurately • names objects • recognizes letter sounds and blends • can trace letters using various media	• strengthens fine-motor skills • begins to show interest in the most effective ways to hold printing objects (i.e., pencils, paint brushes, etc.) • shares books, recording materials, and letter samples for common purposes	• strengthens fine-motor skills • refines speech and volume for various purposes • explains thinking • shows word awareness curiosity	• uses various material to communicate • speaks for specific purposes • uses art materials to respond to text • uses drama and dance forms to respond to text • talks about books and favourite video stories
Mathematics	• uses many sources to find information • shows openness to new experiences • sorts objects by common criteria • uses Venn diagrams for sorting • can draw to show sorting • can explain sorting diagrams by referring to similarities and differences	• sorts by single criterion • collects like objects into sets • describes and discusses objects and sorting pattern • understands the results of taking away an object from a group and adding an object to a group (i.e., one less, two less, one more, two more) • describes linear attributes (i.e., longer, shorter, taller, etc.) • identifies, sorts, and describes 3D objects	• explores and investigates • names symbols and shapes • can name properties of objects • can name environmental events (e.g., "It's raining.") • can ask questions and generalize about environmental events (e.g., "It's cold in winter.")	• is persistent in learning contexts • is curious and interested in learning opportunities • seeks support and assistance as needed, including peer support • engages in and completes some self-directed and self-selected activities • acknowledges feedback • provides positive feedback to peers	• develops fine-motor skills to manipulate objects • develops and improves hand–eye coordination • demonstrates spatial awareness • manages working space	• explores patterns, movement, rhythms, sound, music • participates in creating various forms of patterns, movements, rhythms, sounds, and music • engages in problems that are posed in a variety of ways • attempts to solve problems • experiments with art materials

(Continued)

Table 9.3 *Planning Centres for Rich Integration, continued*

Centre Type	To Integrate Literacy Activities	To Integrate Math Activities	To Integrate Science, Environmental, and Technology Activities	To Integrate Personal and Social Development Activities	To Integrate Physical Skills and Well-Being Activities	To Integrate Creativity Activities
Art	• draws • records • uses colour, print, and sketches to explain • explains personal drawings	• creates patterns • builds 3D objects • sorts • states sorting criteria • uses relative vocabulary (e.g., *behind*, *beside*, *on top of*, etc.)	• solves problems • contributes ideas • differentiates between use and waste • selects and uses materials appropriate to tasks • shows awareness of colour, shape, pattern, and texture • engages in conversations about design features; explores variations	• shares • participates • engages fully and completes tasks • develops social skills related to productive cooperation • seeks help and guidance as needed • expresses specific needs	• advances fine-motor skills • builds hand–eye coordination skills • develops spatial awareness skills	• expresses ideas, thoughts, and feelings • responds to visual images • creates 2- and 3D items • openly experiments with artistic elements (i.e., line, colour, space, shape, texture, pattern)
Building blocks and large manipulatives	• connects ideas • shares ideas and information orally • participates • listens and responds appropriately to the ideas of others	• builds • recognizes and discusses characteristics of building projects • creates and extends patterns • compares size, height, length, width orally	• selects appropriate materials • organizes material options for a purpose • generates ideas and options for specified purposes • can relate personal structures to structures outside of the classroom • uses related construction terms accurately (i.e., *move*, *carry*, *place*, *support*)	• can work independently • can work cooperatively • can seek assistance as needed • can seek and accept help • can consider alternatives • can select and complete tasks • can express concerns and frustrations in appropriate ways	• can manipulate objects of various sizes to achieve a purpose • develops manipulative skills with objects of various sizes • develops spatial awareness • uses body strategically for tasks of building and manipulating	• engages in dramatic play • asks questions • identifies problems • solves problems posed by self and others • expresses thoughts and feelings in a variety of ways • uses appropriate caution when handling large or heavy objects
Computers and technology	• engages in talk about books and media • listens to others' views and opinions • assesses information using a variety of communication cues	• recognizes patterns • repeats and extends patterns • can use a computer or calculator to represent numbers	• uses sources to find information • uses technology as a learning tool • participates in age-appropriate problem solving • names shapes and symbols	• is curious, persistent, and focused in learning • expresses needs and wants clearly and appropriately • follows direction • sequences tasks productively	• is developing hand–eye coordination • is developing fine- and gross-motor skills as appropriate • interacts as expected • responds in acceptable ways	• uses creative software with guidance • is open to exploring on the computer

(*Continued*)

Table 9.3 *Planning Centres for Rich Integration, continued*

Centre Type	To Integrate Literacy Activities	To Integrate Math Activities	To Integrate Science, Environmental, and Technology Activities	To Integrate Personal and Social Development Activities	To Integrate Physical Skills and Well-Being Activities	To Integrate Creativity Activities
Computers and technology, (*continued*)	• uses sketches, objects, photographs, print, stories, and other media forms to gather information • recognizes the purpose and layout of a computer keyboard	• uses comparison language correctly (e.g., *more*, *less*, *same*, *different*, *greater than*, *less than*)		• shows effort to adapt to new situations and requirements • begins to understand sustainability concepts • participates in recycling efforts		
Home Centre	• uses print and pictures to extend oral communication • focuses on a topic • explores text concepts • demonstrates willingness to be inclusive • can retell, reflect, and relate text to self to make connections • explores texts in various forms	• uses comparative vocabulary • uses correct vocabulary to discuss measurement concepts (e.g., length, weight, capacity, height, volume, temperature) • uses comparative forms of common describing words (e.g., *cold*, *colder*, *coldest*)	• participates in problem solving • uses descriptive words correctly • conserves resources • shares resources • recognizes safety issues and practices • uses simple tools appropriately • recognizes the function of common objects found in the classroom and school yard • considers alternate uses for common objects	• participates • shows a sense of responsibility for tasks • asks questions • seeks help • rephrases to ensure understanding • acknowledges input appropriately	• develops coordination • recognizes healthy and unhealthy food choices • observes safety rules • follows rules and routines • can sort foods by common labels (e.g., fruits, vegetables, etc.) • can select most healthy options from choices • follows hygiene routines	• adapts materials • demonstrates creativity in the use of materials • shares stories about traditions and family practices • recognizes traditions • recognizes cultural influences of representative traditions • can distinguish between traditions and celebrations • participates in celebrations
Drama and dance	• describes experiences and related ideas • can portray and imitate actions • can follow along and repeat physical movements	• uses descriptive terms as might be found in children's stories (e.g., time, place, events, etc.) • uses measurement vocabulary in descriptions	• recognizes common ways to express feelings • understands some cultural influences on expressions • identifies community resources • identifies community workers	• explores spatial concepts • is willing to take reasonable risks to explore new situations • is adaptable and flexible	• listens • responds appropriately • is aware of safety considerations when doing physical activity • understands what fairness means in different contexts	• engages in creative activities • engages in imaginative play • uses costumes and props • sees drama and dance as forms of expression

(*Continued*)

Table 9.3 *Planning Centres for Rich Integration, continued*

Centre Type	To Integrate Literacy Activities	To Integrate Math Activities	To Integrate Science, Environmental, and Technology Activities	To Integrate Personal and Social Development Activities	To Integrate Physical Skills and Well-Being Activities	To Integrate Creativity Activities
Drama and dance, (*continued*)	• can describe and elaborate on drawings and pictures	• trades and exchanges • engages in representative play (e.g., house, store, school, construction, etc.) • compares objects with appropriate vocabulary	• engages in role play in representative play contexts • recognizes and names common household objects • recognizes and describes roles and responsibilities	• names desirable human qualities (e.g., honest, trustworthy, kind, etc.) • can describe family roles, responsibilities, and relationships • considers choices when interacting with others • resolves conflicts productively • negotiates • shows respect for peers and adults	• follows rules • can help establish rules for cooperative play • cares for others' space and property • respects personal space • takes appropriate hygiene measures with minimal direction	• expresses feelings and thoughts through dramatic means
Gross motor and outdoors	• connects to text • asks questions • responds to questions • takes turns • recognizes game rules • shares ideas	• recognizes and uses vocabulary that shows relative location and position • makes and extends patterns • orders materials by single criteria • uses comparative words	• understands causal relationships /cause–effect • sees alternatives and options in possible responses • demonstrates body awareness • can name body parts • differentiates between needs and wants • expresses needs appropriately	• expresses self positively • acknowledges feedback • recognizes sources of frustration • expresses frustration appropriately • moves around the classroom and school appropriately • engages in exercise • engages in a variety of play formats • understands the meaning of fairness and taking turns • participates without competing	• uses and develops large-muscle coordination • expends effort in physical activities • gets involved • participates actively in the outdoor environment	• experiences, explores, and experiments with increasing confidence • dances • engages in drama activities

(*Continued*)

Table 9.3 Planning Centres for Rich Integration, continued

Centre Type	To Integrate Literacy Activities	To Integrate Math Activities	To Integrate Science, Environmental, and Technology Activities	To Integrate Personal and Social Development Activities	To Integrate Physical Skills and Well-Being Activities	To Integrate Creativity Activities
Music	• connects to texts by speaking about personal experiences with music • experiments with sounds • creates various sound-making instruments with support • shows interest in the qualities of intonation applied to oral text • engages in wordplay and sound experiments • participates in singing and rhyming activities • can memorize and repeat children's rhymes	• reproduces patterns in sounds • creates and extends sound patterns • describes patterns in sound • makes sound-producing toys	• identifies personal preferences when choices are available • understands circumstances when options may be limited • uses all senses for exploration as suitable • recognizes and imitates familiar sounds (e.g., "The car makes a honking sound.") • recognizes a range of ways in which feelings and preferences may be expressed	• follows directions • participates when appropriate in group activities • shows confidence when engaging in musical imitation or creation • uses appropriate methods to show personal feelings and preferences	• is aware of safety issues when moving • is sensitive to the needs of others for personal space • develops and uses all senses as appropriate to explore and create	• expresses feelings and thoughts through musical forms • can reproduce beat and rhythm • learns songs and rhymes • responds to music
Water	• uses language related to water accurately • explores new ideas with water experiments	• shows curiosity about new apparatus introduced to water resource play areas • uses and explores with objects related to capacity and volume • reads and imitates numbers related to volume from containers	• shares resources • makes observations related to cause and effect • solves problems • uses language to explore the effects of water on other objects	• follows safety rules • reorganizes materials and resources after play • tidies and cleans up • shows careful use of resources	• develops improved coordination • perceives and names problems • seeks workable solutions • is receptive to questions about personal explorations	• creates new experiments with water and related resource • adapts materials

(*Continued*)

Table 9.3 *Planning Centres for Rich Integration, continued*

Centre Type	To Integrate Literacy Activities	To Integrate Math Activities	To Integrate Science, Environmental, and Technology Activities	To Integrate Personal and Social Development Activities	To Integrate Physical Skills and Well-Being Activities	To Integrate Creativity Activities
Sand	• explains experiences with sand creations • retells and relates to share ideas • supports the work of peers as they create in sand • questions others about their sand projects	• uses comparative words to describe • creates and extends patterns • describes patterns and creations • can describe characteristics of volume and capacity in simple language (e.g., "This is full.")	• explores using sand • creates using sand • mixes sand and other objects to create interest and diversity • explores cause and effect as constructions are made • makes purposeful choices about resources • creates structures with multi-sensory appeal	• shows persistence • shows interest in the ideas of peers as they create structures with sand • engages in cooperative play to share resources to complete tasks	• develops fine-motor skills • develops improved coordination • follows safety rules when working with sand • shows curiosity and initiative when new elements are introducing to the sand table	• shows adaptive capabilities when using resources • is open to suggestions from peers and adults • solves problems • seeks help when needed
Writing and bookmaking	• shows developing awareness of word concepts • holds books properly • tracks eye and finger movement from top to bottom and left to right on a page or computer screen • uses various materials to write • shows interest in unique forms of books (e.g., pop-up books, flip books) created by others • begins to show some understanding of the connections among sounds, letters, and words	• uses numbers as patterns for writing • restates rhymes using numbers • sees the purpose of sequential numbering when writing or in books (i.e., page numbers)	• engages books from many cultures • understands the concept of different languages • shows interest in print forms from other languages • talks about picture book depictions	• is open to book exposure • chooses books for "rereading" during play time • works cooperatively with an adult to tell a story that can be made into a book • contributes ideas for a class book about a selected theme • recognizes what fits and does not fit a theme	• holds writing objects firmly • follows patterns and reproduces print • perceives words that are oriented wrongly (e.g., letters upside down or backwards)	• uses letters and numbers in art forms • plays with creative ways to represent letters and numbers • chooses appropriate media for making picture and word books

9.9 Work play can happen outdoors as well as at classroom centres.

As children engage in work play at centres, educators will want to observe how they plan and follow through on plans to complete tasks. Observation sheets at centres can be designed to reflect various stages of their planning that may be evident as children spend time at a centre (see Figure 9.6).

Child's Name	Date: Centre: Activity Purpose:
Play Status	Observations
• Starting a plan	
• Continuing a plan	
• Interrupting a plan	
• Completing a plan	
• Changing a plan	

Figure 9.6 *Observing Children's Play Status during Work Play*

During these times, educator team members will engage children by participating in their play in a relaxed and joyful way; observing their play for the purpose of supporting extensions; conversing with children as they play, to challenge, respond, and extend thinking; encouraging children as they attempt to solve problems and resolving issues as they play; or recording dialogue of ordinary moments for later professional reflection about what each dialogue reveals about the child's learning. The supports that the team provides will be context dependent and will be designed to support each child's learning.

These supports can take any of the following forms:

- Providing spaces for play and work play
  - Allowing choice
  - Providing for differentiation
  - Monitoring safety issues
  - Managing resources (suitability and replenishing)
  - Monitoring work zones (quiet, noisy, wet, dry)
- Observing and monitoring
  - Looking for ordinary moments when learning is happening
  - Determining the child's play status (see Figure 9.6)
  - Supporting social interactions
  - Observing types of play and monitoring for patterns
  - Looking for openings to respond to, challenge, or extend thinking
  - Showing initiative in questioning, responding, and extending
  - Recording and interpreting observations
- Intervening
  - Reflecting children's concerns
  - Monitoring conflict
  - Suggesting options
  - Providing comfort
  - Regrouping
- Participating in children's play
  - Waiting to be invited to play
  - Monitoring for natural openings where play scope can be extended
  - Engaging in parallel or partner play
  - Supporting a child who has become isolated
  - Inserting new play materials to extend play
  - Offering ideas
  - Monitoring reactions to new circumstances and input
- Having ordinary-moment conversations with children as they engage in various forms of play
  - Responding to children's comments as they play
  - Initiating a discussion about a play process or product
  - Introducing children to each other
  - Explaining a child's interests to another child
  - Asking questions
  - Providing non-judgmental feedback
  - Mirroring children's comments back to them (e.g., "So you think…")
  - Conversing as a play partner or from a parallel play situation
  - Asking *why* and *how* questions

- Encouraging resolutions and problem solving
  - Seeing conflicts as inevitable aspects of group situations
  - Speaking to children about productive ways to manage social conflicts
  - Teaching children what social skills look and sound like (e.g., ways to disagree in agreeable ways)
  - Providing support and time as children try to resolve problems
  - Inviting children to seek options when problems arise
  - Teaching children the difference between telling (to get someone out of trouble) and tattling (to get someone in trouble)
  - Modeling calm problem-solving approaches
  - Providing comfort
  - Interacting
  - Providing breaks
- Managing productive transitions
  - Teaching cleanup standards and practices
  - Clarifying expectations that are realistic and age appropriate
  - Providing regular nutrition and rest
  - Modeling teamwork

By considering all of the roles that educator team members might have during centre times and free play activities, they can plan to maximize on the strengths of each team member to ensure that all children have optimal opportunities to engage in play and work play that will be fulfilling.

9.10 *By interacting with adults during play, the older children in a JK/SK group may engage in their highest levels of play. Children engage in their highest levels of play when they work in pairs.*

CHAPTER SUMMARY

Play-based learning supports neural development and rejuvenation, promotes curiosity and alert observation, provides socialization, teaches about culture, and supports the growth of communication and understanding. By providing many modes of play and supporting many forms of social play in a variety of indoor and outdoor areas, educator teams optimize play-based learning in the JK/SK context. Diversity in resources and support for learning through different learning styles provides optimal opportunities for children to use imagination and creativity during play.

More structured approaches for learning interspersed in the JK/SK day provide opportunities for differentiation for young learners, based on their readiness for new learning challenges. Pedagogical narratives provide children with support as they explore, consolidate, and apply new learning in new play contexts.

THINKING AHEAD: Opportunities for Professional Reflection

- Outdoor time serves many purposes during the JK/SK day. Team members may plan to extend some indoor goals to outdoor contexts, but many times the nature of outdoor play will be very different from indoor play and work play. Play spaces need to be checked daily for potential dangers, since many areas are open to the public outside of school hours. Children will initiate much of the outdoor play, but this can be supported by making some suitable outdoor equipment available for various seasons of the year. Many pieces of equipment can be purchased in forms that are suitable for four- and five-year-olds (see Table 9.4).

Table 9.4 *Outdoor Play Items that are Suitable for Different Seasons*

Autumn	Winter	Spring
Sand boxes	Shovels	Water buckets
Shovels and hand trowels	Sleds	Hoses
Bird feeders	Birdfeeders	Sandboxes
Balls	Cardboard boxes	Shallow pools
Skipping ropes	Music source (for movement games)	Rubber boots
Playground chalk		Skipping ropes
Sponge bats		Playground chalk
Swings		Sponge bats
Slides		Balls
Tricycles		Slides
Rakes		Tricycles
Cardboard		Cardboard
Children's gardens		Children's gardens
Wagons		Magnifying glasses
Music source (for movement games)		Wagons
Parachute		Hula hoops
Collection bags		Music source (for movement games)
		Parachutes
		Bug cages

- Many outdoor play items for schools should be purchased from school suppliers, because they are often made of more durable materials than may be available from public sources. Using Table 9.4 as a starting point, add other outdoor play items that you think would be suitable for each season in your area.
- Locate samples of observation sheets you have seen used in JK/SK classrooms for recording what children do and say during play and work play times of the day. Examine the samples you have collected and determine the features of the ones you like best. Use these features to design an observation recording sheet that you might want to use in your own classroom.
- Table 9.1 provides a summary of eight types of play that children may prefer because of their interests, strengths, and learning styles. Consider each type of play and identify ways you could respond to, question, challenge, and extend each type. Discuss your ideas in a small group.
- Consider how you will teach young children the difference between play and work play. Work play should allow time for children to play with purpose, carry out their planning intentions, socialize, observe, support peers, solve problems, and be exposed to new ideas.
- Consider ways that are appropriate for the educator team members to get involved in children's play. How would you initiate involvement? Why?
- Gather a group of young children and develop at least six strategies you could use to teach these children any one of the songs or poems found at www.kinderthemes.com/Songsideasandchecklists.htlm. Videotape your interactions and share your strategies with colleagues. Discuss how you might use this song or poem in your classroom (i.e., as a transition, a pre-rest gathering, a theme, etc.).

ADDITIONAL READING SUGGESTIONS

This site provides a wealth of references related to resources and exemplars for early learning contexts. It is a New Zealand site but many ideas are easily adaptable to any Canadian classroom for JK/SK children:
www.educate.ece.govt.nz/learning/CurriculumAndLearning/Assessmentforlearning/KeiTuaotePae.aspx.

10 Assessing Early Learning

"...full-day kindergartners exhibited more independent learning, classroom involvement, productivity in work with peers and reflectivity than half-day kindergartners. They were also more likely to approach their teachers and they expressed less withdrawal, anger, shyness, and blaming behaviour than half-day kindergartners."

(A. Miller, 2001)

10.1 *With young children, observation is the main strategy used for the assessment of learning.*

In this chapter, educator team members will learn about

- observation: pedagogical narrative and the early learner
- Kei Tua o te Pae / assessment for early learning: early childhood exemplars
- action research to support early learners
- portfolios: picturing growth over time
- structured growth planning and observation
- reporting to the parent
- reporting to the ELL parent
- reporting to the child
- arranging support services

At the end of this chapter, educator team members can reflect on their personal growth through

- CHAPTER SUMMARY
- THINKING AHEAD: Opportunities for Professional Reflection
- ADDITIONAL READING SUGGESTIONS

The quality of the observations made by the educator team members as young children engage learning opportunities is crucial to the quality of subsequent learning opportunities that are offered. When professional observations lead to valid interpretations of the child's thinking, educators are able to plan for and provide more appropriate resources for the next learning episodes. As the educator team members observe children at **work play**, they begin to track what the child's intentions are for their activity and position themselves to respond, question, challenge, and extend thinking to support each child's growth.

OBSERVATION: PEDAGOGICAL NARRATIVE AND THE EARLY LEARNER

The early learning JK/SK classroom should be characterized by many features that have been proven to benefit the early learner (Miller, 2001). These features include:

- new learning that is integrated with prior experiences
- learning experiences that include project work
- learning structured with flexible groupings of children so that they experience mixed-ability and mixed-age groups (Drew and Law, 1995)
- an unhurried setting
- experiential approaches
- informal interactions with educator team members, volunteers, other children, and objects (Housden and Kam, 1992)
- pre-literacy experiences and an emphasis on language development,including numeracy concepts
- partnership among the parents, extended family members, and the educator team
- complementary roles between educators and families
- focus on books in the classroom and home
- balanced grouping arrangements throughout the day, including individual activities, small group activities, and whole group instruction (Katz, 1995)
- focus on social skills development and conflict management skills (Rothenberg, 1995)
- close observation of children's learning and systematic collection and examination of work samples

10.2 Some pedagogical narratives will be recorded so that they can be analyzed later.

Through close observation, educator teams can support children as they engage in a wide range of classroom and outdoor activities. Through work play children engage in activities that become opportunities for their own experiences and help them advance their understanding in many areas. Their activities become self-education opportunities. By engaging children in **pedagogical narrative** during these activities, adults can support children's evolving understandings. Pedagogical narrative is an adult-supported conversation, led by the child, to discuss the child's learning. These discussions between children and educator team members serve to respond to, challenge, or extend children's thinking as they engage in play.

During work play, children use language to communicate, build social relationships with adults and peers, build self-confidence to explore options, develop initiative, discover new language, discover relationships and connections to explain how things work, extend their mental **schema** by accommodating or adapting it to new experiences, and learn to use representations as they imitate and engage in various forms of play.

Educator team members will need to be skilled in listening to, engaging in, and interpreting meaning from children's play in order to understand the area of growth that is being represented as children participate in conversations about what they are doing. By recording these conversations (pedagogical narratives) educator teams can examine them more closely and compare daily experiences and the growth they represent (see Table 10.1).

Through pedagogical narrative, the adult can create openings for the child to consider the consequences of specific actions and encourage purposeful

Table 10.1 *Growth Represented in Pedagogical Narratives over Time*

Tuesday's Pedagogical Narrative at the Water Table	Wednesday's Pedagogical Narrative at the Water Table
Child: "This is my boat." Adult: "What is your boat doing?" Child: "It's on top of the water. I am pushing it." Adult: "I see something in your boat." Child: (after a long pause) "I got it from over there." (pointing) Adult: "Is your boat taking it somewhere?" Child: "Uh-huh."	Adult: "You're taking things somewhere in your boat again today." Child: "Yep." Adult: "The boat is going somewhere today." Child: (points) "I can make it move when I slap the top of the water." Adult : "Yes. Is it going where you want it to go?" Child: (after a long pause) "I can make it." (pushes boat from behind)

experimentation. Over time, these narratives can introduce new vocabulary so that children expand their **conceptual language** about things they are investigating (e.g., floating, sinking, direction). As adults interact with children engaged in work play, they can introduce new terms and reinforce them through repetition.

Example:

Child: "It's on top of the water. I am pushing it."

Adult: "It's floating on the water."

Child: "Floating."

The pedagogical narrative is a purposeful interaction; the adult has many roles before, during, and after the narrative. The adult will provide work play places for children to explore, monitoring the choices children make during work play times of the day, observing to gain a perspective on the children they intend to interact with, initiating interaction by responding, questioning, or extending children's ideas, participating in the child-initiated work play, conversing about what the children are doing, encouraging problem solving through dialogue, recording observations and the progress of work play narratives, and interpreting pedagogical narratives so that children have support for their next work play episode.

To be purposeful, the pedagogical narrative should be initiated with full awareness of where the child appears to be in the process of their own work plan for the work play period. Educators should consider

- Has the child developed a plan?
- How can you tell?
- Has the plan been started?
- At what stage is the plan (i.e., just started or well under way)?
- Is the child appropriately focused on the task they have initiated?
- Has the child interrupted the work plan? Why?
- Are new resources needed? Would prompts from responses, questions, or discussion overtures be appropriate?
- Is the child completing the plan?
- Has the child changed or improved the plan?

10.3 *Analysis of taped conversations with children and among groups of children can provide valuable direction for further program support choices.*

Engagement in pedagogical narrative approaches to children's work play will provide valuable information about how to support the extension of the child's learning. These narratives will produce supportive relationships with children, create learning partnerships, and encourage children to pursue their interests as they take initiative, exercise control, and gain confidence in their ability and competence in determining their direction. To create these engaging pedagogical narratives, educator teams must agree that children think and reason differently from adults; that problem-solving conversations are worthwhile opportunities to support individual growth; that opportunities to grow in developmentally appropriate ways and areas are essential for young children; that experimentation is essential to the learning process and the developing understanding of new concepts, new vocabulary, and new relationships; and that play contexts support the growth of independence and competence. By sharing these beliefs, educator team members can set the stage for play-based learning that will provide growth opportunities for each child. Recordings of conversations with children or among groups of children may be made to provide educators with details that they may want to revisit or examine more closely.

Educators must remember that observation records are highly confidential evaluation documents and should be shared only with other members of the educator team, parents, and with the child as appropriate.

KEI TUA O TE PAE – ASSESSMENT FOR EARLY LEARNING: EARLY CHILDHOOD EXEMPLARS

New Zealand has been a leader in the work being done to develop early learning programs for children. Kindergarten in New Zealand can include children as young as three and a half years of age and extend until five and a half. *Kei Tua o te Pae* is the Maori phrase used to describe the New Zealand early learning website, resources and supports for teachers. This phrase means "beyond the horizon." The phrase provides a metaphor for teachers with a focus on helping them to improve their teaching by showing them examples of best practice.

Kei Tua o te Pae is a phrase from a lullaby by Hirini Melbourne. The lullaby displays the symbolic horizon in three comparisons. First, the horizon is a metaphor for the limitless possibilities for the direction of each child's learning. Second, the metaphor addresses the horizon of possibilities for the growth, development and learning of each child in relation to their body, mind, and spirit. Finally, the horizon metaphor addresses the reciprocal relationships of children in a learning context with people, places, and things. In this final metaphor, the child and the world relate to each other as the world shapes their learning and their learning in turn shapes the world.

Kei Tua o te Pae (www.educate.ece.govt.nz/learning/curriculumAndLearning/Assessmentforlearning/KeiTuaotePae.aspx) provides teachers with many exemplars or examples of assessment practices and their meanings from many early learning contexts. Exemplars make valued learning visible for children, educators, families, and community services staff, so that learning can be supported to its full extent. As educators collect, examine, and interpret exemplars, they are

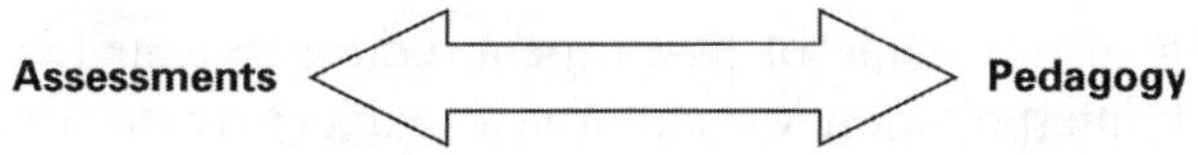

Figure 10.1 *Assessment Practices and the Resulting Pedagogy are Reciprocal*

able to support diverse learning pathways for children and effectively differentiate learning for the unique needs of each child.

By using exemplars, educators are able to make the link between the assessments they collect, examine, and interpret and the next steps in their pedagogical choices to support the learner. Assessment and **pedagogy** become reciprocal (see Figure 10.1).

Once educators collect, examine, and interpret exemplars, they can work with children's interests, strengths, and learning profiles to develop a pathway for learning and provide supports that are ongoing and diversified to ensure the children's learning success. Educators are constantly within the cycle of observation of children's learning, recognizing and interpreting what they observe, and responding to the learning by providing the children with feedback and access to new learning pathways (see Figure 10.2).

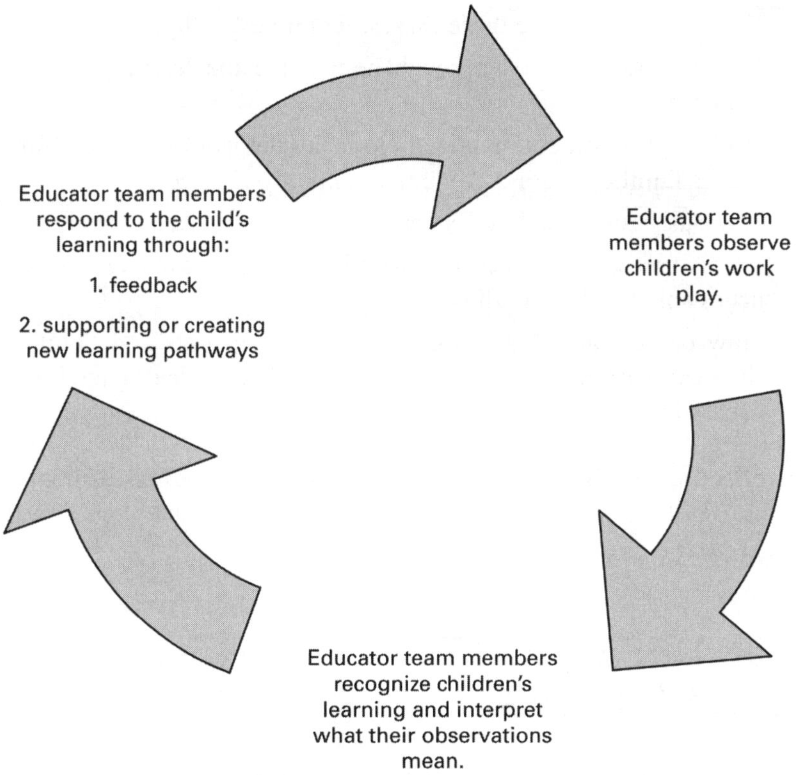

Figure 10.2 *The Cycle of Assessment in the Early Learning JK/SK Context*

By engaging in this cycle of assessment, educator teams can support their recognition and interpretation of children's work play to implement timely and appropriate responses through feedback and pathways to learning. In this cycle, feedback will sometimes be documented in the form of examples and portfolio entries, on **growth schemes**, or through open-ended observation notes. Feedback will frequently be oral and incidental as children engage in various forms of work play throughout the day, and may consist of nods, brief comments, or approval signals such as smiles. Feedback in different forms helps children recognize that the outcomes they are achieving are valued and significant.

Assessment should always make a difference in children's learning. It should invite participation in learning from the children, their families, and the broader learning-support community. It should celebrate the children's competence as they make their learning visible and strive to achieve learning that is valued in their community. It should create a sense of continuity as children receive supports for their ongoing learning through many pathways.

To assess effectively, educators must see assessment as a reflective exercise with the single goal of improving instruction. To promote reflection, they should consider the following questions:

- Who will need to use these assessment notes? Why?
- Will this assessment approach help make the learning visible for the children?
- Will this assessment practice help make the learning visible for the children's families or for community support personnel?
- Is the assessment culturally sensitive?
- Is this assessment accessible to all families? How can I make it more accessible to ELL families?
- How can I make this assessment open to parents and families so that they can participate in responding, questioning, and extending the children's learning?

By reflecting on these questions for the documented assessments that are used in the JK/SK classroom, educator teams can ensure that their approaches to assessment extend all possible horizons for learning.

ACTION RESEARCH TO SUPPORT EARLY LEARNERS

Action research refers to an *in situ* approach to learning more about one's own professional practice. In the context of the JK/SK classroom, educator team members engage in action research when they ask questions about the impact of their own practice. Through critical observation of the impacts of changes in practice on children's learning, they determine the value of the change.

To engage in action research in the JK/SK classroom, educators must find many ways to engage children through their play. Their involvement in children's play must be responsive to the child's initiation of a play sequence. There are often opportunities to become involved in children's play in the initial moments of play when children may be most open to participating with a play partner. These are ideal moments for the educator team members to join play in unobtrusive and supportive ways. These opportunities may provide a context for action research.

As well, educators must be aware that some types of play will be more readily engaged in by adults than others. For example, play that is based on imagination is expandable to include a wider cast of participants. Games and pretend play often can expand to include adult players. Table 10.2 provides some guidance for opportunities that should be considered for action research related to children's play.

Table 10.2 *When Adults Participate in Children's Play*

How to Participate in Children's Play	Examples of Things to Attend to in Order to Participate in This Way	Action Research Foci That Could Be Engaged in Play Participation
Look for natural play openings	• Explore the same materials the child is exploring. • Join in games. • Take a role in pretend play. • Consider carefully when it may not be appropriate to engage in play with the child (e.g., construction play).	• How do the children respond to you as a play partner in various forms of play? • What seems to be the most effective way for adults to engage in play with children? • Are there times when children seem to resist adult involvement in their play? • How is leadership during play influenced by adult involvement?
Play at the children's physical level	• Gain perspective by getting a child's view of the play area and resources. • Let the child(ren) lead your involvement. • Engage respectfully by following the leads given by the child. • Build trust through respectful play participation. • Use pedagogical narrative sensitively; look for natural openings and take cues from the child's responses.	• Do children engage in play more readily with some adults than with others? Why? • What cues do children provide when they want to lead play? • How do children invite adults into their play? • How do children end play when adults are involved? Is it different from how they end play when no adults are involved?
Join play as a play partner	• Engage in pretend or game play as an equal. • Follow the child(ren)'s lead. • Adopt the tone of the play you are joining. • Adopt assigned roles as determined by the child(ren). • Follow directions from the child(ren).	• How do children experiment with new language and phrases as adults enter their games and pretend play? • How do children invite adults to join pretend play and games? • Do children use different directive language with adults than they do with their peers?

(*Continued*)

Table 10.2 *When Adults Participate in Children's Play, continued*

How to Participate in Children's Play	Examples of Things to Attend to in Order to Participate in This Way	Action Research Foci That Could Be Engaged in Play Participation
Support children making connections to other children as play partners	• Refer children to other children for support and expansion. • Introduce new vocabulary to a child by commenting on the work of peers and inviting them to comment. • Recognize imitative behaviour as a form of exploring new ideas and new perspectives.	• Are established social groups in the classroom more effective for making play partner connections than introductions and references to play partners across existing social groups? • Whom do children imitate as they play? • What adult characteristics do children imitate as they play?
Support play extensions	• Respond, question, challenge, and extend, in that order. • Introduce play variants gently and gradually. • Follow; don't lead.	• Are natural growth patterns evident in the play when responses, questions, challenges, and extensions are introduced? • What evidence do you have that the play includes learning? • How do children respond to play extensions introduced by an adult player?

Used with permission of Nancy Maynes

As educators engage in children's work play, they will find many opportunities to question the impact of their engagement and interactions with the children. Each question provides an opportunity to engage in new aspects of action research and to learn more about the effects of professional actions on the child's learning and growth.

PORTFOLIOS: PICTURING GROWTH OVER TIME

Portfolios provide images and anecdotes about a children's learning over time. Portfolios are used to collect, monitor, track, and report children's growth. Well managed portfolios show trends over time and across circumstances. They can be used for formative and summative purposes (see Chapter 9) and allow educator team members to develop a sense of "before and after" as children's understanding evolves.

Portfolios are also reporting and historical references for parents and guardians. Educator teams can use a portfolio of a child's work to provide examples that will support conversations with parents and with the child. Portfolios can be designed to provide evidence of growing literacy and numeracy concepts, engagement in tasks, and social interactions. They provide a storage space for the records of pedagogical narratives and their interpretations. These records support the efforts of the educator team to expand the child's learning by providing appropriate new experiences in the child's **zone of proximal development** (Vygotsky, 1978).

Photographs are an important element of the child's developing portfolio. Photographs can capture ordinary moments in the child's work play that provide evidence of learning and guidance for new learning extensions. These visual records can create platforms for discussions among educator team members and between the educator team and parents. They can create common ground that supports discussion about how the school and home can work together to support the child's further growth. Well-organized portfolios can also provide a testament to the child's physical growth and growth in dexterity and social breadth over the course of the program. They can be used effectively as transition documents for teachers in grade school programs to learn more about the strengths and interests of the child before they enter Grade 1.

A child's portfolio should be easily accessible to educators and the child during the school day. Easy accessibility will encourage children to participate in selecting items to store in the portfolio over time. Easily accessible portfolios will also allow educators to support children's recall of earlier learning and use this as an opportunity to extend learning. Children can participate in designing and decorating their portfolios with their personal art to create a stronger sense of ownership of the portfolio. By ensuring that portfolios are easily accessible, educators can ensure that they take their rightful place in the classroom as evolving records of growth and celebrations of successes.

Zone of proximal development is Vygotsky's term for the range of tasks that

1. a child can complete independently; and
2. those completed with the guidance and assistance of adults or more-skilled children.

The lower limit of this zone is the level of skill reached by the child working independently. The upper limit is the level of new understanding that the child can achieve with the assistance of another person, as the child's cognitive skills are in the process of maturing.

STRUCTURED GROWTH PLANNING AND OBSERVATION

Most jurisdictions that offer full-day JK/SK school programs will also provide curriculum support documents that give educators direction about the goals of the program. As we saw in earlier chapters, social goals for early learning, followed by problem-solving goals, are typically the most valued by parents who choose JK/SK and early learning settings for their children. Literacy concepts and numeracy are also often a focus for early learning curriculum. Educator team members must be very familiar with local curriculum guidelines and the mandate provided within guidelines as a starting point for planning their programs.

Once the educator team is familiar with the guidelines, and any support documents that may be available to expand on the guidelines, these will be used to plan the program. Earlier chapters provided templates for planning across the school year and for considering ways to integrate learning through activity centre approaches.

Planning for learning after the general structure of the year has been determined is a responsive activity. Once educators begin to engage with the children, the current status of each child's learning in relation to the direction provided by curriculum guidelines will direct the next steps that the educator team will need to take. Part of this next stage of planning for learning involves imagining the various steps that most children will go through to achieve the learning goals as they are described in local guidelines. This process is referred to as *growth scheming*. A **growth scheme** starts with the mandated learning expectation and then identifies all of the various aspects (or criteria) of that learning expectation that might be achieved separately and thereby contribute to achieving learning of the overall expectation. Once the various aspects are identified, the full range of possible iterations of each aspect is identified in order from the least mature or sophisticated to the most sophisticated level. An example for a common JK/SK learning expectation is shown in Table 10.3. The number of growth steps that can be imagined for a learner will vary with the aspect or criteria under consideration.

By developing growth schemes of this type for each of the learning expectations for the early learning JK/SK program, educator teams can

- envision the possible levels of learning that may be demonstrated by the children as they move toward full understanding,
- plan ahead for resources that may be needed to support learning,
- plan small learning steps that will require consolidation and application (see Chapter 9) support as children learn, and
- plan specific activities for centres to support further consolidation and application of skills as children become increasingly independent with each aspect of a learning goal.

Growth schemes can also be shared with parents and guardians to support their active partnership in the child's learning. When home supports are provided for children to repeat new words and apply new school learning to everyday applications outside of the school, the children will be more motivated to acquire the new ideas and use them appropriately.

Observation is the main form of assessment used with learners who are still learning print concepts and are not yet independent readers. Well-developed growth schemes can become the observation recording sheets for learning expectations. Educator teams can circle and date the most accurate descriptor of the child's learning in relation to the learning expectation outlined on the growth scheme and the page can be reused over several weeks as children have further opportunities to practise the new learning. Using growth schemes as observation record sheets has the added advantage of allowing the educator team ready access to each person's notes and ease of access to records of changes related to time. This will provide educator team members with an easy-to-use glance at how children are progressing in comparison to their peers, while still ensuring that supports for growth are provided on an individual basis.

REPORTING TO THE PARENT

A student's progress reports should never be a surprise to a parent or guardian. In the JK/SK context, parents and guardians will have many opportunities to make contact with the educator team during drop-off and pickup times of the day.

These are times when the teacher should be available for casual chats with parents about the child's learning. If the educator team makes regular efforts to speak to parents about the learning that is happening in the classroom, a formal progress report is merely a confirmation of those earlier discussions.

Table 10.3 Example of a Growth Scheme

Learning Expectation:
Learners will be able to name, correspond, and print the cardinal numbers from 1 to 10.

Least sophisticated acquisition of this learning	Aspects or criteria for this learning expectation	→		
↓	• Ability to understand one-to-one correspondence	- Watches correspondence demonstrations with interest	- Uses oral counting imitatively to correspond objects and numbers	- Is able to describe an object by number as it is counted independently
	• Ability to name numbers	- Can say the words for numbers 1 to 10 but guesses as to their applicability when asked to count	- Can name some numbers from 1 to 10 but without confidence or with some errors	- Can name the numbers from 1 to 10 on sight of their cardinal symbols
	• Ability to print numbers	- Scribble writes to represent numbers	- Can print numbers randomly but does not match printed numbers to their value or correspondence to quantity of objects	- Can print all numbers from 1 to 10 and matches each to its correct value or correspondence to quantity of objects
	• Ability to sequence numbers by increasing size	- Does not understand the sequenced value of numbers from 1 to 10	- Understands the concepts of more than and less than but cannot sequence numbers from 1 to 10 to represent relative value	- Can sequence numbers 1 to 10 in order to represent their relative value
Most sophisticated acquisition of this learning	• Ability to count objects and represent their count result as a number from 1 to 10	- Says number words but does not relate then to counting objects	- Can count objects sequentially from 1 to 10	- Can pick up a count sequence and complete it to correspond objects to numbers from 1 to 10

Sharing progress records for people is governed by many laws, including the FOI Act. Canada's Freedom of Information and Protection of Privacy Act can be accessed at www.gov.pe.ca/law/statutes/pdf/f-15_01.pdf

Reporting is a part of the teacher's job. While the collection of information as evidence of students' learning is shared by the educator team, it is the professional role of the teacher to interpret that evidence and to use their professional judgment to evaluate the learning. Educator teams should address conferencing with parents as a team whenever possible because both members of the team will have many examples and anecdotes they can share with parents to help them understand what the child has learned, what learning is in progress, and what the parents can do in the home environment to support further learning.

Technology should be used to full advantage in reporting to parents. Video segments that illustrate key learning episodes can be used as a support for reporting. Each child's portfolio can provide several samples of work that indicate levels of achievement for the child. Educator teams may decide to post daily secure website segments describing events in the classroom for that day, so that parents know what children are learning. Educators must be careful when using this technology that they protect the privacy of all children and families and align their practices with local school board policies and Freedom of Information and Protection of Privacy legislation.

Most school boards will identify specific times throughout the school year when formal reporting must be provided for parents. Forms that can be used for this reporting vary by jurisdiction and often are unique for the JK/SK context. Educator team members should research forms that will be used in their jurisdiction early in the school year. Parents should also be notified of formal reporting times in the year as soon as these are known to the educator team. This will help parents plan for those meetings and avoid other commitments at these times. Figure 10.3 shows a sample of a typical reporting form that might be used for early reporting purposes in the JK/SK school year. Educators should understand that the term *Next Steps* as used on formal reports refers to identification of the next steps they will take as educators to ensure that learning continues.

The purpose of this formal report is to inform parents and guardians about the progress of their child. A conference with their child's teacher and other educators will also assist parents and guardians in understanding the assessment process and the school's focus on individual developmental progress. This includes the ways in which assessment helps identify the child's strengths and, based on needs, the next steps for program planning.

While reporting creates a formal record of the students' progress, ongoing communication with parents is necessary to ensure that they are always partnered in supporting their child's progress. There should be many times throughout the school year when parents and educators make contact and create opportunities to discuss the child's progress.

To make reporting successful as an aspect of communication with parents, it should be seamless. That is, reporting should not be an event that has the potential to cause anxiety and stress for children and their families. Rather, it should be confirmation of what is already known, sensitive to family issues and structures, and positive in tone. During reporting conferences, educator teams should work to ensure that parents feel welcomed, respected, and partnered in their child's education.

Personal and Social Development
• **Strengths**
• **Next Steps**

Language
• **Strengths**
• **Next Steps**

Mathematics
• **Strengths**
• **Next Steps**

Figure 10.3 *Reporting forms that are used for formal reporting in JK/SK classes may limit the focus of reporting to physical and social development, literacy and numeracy.*

Terminology is important for setting the tone of formal reporting. If the term *progress report* is used rather than *report card*, the positive connotations and underlying focus on individuals is evident. The term *progress report* suggests that the school is working toward meeting the needs of the child. In contrast, the term *report card* suggests that the child is expected to meet the needs of the school. These are subtle but important differences.

Many schools make progress conferencing a family night and create a celebratory tone for the classroom so that children are welcomed along with their parents. It works well to engage young children from the class and other children from the family in a pajama reading series in the classroom, or with larger groups in another area of the school, as parents meet with the educator team. Many schools have found that parent attendance increases when children are welcomed. Also, children are eager to attend a special event at the school, and what can be more special to a young child than getting to come to school in your pajamas?

REPORTING TO THE ELL PARENT

All parents appreciate clarity when they discuss the progress of their child with a teacher or the educator team. Achieving clarity in communication can be very difficult when some parents may be new to Canada and their first language is not

English. These families may be more reluctant to visit the school informally as well because of language barriers and their culturally embedded relationships to teachers in other countries. It is the duty of the educator team to bridge this situation by working toward removing barriers to easy and regular communication with every parent.

In Chapter 6, we addressed communication as a general topic for the early learning educator to monitor. To communicate effectively with all parents of the JK/SK children, educators must remember that schools can be very intimidating to some parents. By recognizing this, educators can make plans to bridge any discomfort and ensure that all parents and families feel welcome in the school. Parents who have engaged in preschool contacts during earlier years may expect similar contacts that may be less manageable in the school context. Awareness of this will help educators make successful connections with all families and help to connect the child's needs to the family context.

Communications with families of ELL learners will need special attention in the communication planning considered by the educator team. As with any family, the communication should be ongoing and continuous. Parents should never have to wonder how or what the children are learning in their JK/SK program. Strong communication practices will allow all parents easy access to this information. Communications need to be open, honest, and bidirectional. Parents need to be able to initiate communication and feel that their efforts are respected.

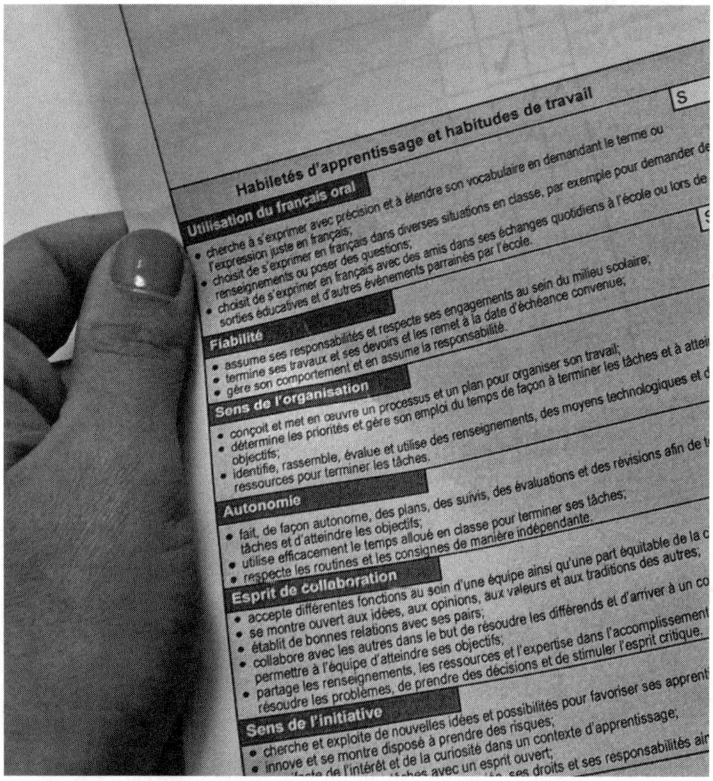

10.4 *Progress reports can be translated to help parents from other first cultures understand their child's progress.*

Educator teams need to provide a wide range of written materials (see Chapter 6) that explain the JK/SK program in ways that are both useful and comprehensible. Many school boards provide centralized access to translation services, so that written materials can be available to non-English speaking parents in their first language. Translation services personnel can also provide educator teams with information about ensuring that communications are culturally sensitive and make respectful connections with parents of other first cultures.

REPORTING TO THE CHILD

Children should not be overlooked in the process of reporting their learning progress. In Chapter 9, Figure 9.5 introduced the concept of assessment *as* learning. This form of assessment requires that children become increasingly aware of the learning goals that guide their school work play and, over time, begin to understand the criteria for assessment of their learning. To be able to take an assessment stance with their own learning, young children need many opportunities to engage in discussions with adults about what they are doing and what their activities mean to them.

To engage in discussions that lead to children's initial forays into self-assessment, adults need to structure learning conversations with purpose. Learning conversations or pedagogical narratives should still allow the child to maintain control of the dialogue and should respect the direction they intend for the flow of conversation. Through these dialogues, educators can gradually introduce language and prompts that will serve to direct attention to the children's understandings of their own learning.

Reporting to young children occurs as educator team members engage in conversations during the ordinary learning moments of the day. As they listen to children and engage them in a pedagogical narrative about their activities, the adults need to ensure that they attend to the many principles that should inform their interactions. In so doing, they can optimize their conversations with young learners and ensure that the learners gradually become more aware of their own learning.

First, educators need to look for natural opportunities to engage in conversations with children about their learning. These conversations may include times when children describe what they are doing, engage in pretend play and role playing, explore or imitate, manipulate materials, pause to consider options, initiate talk during games, or alter plans. Educators should allow the children to initiate and sustain these conversations; their involvement should provide support and reinforce issues that the children are considering. This can be done by reflecting the children's language back to them as they ponder things aloud.

Example:

Child:	This doesn't fit.
Adult:	You think it doesn't fit.
Child:	No.

Second, educators should adjust their physical level to engage in a conversation with the child. They should move to the child's level by sitting, squatting, or kneeing. This adjustment of the physical level will make children more comfortable about conversing. From this perspective, engaging in talk about what the child is learning will be less threatening for the child.

Next, educators should ensure that their involvement in the conversation is responsive to the child's conversational leads. To initiate conversations, the adult needs to move close to the physical work space the child is using and observe the activity the child is engaging. This signals to the child that the adult is interested in what they are doing. Then the educator should wait for the child to initiate a conversation about their work. As children are in the process of working on tasks, educators can help them to identify language that applies to the materials, processes, or products they are using. This will expand the children's vocabulary and help them become more aware of their work and the standards that influence reporting.

Example:

Child:	I painted this colour on the other one.
Adult:	Do you like how it turned out?
Child:	Don't like that part (pointing to one area of their work).
Adult:	That's an interesting colour.
Child:	Painted over that when it was wet.
Adult:	Do you think it would be a better colour there if you waited until the first colour was dry?
Child:	Yeah...maybe...(long pause). I'm going to paint over it pretty soon.

Educators should also engage in conversations as the child's partner in the learning. To do this, they must follow the child's conversational direction and respond to topics the child introduces. Comments should be brief and echo the words the child has used. Educators should be aware of the purpose of each of their additions to the conversations and ensure that they intend to respond, question, challenge, or extend as they become involved in work play conversations. If the adult opens the discussion about the child's work, they should note the child's response to their initiation and not pressure the child to engage in the discussion if their focus is elsewhere. By making open-ended comments about what a child is doing during work play, the adult invites, but does not force, a response. The child is able to determine and control the direction of the resulting conversation to highlight the things that capture their interest.

10.5 *The educator team member responds to the child's conversational leads in a non-intrusive manner.*

Example:

Adult:	You've used one of my favourite colours in your work.
Child:	Which one?
Adult:	Right here (points).
Child:	I made that one from this and this (pointing to two other colours).
Adult:	How did you decide that?
Child:	Just did it.
Adult:	You mixed the two colours together.

In this conversation, the adult extends the child's vocabulary by introducing the word *mixed* into a conversation that the child has freely engaged. This conversation may be the starting point for the child to consider the effects of mixing different colours and may lead to more experimentation with colour blends.

Questioning is a method of initiating conversation with young children. Educators need to be aware that questions can sometimes intimidate young children and cause them to avoid risks or avoid conversations about their work. Questions that promote conversation about learning will be incidental and conversational in tone, used infrequently in favour of more natural forms of conversational interaction, relate closely to what work play the child is currently doing, and encourage the child to talk openly about their thought processes. If too many questions characterize the adult involvement in the dialogue, children may find this unnatural or intrusive and may withdraw from the conversation or respond very briefly, rather than engaging in the dialogue in a way that would support further learning. As much as possible, conversations should focus on setting the stage for children to ask and investigate their own questions.

Wood et al. (1980) found several trends in children's responses to adult questions during their learning. Among these were:

- The least conversationally controlling adults who worked with young children asked the fewest questions and made a high proportion of contributions in a conversation.
- Adults who used the least controlling methods (questions) in conversations with young children about their work were more likely to have children ask them questions.
- Adults who used the least controlling methods in conversations with young children about their work were far more likely to have children respond to their infrequent questions with elaborations beyond a simple answer.
- Questions were only one of many effective approaches adults used to initiate and engage children in conversations; children responded to all other forms of adult contributions.
- Less controlled (question-based) conversations provided more openings for children to contribute ideas.
- Pauses and quiet times in a conversation provided time and less pressured contexts, allowing children to become most conversational.

In controlled conversations, adults typically use one of three strategies to engage the conversation. They 1) try to force repetition, 2) ask closed questions that have only one possible answer, or 3) ask open-ended questions. However, when adults try to pass control of the conversation to young children, they are more likely to either make a related comment that contributes to reflection on what the child is doing or acknowledge what the child is doing in a way that does not lead the next stage of the conversation (see Figure 10.4).

Wood et al (1980) identified approaches educators use to either retain control of a work play conversion with a child or to pass control to the child. Approaches include:

To retain control of the conversation

- Require repetition by identifying what should be said by the child (Example: "Say you're sorry").
- Ask closed questions where only one answer is possible (Example: "Are you painting?").
- Ask frequent open questions that may not relate directly to the child's work (Example: As the child builds something the educator team member asks, "Who is picking you up today?").

To pass control to the child so they can lead the conversation

- Contribute to the conversation by making a comment related to the child's work (Example: "You've made a colour I really like.").
- Acknowledge the child's work in a neutral way so the child can direct the next stage of the conversation (Example: "I see.").

Figure 10.4 *Wood el al. Framework for Sharing Conversational Control with Young Children*

Used with permission of Nancy Maynes

These approaches can be used to optimize the conversations educators have with children as they work. These conversations lead children to develop a stronger sense of their own learning and open the door to including them in the assessment of their work.

ARRANGING SUPPORT SERVICES

In many school communities, additional support services are available to help educators teach and evaluate children as they grow and learn. Some of these services relate to physical development and nutrition, some to home and community safety, and some to supports for cognitive and social development (see Table 10.4). These services vary in name and function across jurisdictions, but the general trend is toward increased focus on the school location and school day structure as a hub of services for young children (see Chapter 4).

Table 10.4 *School- and Community-Based Services Available for Young Children*

Physical Development and Nutrition	Home and Community Safety	Cognitive and Social Development
School nurse	Community helper visits (e.g., firefighters, police)	Speech therapy
Immunizations	Safety village/street-proofing programs	Early years programs that focus on stimulation, group play, and literacy concepts
Dental hygiene and checkups	Home safety programs	Learning resource teacher support
Nutritionist consultations for families	Subsidized swimming instruction programs	Child development counsellors
Subsidized school lunch and snack programs	Internet proofing	Child and family protection services
Physiotherapy		Toy-lending libraries
Occupational therapy		Mobile book libraries
One-on-one disability supports (e.g., through an educational assistant)		Parent support groups
Parks and services camp programs		

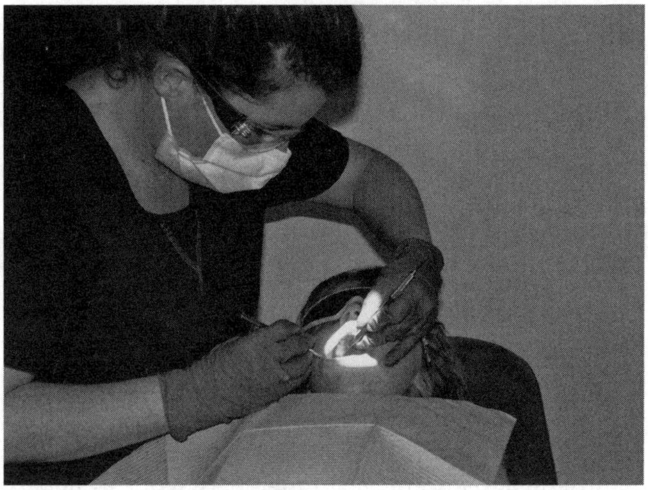

10.6 Community support personnel may work with individual children in the classroom to provide additional services.

Where community hub supports are available for children and their families, these can be available in two distinct models. Often, services are provided equally to all schools in a jurisdiction through a centralized source at the school board level. In this case there is usually an articulation agreement between the school authority and the service organization. Articulation agreements define the services that the organization will provide and any associated costs. They may also define frequency of access and identify target groups of children to receive a specific service. These types of services may be subject to grant-based funding, so programs may not have a long life if funding is short-term. Other services may be available in the community on a regular basis because they are a mandate of the organization. For example, public health units typically have an oral hygiene and immunization program mandate, and these services are of long standing and less subject to fluctuations in funding.

Some services may be available to schools on a request basis. For example, educators can make individual requests to local police services to speak to children about community safety issues or to visit the school as a community helper for the purpose of acquainting young children with the uniformed helpers they may encounter as they move around the community. These types of services may also be made available to children by arranging visits to sites in the community (e.g., a safety village). Educators need to be familiar with the regulations and practices governing the arrangement of school trips, if they choose to access these services by taking children out of the school building (e.g., a hospital visit).

While many of these services are made available to all children in the JK/SK program, some services are arranged on a consultative basis to support age-appropriate development. In order to access services that support development, educators need to make the case that such services are required. Physiotherapy would be an example. If educators observe the child during the JK program and find that there are specific issues related to physical development that have not been previously identified, they can request assessments from outside agencies. To start this assessment process to determine service needs, educators would speak to their in-school support team and access any diagnostic services that may be available through the team. An in-school support team usually comprises an administrator, a school resource teacher, and perhaps one centralized resource teacher. This team can provide additional assessments, arrange access to outside agencies that can provide further assessments, and negotiate a service model to support the child or family.

In many cases, early access services available in the community will already have served the child before school entry, and appropriate support services will be in place before the child starts the JK/SK program. In some cases, these service agencies want to provide service during the school day on site. They need to negotiate this process directly with the school and classroom staff.

Early educators should remain vigilant and monitor all areas of a child's growth as they are involved in the JK/SK program. Close monitoring can catch issues that may have evolved after school entry.

CHAPTER SUMMARY

Assessment in a JK/SK classroom is based on observation. As children play and work in a play-based environment, educator team members work to understand what the child is learning and the meaning that is being made from observations. Exemplars of child–educator pedagogical narratives can help educators understand and interpret children's thinking and actions.

Portfolios can be used to maintain records and samples of children's products over time. Portfolios can form the basis of discussions with parents, ELL parents, and children about what and how they are learning. Regular, culturally sensitive reporting practices are used to invite parents and guardians to participate in supporting each child's learning in the classroom and to extend it to the home. Observation records and portfolios, including growth scheme records, can provide detailed documentation that will facilitate arrangement of support services for children if they are needed.

THINKING AHEAD: Opportunities for Professional Reflection

- Collect several samples of reporting forms and conferencing forms used in JK/SK programs. Examine these to determine what characteristics they have in common. Compare these to the reporting and conferencing forms used in your local school jurisdiction. Determine the features you would like to see in a reporting or conferencing form. Find out if these forms are mandated across the local jurisdiction or if different schools have the option to design their own forms for these purposes.
- Research to find out how a local school addresses the needs of parents whose first language is not English when they hold parent conferences for reporting purposes.
- Some schools provide parent handbooks to encourage parent involvement in the school. Typical handbooks invite parents to:
    - attend council meetings,
    - watch for notices by email or delivered by the students advertising for volunteers, and
    - belong to the parents' email distribution list.

  Discuss in a small group how these approaches work in your local jurisdiction. Consider if there are other ways you would want to involve JK/SK parents and families in your classroom.

- Record an exchange between a young child and an educator team member. Analyze the conversation to determine strategies used by the educator to maintain flow in the conversation by passing conversational control to the child.
- Educator teams determine the learning environment of their JK/SK classrooms through the many decisions they make about how they will interact with the children. The environment can be described on a continuum from a preschool environment to a teacher-directed climate.

Pre-School Climate	Supportive Learning Environment	Teacher Directed Learning Environment
• Adults supervise as children play	• Children and adults share control of the learning focus and direction	• Adults control what children do
• Adults intervene only if conflicts arise	• Adults observe and engage children in their work play	• Adults direct and inform
• Adults provide information only as requested	• Adults support children's intentions as they engage in work play	
• Play is the curriculum	• Expectations for learning are identified as developmental indicators and play environments are designed to support children as they develop in these areas	• Curriculum content comes from adult expectations that are set for all children
• Adults value free play	• Adults value learning through play-based approaches	• Adults limit play opportunities in favour of drill and practice work to master basic academic skills

Using this continuum, observe in a local JK/SK classroom to determine where the approach used in that classroom sits on this continuum. Decide which approach best represents the philosophy for early learning in JK/SK classrooms in your jurisdiction.

- Find an online Parents' Handbook from your local school jurisdiction. Find out what the handbook says about ways to contact school staff and ways for parents to get involved in the local school. Consider whether the handbook is friendly and invitational and how it might be improved to be culturally sensitive.

ADDITIONAL READING SUGGESTIONS

- Carr, M. and B. Cowie. 2003. "The Consequences of Sociocultural Assessment in Early Childhood Settings: Community, Competence and Continuity," in *Early Childhood Education: Society and Culture,* ed. A. Anning, J. Cullen, and M. Fleer. London: Sage.

- Frome, P. and J. Eccles. 1998. "Parents' Influence on Children's Achievement-Related Perceptions." *Journal of Personality and Social Psychology,* 74 (2):435–452.
- Paley, V. G. 2001. *In Mrs. Tully's Room: A Childcare Portrait.* Cambridge, MA: Harvard University Press.
- Robinson, F., W. Croxall, P. Kenny, and D. Klingspon, D. 2010. *Fostering Human Development and Empowerment: A Conceptual Bridge Between Vision and Action.* North Bay, ON: The Human Development and Empowerment Group.
- Wood, D., L. McMahon, and Y. Cranstoun. 1980. *Working With Under Fives.* Ypsilanti, MI: High/Scope Press.

11 Community Support for Early Learning

"It appears that in the most effective settings educators supported children in being assertive, at the same time as rationalizing and talking through their conflicts."

(Siraj-Blatchford et al., 2002)

11.1 *Young children need several opportunities during the day to play outdoors.*

In this chapter, educator team members will learn about

- outside time
- community trips for early learners
- preparing for classroom visitors
- coordinated community services to support early learning

At the end of this chapter, educator team members can reflect on their personal growth through

- CHAPTER SUMMARY
- THINKING AHEAD: Opportunities for Professional Reflection
- ADDITIONAL READING SUGGESTIONS

While much of the learning in a JK/SK context will happen inside the classroom, there are other areas that should also be used as resources to optimize early learning: the outdoors, areas of the community that can be visited, or areas of the school where school visitors can engage the children. Events coordinated through a variety of community services are also potentially rich learning opportunities for children. Each of these opportunities requires special consideration to optimize learning and to ensure children's safety. The daily routines of the classroom can be balanced by providing opportunities for children to learn in these other contexts during the schooling years in JK/SK.

The daily routines both inside the classroom and in these other contexts should include many opportunities to interact in a variety of groupings. Groupings may be either structured or spontaneous, include play both indoors and outdoors, re-engage play and work play from previous days, and start new adventures. These groupings will help children to face new challenges and play within their comfort zone, and to be actively involved in exploration and investigation in preferred play styles. The flexibility of the full-day JK/SK program provides many opportunities to use various groupings and additional resources to support children's growth and development.

OUTSIDE TIME

In Chapter 7, three types of outdoor play were introduced. These were

- creative play (e.g., assembling activities with sand, wood, clay, or water),
- challenging play (e.g., motion equipment such as slides and swings, and tilting equipment such as seesaws), and
- social play (e.g., equipment that requires social interaction or that might be constrained in play by usual use, such as cooking utensils, clothes, dolls, or models).

Also, many types of equipment suitable for outdoor settings were considered. Revisit Table 7.2 in Chapter 7 to review these ideas.

Outside play time during the JK/SK day may vary considerably, based on several criteria. The condition and exclusive availability of the outdoor play space must be considered when determining when to arrange outdoor play. Ideally, young children should have three to four play opportunities outdoors each day. Weather will most certainly have an impact on the use of the outdoors for play. As well, several blocks of the school timetable should be set aside for the JK/SK children to have access to the school's gymnasium. A 60-minute block per day would be ideal, but generous amounts of time may not be possible because of the needs of other classes.

In many JK/SK classes, outdoor time is organized to break up the more intensive work play tasks of the day and to support transitions from the parents' care to the educator teams' care and back again. Outdoor time should become part of the predictable routine of the classroom. When outdoor time is part of the

11.2 *Outdoor play provides opportunities for energetic participation in creative play, challenging play, and social play.*

routine in the JK/SK day, children benefit in many ways. Aside from the health benefits of fresh air and opportunities for vigorous activity, daily routines support each child's sense of initiative, create a predictable social context for interaction among peers, create opportunities for less demanding and intense focus within the flexible outdoor context, and support curriculum and learning goals through pleasurable contexts.

Reflection Point

Investigate the amount of outside time available in your local JK/SK classroom. Is the time outside adequate? What limitations are there on the ability to use the outdoors for extended learning opportunities? How much gym time is allotted to the JK/SK classroom? Is it adequate?

The diversity of play and the possibilities for spontaneous groupings for various play episodes create many opportunities for children to choose and to experience the results of their choices. Space provides freedom for more imaginative, energetic, and noisy play than is possible indoors. The sights, sounds, range of textures, weather differences, and range of outdoor play materials each provide more opportunities for new explorations. Because play equipment outdoors can be large and therefore easy to share, outdoor experiences can help children socialize and learn how to play in cooperative contexts. The different contexts available through outdoor play provide additional scope for the educator team to interact with and respond to children's learning.

During outdoor play, children continue to interact with peers and adults, but may do so in completely different ways than is typical indoors. In the outdoor context, they can explore more widely, be noisier, and vary their activities more quickly. They have many opportunities to use and develop more large muscles as they run, jump, skip, swing, and use different pieces of large equipment. Because there is ease of access to many materials that support a variety of ways to play outdoors, children will engage in a wider range of explorations and interactions.

In the outdoors, adults can continue to support children's play by helping children locate and select materials for play (see Figure 11.1), maintaining play materials in safe condition, providing carrying and storage containers for play items that need to be transported from indoors to outdoors, and supporting transitions between the indoors and outdoors.

Educator team members can support the range of play materials that children have access to outdoors by:

- Providing a variety of flexible and easy to carry containers for outdoor items;
- Arranging JK/SK outdoor play times so the children have exclusive access to some play areas;
- Providing outdoor play materials for early arrivers and late leavers so that materials are always available to stimulate exploration;
- Maintaining the safety of all equipment by inspecting it regularly; and
- Teaching children routines for moving and sharing outdoor equipment.

Figure 11.1 *Supporting Play Materials for the Outdoors*

Outdoor time with young children can be challenging in weather that requires layers of special clothing for outdoors. Parents can be very supportive by helping the child learn to dress and undress for outdoor weather, but this will always be a very time-consuming transition in the classroom. The educator team can do many things to make the outdoor-to-indoor (and the reverse) transitions run smoothly. These include the following:

- Teach children to store their personal things in a particular area (a basket or cubby).
- Ask parents to label their child's belongings appropriately and to teach the child to check for the labels on their belongings.

- Be consistent, so that children know what to expect and how they fit into these expectations.
- Reduce the number of transitions during the day.
- Manage transitions calmly and with purpose.
- Explain the day's agenda to the children every morning (to create an anticipatory mindset).
- Plan indoor-to-outdoor transitions after activities that have already interrupted work play (e.g., after a snack time rather than after activity centres).
- Eliminate waiting time during transitions by using the skills and involvement of all available adults.
- Start each new activity immediately, and allow children to join it as they are ready; this will ease transitions for those who take longer.
- Fill unavoidable wait time with enjoyable activities.
- Add new and creative elements to transition times, so they are always capable of stimulating children's interest (e.g., songs, movements, and imitations).
- Avoid overly regimented movement in favour of creativity and interest.

Reflection Point

What in-class activities would you use in a JK/SK classroom to promote children's increasing independence with transitions from indoors to outdoors?

Outdoor time can be a rewarding and valuable part of the instructional day when effective approaches are used to plan and engage this time.

To plan for the most effective use of time, educator teams need to consider how they manage all of the details of the day, so that they are always supporting each other in the flow of the day. These details might relate to how the day is planned for the children, how the physical space in the classroom and yard is prepared for the planned day, how and when transitions will occur throughout the day, and how the team members will ensure that their actions support each other in making the day function smoothly. Educators should discuss these points:

11.3 *Children can learn increasing independence as they prepare for transitions from the indoors to outdoors.*

How the day is planned for the children, including

- What part of the day is set aside for team planning?
- How are plans displayed for the team? For the children? For volunteers?
- How is flexibility built into the plan to account for unexpected events and for creating opportunities to follow children's interests?

How the physical space in the classroom and yard is prepared for the planned day

- What time can children be dropped off to the care of the educator team?
- What things need to be rearranged after the room has been cleaned by school caretakers (e.g., taking chairs off tables, removing dust covers, etc.)?
- What consumable supplies need to be restocked or refreshed for the day (e.g., paints, paste, papers, chart paper, sand table, water table, etc.)?
- Who waters plants and feeds class pets?
- Who prepares snacks and snack areas?
- Who does purchasing of consumables and food supplies?
- Who checks on the condition of each centre?
- Who sets out and collects and records daily observation sheets for each area of the room?
- Who tidies and maintains the classroom library?
- Who checks on the condition of the in-class washrooms throughout the day?
- Who takes the outdoor equipment out at the start of the day and returns it to the classroom area at the end of the day?
- How do these tasks get done if one member of the educator team is absent for the day?

How and when transitions will occur throughout the day

- Who is on the yard to greet the children and families each morning?
- Who meets the bus(es) and escorts the children to a safe play area?
- Who is available to speak to parents at drop-off times?
- Who deals with small accidents that may need attention (e.g., bumps and bruises)?
- Who reports small accidents to parents?
- Who helps a child who becomes ill during the day?
- Who contacts parents when a child becomes ill? How?

- Where are ill children cared for safely before parents arrive to pick them up?
- Who leads the transition? Who follows, so that stragglers are also supervised and assisted?

How each educator team member can be flexible to evolving needs throughout the day

- What do you do to cover the absence of the other team member?
- How do you manage when one team member is still working with a child or speaking to a parent when help is needed in other places?
- How do you manage conflict between team members?
- How do you handle a child who favours working with one team member to the exclusion of the other?
- How do team members handle unexpected events and needs that arise and disrupt the plan for the day?

These questions are not exhaustive, but they do point to the need to ensure that all of the possibilities and responsibilities that may arise during the day have been considered by team members as they work together both indoors and outside.

COMMUNITY TRIPS FOR EARLY LEARNERS

There are many types of class trips (see Table 11.1) that can be arranged for children depending on their learning purpose.

Table 11.1 *Types of Class Trips*

To create a common base of experience	A group of JK/SK students from an urban school visits a mixed-produce farm to explore ways that the farm serves the local urban community. Two-thirds of the students in the class have never been on a farm, so this trip is planned primarily to strengthen their common understanding of what a farm is and how a farm is worked to produce food items.
To discover new learning in a structured way	Children from a rural environment are learning about irrigation systems used on local farms. One local farm has a new automated overhead irrigation system. The students are visiting this farm to see how this system works and to compare its advantages and disadvantages to more usual ditch or underground irrigation approaches. The children have been talking about adding water to their outdoor constructions during pretend play.

(Continued)

Table 11.1 *Types of Class Trips, continued*

To provide opportunities for students to practise new learning in context	JK/SK children have been learning about planting and harvesting cycles on farms. They understand that different crops are ready for harvesting at different times and that farmers are able to test crops to determine the best time to start harvesting. However, this is an abstract concept. This field trip will allow young students to walk through corn fields with the farmer and witness and participate in the testing being done to determine when harvesting should begin.
To provide opportunities for students to solidify learning through experiences not available in the classroom	This field trip is designed to allow young children to track the process of preparing fields for planting, rotating crops, tending fields during growth, harvesting, and marketing crops. The children will engage in a field trip to the manager of a large cooperative mixed farm. Through visits to the various buildings on the farm, children will be able to see the complex interaction of people who manage the different aspects of the farm.

In the JK/SK context, trips outside of the classroom are likely to be relatively rare for many reasons. For four- and five-year-olds, new situations can be a source of anxiety and even fear. Since out-of-class trips disrupt the routine of the school day, children can lose the sense of security and predictability, because new contexts are introduced. As well, classroom trips may be focused on one aspect of the program that may not engage the current interests of the child. Local policies may also address the use and types of trips recommended for young children, so educators must be aware of these policies.

Despite these cautions, trips outside of the classroom can also be highly engaging and enriching for young children. To achieve these benefits, class trips will need to be well planned, capably supervised, and reviewed in the classroom to identify resultant learning. By ensuring that these steps are taken, educator teams can gradually introduce trips into their early learning program to great benefit. The following sections will outline many of the considerations that the educator team must examine before, during, and after a class trip (see Table 11.2).

11.4 School trips may require the use of bus transportation. Consider the value of the trip against its potential for learning in the early stage of planning. Trips outside of the classroom must be well supervised.

Suitable trips for JK/SK children might include

- the local fire hall
- the local police station
- local markets
- venues for science and history exhibits, especially with hands-on displays
- local government chambers (e.g., mayor's office)
- local parks
- local wetlands
- petting zoos
- aquariums

Table 11.2 *Planning Field Trips for Young Children*

PLANNING TRIPS FOR YOUR JK/SK CHILDREN: Before the Trip Begins
• Identify grade, date of trip, time and location. • Determine the expectations of the trip, and state for your planning purposes exactly what learning goals will be met or enriched by the trip. • Plan to teach skills that will be needed by children during the trip. • Check Board Policy to ensure that the trip is allowed in this jurisdiction. • Preview any site-based resources that will help you with planning for this trip. • Plan and teach pre-trip activities and skills. • Determine risks and follow recommendations for safety. • Get permission from school principal, superintendent or director (if necessary) in a timely way; application timelines may apply under Board policy. • Book the venue. • Book transportation. • Calculate the individual cost per student for the trip. • Consider if fundraising will be involved or if requests for funding are being made (from school funds, School Council, etc.). • Anticipate any students who may be unable to pay for their trip and have a plan for addressing this. • Acquire volunteers to supervise the trip; be aware of supervision ratios required by the Board. • Boards often require volunteers to have a criminal reference check for vulnerable sector screening. • Determine how meals or snacks will be arranged or planned for during the trip. • Consider physical needs that are responsive to the length of the trip (e.g., meals, sun block, medications, sunglasses, clothing). • Determine on-site accessibility for every child. • Determine how parents and guardians could contact you during the trip, should an emergency arise. • Visit the trip site if possible. • Develop a permission letter for parents and guardians. • Set a due date for return of all permission forms and any health forms you may require; communicate this to parents. • Roll and count funds for submission to the main office; complete fund submission forms as required. • Confirm the venue a few days prior to the trip. • Get a cheque from the school to pay door fees or get a bill from the venue to be paid after the trip. • Discuss, teach, and anchor social skills and behaviours you expect to see during the trip. • Consider a "uniform" for the trip so that students are readily visible in crowds (e.g., red baseball caps). • Have a plan for how you will address unacceptable behaviour during the trip; ensure that children know the plan well ahead of the trip date. Follow the plan! (Example: The school principal will be available by phone and will come and get any child(ren) who is (are) not managing the responsibilities of the trip well.) • Discuss bus safety (or other transportation) rules well before the trip; use key phrases (e.g., "nothing that distracts the driver"). • Create a quick attendance check technique, so that you can ensure all students are present several times during the day and do so in 30 seconds or so (e.g., number off or buddies). • Ensure that supervision volunteers understand the academic tasks and the behaviour expectations for your trip well before the trip; it's a good idea to have this reviewed with volunteers in front of children so everyone has the same understanding. • Photocopy medical record pages for each child; take these copies with you in a confidential file you keep securely in your possession. • Know how to contact a school administrator on the day of the trip, should the need arise. • Divide students into workable groups for supervision during the trip (Note: Most jurisdictions require a high ratio of adults to JK/SK-aged children on trips, e.g., 1:5). • Ensure that children have some time for team building and socializing as a group before the trip; teach the social skills that may be needed for productive interaction.

(Continued)

Table 11.2 *Planning Field Trips for Young Children, continued*

PLANNING TRIPS FOR YOUR JK/SK CHILDREN: Before the Trip Begins	
• Provide a copy of the permission letter to the main office or principal (so that office personnel can answer questions about the trip if or when you are not available). • Check children's school records for any medical conditions that may be affected by the trip (e.g., anaphylactic reactions); note any medications that need to be taken along; invite parents of children with special needs or timid reactions to new situations to participate in supervision of the trip. • Collect permission forms and fees at least a week before the trip. • Create a class list record of fees and permission forms collected.	• Create workable academic tasks for the trip, so that children are responsible for some product following the trip. • Develop a communication phone tree so that children's parents and guardians can be contacted readily if buses are late or there is some unanticipated disruption in the plans for the day.
PLANNING TRIPS FOR YOUR JK/SK CHILDREN: During the Trip	
• Remind children of expectations for the trip (e.g., academic learning and social behaviour). • Don't give second chances on social behaviour; if you have prepared children well, they will need to see you being firm and fair, but inflexible, about your expectations. • Plan for rest times during the trip.	• Have a predetermined and commonly understood method for having children, led by their group supervisor, complete the tasks that you have required during the trip. • Bring pencils, markers, clipboards, etc., as required; store them safely near you during transportation and collect them again at the end of the day before getting back on transportation. • Collect completed academic work before boarding transportation for home.
PLANNING TRIPS FOR YOUR JK/SK CHILDREN: After the Trip	
• Send appropriate thank you letters to hosts and volunteers. • Review children's academic tasks and provide immediate feedback about the work during class after the trip. • Review social skills that you found students may have needed and were not prepared for prior to the trip; teach these skills and create opportunities to practise them. • Pay bills.	• Destroy or store the confidential medical record portfolio in an appropriately secure location. (Note: Be sure these are reviewed and refreshed before using them again.) • Teach follow-up lessons to ensure that the learning from the trip connects to the learning from the classroom. • Make, date, and sign any records of accidents, injury, or severe incidents during the trip.

Each location will have special local exhibits and activities that signify celebration of the natural environment and features of the area. Educator team members may find it helpful to maintain a reference file of local places that welcome young children and provide programs specific to their needs.

Reflection Point

What other trips might be suitable for young children in your area?

Many educators may want to limit class trips, because of the age and experience of their students. While these trips can have considerable value and have the potential to broaden children's learning in many ways, they can be problematic and create unnecessary tension relative to the potential learning benefits that may accrue. Instead of taking children out of the classroom for trips, educator teams may decide to invite visitors into the classroom to speak to children about some aspect of a topic they are studying or to provide a unique activity for them.

PREPARING FOR CLASSROOM VISITORS

It can be very difficult to connect with suitable guests who can be effective contributors in the JK/SK classroom. In this context, guest speakers need a unique variety of skills in order to provide a learning experience that is more valuable than what can be provided by the day-to-day classroom experience. A passionate and detailed knowledge of their topic would be critical to ensuring the effective use of learning time guided by a guest speaker. As well, it is critical that the guest speaker has previous successful interaction with young children, who can be a ruthlessly critical audience when their interest is not engaged. With these criteria in place, a guest speaker can engage and encourage young learners to examine ideas from new perspectives and through new ways of knowing.

11.5 Classroom visitors can offer new learning opportunities if they engage the children in focused tasks through activity centre approaches.

With four- and five-year-olds, a group presentation by a classroom guest is often not effective. This may have less to do with the skills of the guest than the relation of the topic and ideas to the immediate learning plans of the children. If the topic is out of step with the children's immediate interests, they may become restless and distracted very quickly and may cause attention challenges in the class group. For these reasons, guests to the JK/SK classroom may be more effective if they visit as a unique learning centre opportunity that children can choose to engage.

Preparing for the visit of a guest speaker in the classroom is key to ensuring the success of the learning opportunity. Ideally, the guest speaker will know and understand the learning expectation(s) that should result from their visit. They should have opportunities to plan with the classroom teacher and to adjust their preparations and resources to the special needs of the class. Small rotating groups of children to engage with the guest speaker will usually be more effective than trying to focus every child on what guests have to offer during a fixed presentation. When interactions can be play based and engage children through many learning styles, four- and five-year-olds are most likely to choose involvement.

Children should also understand exactly what they are to learn from the guest speaker. A presentation by a guest speaker should include a warm-up activity that introduces the speaker to the students and opens up communication by creating comfortable interaction. An introductory activity can be planned by the educator team, but the guest speaker needs to know and understand its purpose. At the end of an effective introductory activity, a level of trust and comfort should be established that will allow children to participate in questioning and open discussion.

Reflection Point

What topics within the JK/SK curriculum in your area might be suitable to include a guest speaker in the classroom? Identify whom you might include and why.

If the guest is presenting something to the whole class, the children should have a clearly defined task to complete during the time period and should have several questions about the topic in hand before the speaker arrives. An effective guest speaker will be able to weave the children's questions into their presentation if they are given access to the questions before they visit the classroom. Guest speakers may also come to the classroom to be interviewed by children rather than to present to them. Community helpers (i.e., police, firefighters, nurses, dentists, etc.) may visit the classroom in work uniforms to help young children relate to their roles in the community.

Following the visitor's time in the classroom, young children will benefit from having time to discuss what they have learned from the visitor. Educator teams can structure group discussion time and, dependent on children's level of print awareness, use a graphic organizer that allows them to relate interview questions and the responses of the speaker (see Figure 11.2).

11.6 *Well-designed early learning computer simulations offer alternatives to class trips. Simulations can be stimulating and engaging for children if they are designed with literacy levels in mind.*

INTERVIEW ORGANIZER
Our guest ____________ will talk about ______________________________
I know these things about this topic:

Our guest speaker knows about this topic because:

I want to find out about these things:

I will ask the guest speaker:
Question ____?
Answer ____
Question ____?
Answer ____

Figure 11.2 *Discussing What Children Will Learn or Have Learned from Classroom Vistors*

After the guest speaker's presentation, children can be engaged in helping to write a thank you letter to the speaker, with educator team members as scribes. This will help children be more aware of what they learned from the speaker and will support their **metacognitive** development. Expressions of appreciation provide a good social model for how to interact with people who help us and provide an authentic opportunity for children to practise print skills if they can sign the thank you letter. Many local businesses display children's letters of appreciation proudly and appreciate being recognized for their contribution to the community.

Most jurisdictions will require that all adults coming into contact with children under the auspices of the school have a vulnerable sector criminal reference check completed. If the adult is a regular contributor to the classroom, many schools will make arrangements to pay the visitor for the costs related to maintaining an up-to-date reference check.

Young children should also have both pre- and post-visitor opportunities to express their thinking about a classroom visitor's presentation or activity through non-print means. Artistic and physical activities should be offered to help children express what they have learned and to explore new perspectives and ideas during and after times when classroom visitors have contributed to the program.

When considering classroom trips and classroom visitors for JK/SK classes, educator teams should also examine the potential of electronic simulations to engage children in new learning experiences. Simulations have many of the benefits of trips and visitors without the difficulties of trips or the limitations of finding suitable guest speakers.

11.7 *Simulations that engage children through physical activity can also provide strong learning contexts.*

COORDINATED COMMUNITY SERVICES TO SUPPORT EARLY LEARNING

Earlier chapters of this book have provided a vision of coordinated supports for early learners that start with the family and extend to the first years of early learning in the JK/SKclassroom. The success that children experience in JK/SK contexts is partially based on how ready they are to learn when they start the JK program. Parents, caregivers, and early childhood educators have all contributed to the attitudes, skills, and knowledge that the children bring to their first formal school experience. Engaging young children to learn through talking, singing, playing, sharing, experimenting, and reading will support children's transitions into the JK/SK context. When parents use these strategies with children from birth onward, the children are supported to enter school, ready to learn in another context that will extend and enrich previous growth.

Quite a few four-year-olds entering Junior Kindergarten will have many of the basic skills to support their success (see Table 11.3). However, educator teams need to be aware that not all children have equal access to early learning resources. If the child is a new immigrant, has lived in a remote area, or has had limited access to services because of parents' lack of familiarity with offerings or reticence to avail the services, the child's school entry background may be quite different. For this reason, an early learning profile should be developed for each child, in order to record and assess the child's pre-school strengths and areas for development and early attention in the JK/SK program.

Table 11.3 *Foundations Many Children Have Acquired before Entry into JK/SK*

Early Literacy Foundations	Physical, Social, and Emotional Foundations
• The child enjoys listening to story books. • The child enjoys discussions about books and TV stories. • The child understands early print concepts. • The child attempts to make marks that represent early attempts at print; may be able to print some letters, or his or her name. • The child is able to identify some signs and labels in their immediate environment. • The child eagerly participates in group activities, including games, choral rhyming, songs, and imitation. • The child recognizes, names, and may print some letters and letter combinations.	• Basic needs for sleep, rest, and food are met. • The child can focus and concentrate when needed. • The child can listen and communicate appropriately. • The child can express feelings appropriately. • The child shows empathy for the feelings of others. • The child can cooperate when needed. • The child understands sharing and taking turns. • The child demonstrates appropriate social **self-regulation** (i.e., can control personal behaviour appropriately in different contexts). • The child attempts to resolve conflicts in productive ways. • The child attempts to solve problems both with support and with appropriate independence. • The child demonstrates self-confidence and self-esteem in appropriate ways.

Reflection Point

Earlier chapters presented the Nipissing District Developmental Screen for young children. Some school boards use this tool, or some variations of it, to screen children entering kindergarten and provide an early identification of additional supports a child or family might need to ensure kindergarten success. What screening tools are used in your local jurisdiction? How are these screening devices or processes used?

As well, early learning supports vary across Canada. While a wide range of supports may be available in some provinces or territories, other areas may offer only minimal supports for family access to preschool learning. Urban areas typically have a higher concentration and variety of resources and supports available for early learning.

CHAPTER SUMMARY

The community can enrich the JK/SK experience for early learners. Outside time, including off-property time, can provide rich contexts for new learning for children. In outdoor play spaces, designs should reflect the needs of young children for safety, adaptability, imaginative play, spontaneous flexible groupings, exploration, and easy transitions throughout the day.

When children are taken off school property for educational trips, educators need to plan carefully and thoroughly. There are many types of class trips; they must be evaluated for their economy of effort, supervision requirements, safety, and planning needed before, during, and after the trip to ensure that each trip contributes to children's learning. Many trip venues may not be suitable for all JK/SK children.

If classroom visitors are used in JK/SK classrooms, educators need to ensure that their engagement is connected to the children's learning in relevant and timely ways.

The JK/SK classroom can be the hub of services for the young child and their family. If services are designed on pre-kindergarten foundations, the school can optimize its service role within the community.

THINKING AHEAD: Opportunities for Professional Reflection

- Locate and examine a local school board policy handbook or manual about out-of-classroom trips for young children. Using the local policy, identify criteria for trips that are considered low, medium, and high risk. Also identify any trip sites or activities that are prohibited in your local school board jurisdiction.
- Work with a group of five other classmates to design a JK/SK manual for out-of-classroom trips; they should meet the following five criteria:

1. They align with board policy.
2. They relate to the JK/SK curriculum.
3. There is potential for new learning for those children who may have been on the trip in their JK year to learn more in their SK year.
4. Children can be actively engaged in learning tasks during the trip.
5. The site promotes play-based approaches and interaction.

- Once a minimum of five trip sites has been identified, develop a trip manual for teachers in your area to address all of the details they need to attend to in order to plan successful trips to these sites. Use the details in Table 11.2 to ensure that all plans are addressed thoroughly. Include site photos with explanations to help educators plan for specific activities in the classroom before the site trip.
- Using the same strategy described above, create an educators' manual for directing teachers and ECEs to people in the local community who can visit classrooms and have experience working with young children, in particular those who can address particular topics (e.g., Risk Watch programs). For each of the classroom visitors identified in your resource manual, include

  1. name and contact information for the guest speaker,
  2. topics and specialties of the speaker,
  3. resources and spaces the speaker will need in the classroom,
  4. preferred warm-up activities the speaker would like to do or to have the educator team arrange before their visit to introduce the children to the speaker, and
  5. activity centre details that children should experience before the visitor comes to the classroom.

  In this "Classroom Visitor's Manual" also include specific details for centre activities you would recommend that educators provide after the visit to help young children consolidate and apply the ideas that were introduced by the visitor.
- Write a sample permission letter to parents to explain a proposed classroom trip. Be sure to include all of the details parents will need to have about transportation, clothing needs, food, departure and return times, supervision, and learning benefits of the proposed trip. Share your draft among colleagues and get their input into how you should improve your letter.
- Visit the websites listed in the section below (Additional Reading Suggestions). With a group of four colleagues, create a jigsaw, so that each person on your five-person team becomes very familiar with one site and is able to walk the other members of the team through the site to show them the resources available for JK/SK classrooms, parents, and communities.

ADDITIONAL READING SUGGESTIONS

Ainsworth, M., D. Salter, M. Blehar, E. Waters, and S. Wall. 1978. *Patterns of Attachment: A Psychological Study of the Strange Situation*. Hillsdale, NJ: Erlbaum.

Evans, B. 2000. "'Bye Mommy!' 'Bye Daddy!' Easing Separation for Preschoolers." *High/Scope Extensions* (September):1–3.

Goleman, D. 1989. "The Roots of Empathy are Traced to Infancy." *New York Times* (March 28): 20–21 (Section B).

The Internet provides a wealth of information and inspiration for educators. Here are some sites you may want to visit:

- www.kinderthemes.com/Songsideasandchecklists.htlm — This site provides a variety of songs and poems to support classroom routines and traditions in early learning contexts.
- www.songs4teachers.com/kindergraduation.html — This site provides access to the online purchase of the e-book "Kindergrads End of the Year: 30 Songs & Poems" ($5.95 US).
- http://members.tripod.com/~patricia_f/poems.html — This site provides a variety of inspirational poems for teachers and parents about their roles in supporting young children.
- www.learn4good.com/games/simulation.htm — This site provides access to several free online simulations for young children.
- www.heidisongs.com — This site provides an outline of many commercially available resources that are valuable for early learning programs. The resources have been developed to appeal to early learners and use song and motion to teach concepts. A sample song demonstrated with children is available for viewing. The approach has multisensory appeal.
- www.smories.com — This site provides access to many stories for children, read by other children from around the world. By clicking on the first-page icons or photographs, users can learn the title of the story, the target age group for the story, and open a video link to see and hear the story being read.
- www.bced.gov.ca/early_learning — This site provides a wide variety of overviews and access links to early learning programs in British Columbia, including Pre-Kindergarten; Strong Start BC; Ready, Set, Learn; Early Learning webcasts on new initiatives; LEAP BC; Readnow BC; Early Childhood Development; and Ministry of Health Services – Children and Youth Health.
- www.readnowbc.ca/early_learners/klp.php?page=about-the-kindergarten-learning-projects — This site provides a variety of literacy resources for both parents and educators.
- http://education.alberta.ca/parents/ecs.aspx — This site is a direct connection to Early Childhood Services available in Alberta. It includes links to a set of Early Childhood Services Fact Sheets and provides information about specialized services, resources, and programs in the community.
- www.edu.gov.on.ca/eng/curriculum/elementary/kinder.html — This site is a direct connection to kindergarten resource documents and curriculum guidelines for full-day kindergarten in Ontario. The site also contains information about access and programs for the extended day for four- and five-year-olds.
- www.earlylearningcommunity.org/ — This site provides background, links, resources, and access to speakers for a variety of foci related to learners from birth to age five.

In closing this book, I offer this credo about young children as a summary of the tone I have tried to achieve throughout the book. It will help us remember as educators that we should never do for children those things which we can teach them to do for themselves, as independence is a priceless gift to a child.

MEMO FROM YOUR CHILD

1. Don't spoil me. I know quite well that I ought not to have all that I ask for. I'm testing you.
2. Don't be afraid to be firm with me. I prefer it; it makes me feel more secure.
3. Don't let me form bad habits. I have to rely on you to detect them in the early stages.
4. Don't make me feel smaller than I really am. It only makes me behave stupidly "big."
5. Don't correct me in front of people if you can help it. I'll take much more notice if you talk to me privately.
6. Don't make me feel my mistakes are sins. It upsets my sense of values.
7. Don't protect me from consequences. I sometimes have to learn the painful way.
8. Don't be too upset when I say, "I hate you." It isn't you I hate, but your power to thwart me.
9. Don't take too much notice of my small ailments. Sometimes they get me the attention I need.
10. Don't nag. If you do, I shall have to protect myself by appearing deaf.
11. Don't forget that I can not explain myself as well as I should like; this is why I'm not always accurate.
12. Don't make rash promises. Remember that I feel badly let down when promises are broken.
13. Don't tax my honesty too much. I am easily frightened into telling lies.
14. Don't be inconsistent. That completely confuses me and makes me lose faith in you.
15. Don't tell me my fears are silly. They are terribly real to me and you can do much to reassure me if you try to understand.
16. Don't put me off when I ask questions. If you do, you will find that I stop asking and get my information elsewhere.
17. Don't ever suggest that you are perfect or infallible. It gives me too great a shock when I discover that you are neither.
18. Don't ever think it is beneath your dignity to apologize to me. An honest apology makes me feel surprisingly warm toward you.

19. Don't forget how quickly I am growing up. It must be difficult to keep pace with me, but please, do try.
20. Don't forget that I love experimenting. I couldn't get along without it so please put up with it.
21. Don't forget that I can't thrive without lots of understanding love, but I don't need to tell you that do I?

Source: Thomas C. Ritt, Jr., *Arizona ACLD Newsletter*. December, 1975. Used with permission of American Council of Learned Societies (ACLS).

Glossary

accommodation – when individuals experience variations from prior experience, they can change their existing concepts to include more expanded criteria

adaptation – the behavioural changes a person makes because environments put pressure on individuals to change what they do and how they perceive what happens around them

assimilation – when individuals experience variations from prior experience, they can include this variation in their existing concepts for the experience

assistive technology – supports to ensure learning success through technology

attachment theory – a view that brain development in children is influenced by both psychological and biological factors

autonomy – a sense of self-containment and separateness from caregivers

biological embedding – contextual influences, such as the neighbourhood interactions that the child experiences, actually become incorporated into the child's organic makeup and influence the child's development at the cellular level

cognitive development – the growth and extension of knowledge in an individual

conceptual language – the names given to abstract ideas or concrete objects that help a person create a mental image of the idea or object

concrete operational stage – at this stage, children may continue to use concrete objects as symbols for actions or a basis for their thinking, use one-to-one correspondence to make symbolic representations (e.g., maps), develop reading, writing, and numeracy skills that symbolize thoughts and relationships they have considered in their thinking; they may rely on objects to help them manage processes such as mathematical operations; the ability to store mental images is expanding

constructivism – the belief that some essential experiences accompanied by opportunities to make meaning of those experiences are essential for learning

co-teaching – teaching in partnerships

critical reflection – the art of thinking deeply about our own fundamental beliefs, with the goal of understanding the various cultural and social forces and factors that shape our professional practices and perspectives

developmental approaches – strategies used at various stages of growth to support learning, based on the belief that age and physical growth roughly correlate with variations in types of things that can be learned at various stages of development

differentiation – instructional practices and strategies that are inclusive and enable all children to have access and succeed in the general education classroom and curriculum

direct instruction – instruction that includes motivation, modeling new learning, consolidation, application, and metacognitive review

duty of care – the legal expectation that adults in certain care roles in relation to children will take their duty to care for those children seriously and be aware of their position of trust within society

ecological theory (Bronfenbrenner, 1979) – emphasizes the relationship between the biological factors (nature) that affect a child's development and the contextual factors (nurture) that may determine or predispose outcomes

educator team – the teacher and the early childhood educator who work together to establish, monitor, and promote learning in a JK/SK classroom

equilibrium – when individuals face new experiences, they seek to make sense of the experience by either assimilating or accommodating the new information to maintain the sense of balance or harmony in their lives

exceptionalities – individual differences in the learning type and/or severity of needs of an individual, such that special provisions are required to ensure learning success

focused teaching – teaching that ensures that each student receives the instruction best suited to his or her current understanding

formal operational stage – at this stage, the person's ability to think abstractly is expanding, reliance on concrete objects to represent thinking is reduced, and logical and deductive abilities are strengthening

goal interdependence – a measure of the extent to which team members believe they are assigned group goals or receive group feedback

growth scheme – a plan for growth that identifies the stages of growth imaginable toward the achievement of an overall expectation for learning

indirect instruction – strategies used to support learning by approaches other than teacher modeling

interanimation – open discussions not limited by a position of authority

Maslow's needs hierarchy – theory that identifies basic human needs and proposes that these needs must be met in a hierarchical order so that the next level of needs can be actualized; basic needs were seen as preconditions to achieving higher-order needs

metacognition – knowing what you know

methodology – the strategies used to promote learning

pedagogy – the intentional instructional actions taken to promote learning

pedagogical narrative – discussions between children and educator team members that may serve to respond to, challenge, or extend children's thinking as they engage in play

play – a wide range of voluntary activities that typically are pleasant to engage

play configurations – the observable differences in the way people relate to objects and other people as they engage in voluntary pleasurable activity

play-based intentional learning – a wide range of voluntary activities that typically are pleasant to engage and are intentionally provided by an educator team member with the intention that the child learn something through the play experience

preoperational stage – at this stage, young children begin to understand symbols, use role play and alternative objects in their play, name and assign roles, use pretend reading strategies and scribble writing in their efforts to communicate, develop relational vocabulary (e.g., *under*, *behind*, *beside*); talk becomes an important part of meaning making

program principles – the beliefs that support the design and implementation of a program of learning

rapport – the tone of the relationship between educators and the children in their care

scaffolding – a range of supporting behaviours designed to help students extend their learning successfully

schema – the mental images people develop to associate ideas

schema theory – all people seek a sense of balance in their understanding of the things they experience in daily living; to achieve this balance, they either expand existing ideas to include new examples (assimilation) or they develop new concepts to explain the new phenomenon (accommodation)

school readiness – measures of the physical health and well-being, social competence, emotional maturity, language and cognitive development, communication skills and general knowledge that may support school success for young children

self-actualization – meeting needs so that one's fullest potential is realized

self-regulation – an awareness and disposition to monitor and control personal responses in social and cognitive contexts

sensorial materials – materials designed to help young learners experience the natural order of the physical environment (e.g., size, colour, shape, dimension, position)

sensorimotor stage – at this stage, young children use the senses of hearing, sight, smell, touch, and taste to distinguish objects and actions in their environment; they begin to "track" moving objects, respond to familiar sounds, and recognize comforting or rewarding smells, movements, and tastes; they begin to look for items or people who disappear from their line of sight

social constructivism – the belief that learning is best accomplished through social interaction in which people can work together to learn and develop a shared sense of meaning

spontaneous differentiation – the provision of on-the-spot supports for children in the time and methods that best suit their individual needs; sometimes referred to as *reflection-in-action*

stage theory – the belief that all children move through predictable ways of learning at fairly standard times in their life

standards of care – the specific standards required in professional practice from teachers and early childhood educators in their interaction with, and care of, children

task interdependence – a measure of the extent to which the individual team members need information, materials, and support from other team members to carry out their job

touchstone books – books that contain messages about values and social behaviour for young children

work play – a form of play that has the embedded intention of learning for the children engaged in it

zone of proximal development – the readiness of a child to learn a new idea with support to transition from their current independent problem-solving capabilities toward their potential development

References

Ainsworth, M., D. Salter, M. Blehar, E. Waters, and S. Wall. 1978. *Patterns of Attachment: A Psychological Study of the Strange Situation*. Hillsdale, NJ: Erlbaum.

Ayoko, O., C. Hartel, and V. Callan. 2004. "Resolving the Puzzle of Productive and Destructive Conflict in Culturally Heterogeneous Workgroups: A Communication Accommodation Theory Approach." *International Journal of Conflict Management* 13: 165–87.

Barinaga, M. 2000. "A Critical Issue for the Brain." *Science* 288: 2116–2119.

Bauwens, J., J.J. Hourcade, and M. Friend. 1989. "Cooperative Teaching: A Model for General and Special Education Integration." *Remedial and Special Education* 10(2):17–22.

Beach, J. and J. Bertrand. 2000. "More than the Sum of the Parts: An Early Learning Development System for Canada." Occasional Paper 12. University of Toronto Centre for Urban and Community Studies.

Blake, R. and J. Mouton. 1964. *The Managerial Grid*. Houston, TX: Gulf.

Bloom, J.W. 2006. *Creating a Classroom Community of Young Scientists*, 2nd edition. New York: Routledge.

Boethel, M. 2003. *Diversity: School, Family and Community Connections*. Annual synthesis 2003. Austin, TX: Southwest Educational Development Laboratory, National Center for Family and Community Connections with Schools.

Brauner, J., B. Cordic, and E. Zigler. 2004. "Putting the Child Back into Child Care: Combining Care and Education for Children ages 3–5." Society for Research in Child Development Social Policy Report, 18 (3): 3–15.

Bridgemohan, R., N. van Wyk, and C. van Staden. 2005. "Home-School Communication in the Early Childhood Development Phase." *Education* 126(1): 60–77.

British Columbia Ministry of Education 2008. Understanding the British Columbia Early Learning Framework: From Theory to Practice.

British Columbia Ministry of Education. 2009. "Making Linkages: How the British Columbia Early Learning Framework Links to the Primary Program: A Framework for Teaching."

Bromer, J. 2001. "Helpers, Mothers, and Preachers: The Multiple Roles and Discourses of Family Child Care Providers in an African-American Community." *Early Childhood Research Quarterly* 16(3): 313–27.

Bronfenbrenner, U. 1979. *The Ecology of Human Development: Experiences by Nature and Design*. Cambridge, MA: Harvard University Press.

Brown, C. 2010. "The Challenges of the New Early Learning Program." *ETFO Voice* 12(4): 35–36.

Brown, S. 2009. *Play: How it Shapes the Brain, Opens the Imagination, and Invigorates the Soul*. New York: Penguin Books.

Bruer, J. 1999. *The Myth of the First Three Years: A New Understanding of Early Brain Development and Lifelong Learning*. New York: Free Press.

Bushnik, T. and R. Garner. 2008. "The Children of Older First-Time Mothers in Canada: Their Health and Development." Children and Youth Research Paper Series. Catalogue no.89-599-M—005. Ottawa, ON: Statistics Canada.

Campion, M., E. Papper, and G. Medsker. 1996. "Relations between Work Group Characteristics and Effectiveness: A Replication and Extension." *Personnel Psychology* 49: 429–52.

Canadian Council of Learning. 2010. "Educational Toys: Learning to Play or Playing to Learn?" Accessed online October 25, 2010.

Canadian Network for Leadership in Education and Early Learning and Care. Available at www.cnleelc.ca/

Carr, M. and B. Cowie, B. 2003. "The Consequences of Sociocultural Assessment in Early Childhood Settings: Community, Competence and Continuity," in *Early Childhood Education: Society and Culture*, eds. A. Anning, J. Cullen, and M. Fleer. London: Sage.

Chen, K. T. 1990. "An Investigation of Young Children's Playing Facilities' Games." *Journal of Chinese Teaching* 85: 37–43.

Child Care Human Resources Sector Council. n.d. "Educational Qualifications of Centre-Based ECEs and Assistants by Province." Available at www.ccsc-cssge.ca/english/pdf/aboutcw/o51118-education-tables.pdf. Accessed July 30, 2007.

Corsaro, W. and L. Molinari. 2000. "Priming Events and Italian Children's Transition from Preschool to Elementary School: Representations and Action." *School Psychology Quarterly* 63(1): 16–33.

Corter, C. and J. Pelletier. 2005. "Parent and Community Involvement in Schools: Policy Panacea or Pandemic?" in *International Handbook of Educational Policy*, eds. N. Bascia, A. Cumming, A. Datnow, K. Leithwood and D. Livingston. Dordrecht, Netherlands: Springer, 295–329.

Craik, F., and E. Bialystok, E., 2006. "Cognition through the Lifespan: Mechanisms of Change." *Trends in Cognitive Science* 10: 131–38.

Crowson, R. and W. Boyd. 1995. "Integration of Services for Children," in *School-Community Connections*, eds. L. Rigsby, M. Reynolds and M. Wang. San Francisco: Jossey-Bass.

Curry, N.E. and C.N. Johnson. 1990. *Beyond Self-Esteem: Developing a Genuine Sense of Human Value*. Washington, DC: NAEYC.

Cyran, J.R., R. Sheehan, J. Wiechel, and I. Bandy-Hedden. 1992. "Success Outcomes of Full-Day Kindergarten: More Positive Behavior and Increased Achievement in the Years After." *Early Childhood Research Quarterly* 72: 187–203.

Dahinten, V. and J. Willms. 2002. "The effects of adolescent childbearing on children's outcomes," in *Vulnerable Children*, ed. J. Willms. Vancouver, BC: Raincoast Books, 229–244.

Davies, D. and V. Johnson, eds. 1996. "Crossing Boundaries: Family, Community and School Partnerships." [Special Issue] *International Journal of Educational Research*, 25(1): 1–105.

Deutsch, M. 1973. *The Resolution of Conflict*. New Haven, CT: Yale University Press.

Dever, M. and Falconer, R. 2008. *Foundations and Change in Early Childhood Education*. John Wiley & Sons.

Dinnebeil, L. 1999. "Defining Parent Education in Early Intervention." *Topics in Early Childhood Special Education*, 19(3): 161–64.

Doherty, G. 1997. "Zero to Six: The Basis for School Readiness." Ottawa: Human Resources and Skills Development Canada.

Dohrmann, K.B., T. Nishida, A. Gartner, D. Lipsky, and K. Grimm. 2007. "High School Outcomes for Students in a Public Montessori Program." *Journal of Research in Childhood Education* 22: 205–217.

Drew, M. and C. Law. 1990. "Making Early Childhood Education Work." *Principal* 69(5): 10–12.

Duke, D., B. Showers, and M. Imber. 1980. "Teachers and Shared Decision-Making: The Costs and Benefits of Involvement." *Educational Administration Quarterly* 16: 93–106.

Early, D., R. Pianta, L. Taylor, and M. Cox. 2001. Transition Practices: Findings from a National Survey of Kindergarten Teachers." *Early Childhood Education Journal* 283: 199–206.

Epstein, A., L. Schweinhart, A. DeBruin-Parecki, and K. Robin. 2005. "Preschool Assessment: A Guide to Developing a Balanced Approach." National Institute for Early Education Research.

Epstein, J., "Epstein's Framework of Six Types of Involvement." Accessed online January 16, 2011.

Epstein, J. and L. Connors. 2002. "Family, School, and Community Partnerships," in *Handbook of Parenting: Practical Issues in Parenting*, 2nd edition, Vol. 5, ed. M.H. Bornstein. Mahwah, NJ: Lawrence Erlbaum Associates, 407–37.

Evans, B. 2000. "'Bye Mommy! Bye Daddy!' Easing Separation for Preschoolers." *High/Scope Extensions* (September): 1–3.

Field, T. 1998. "Maternal Depression Effects on Infants and Early Interventions." *Preventive Medicine* 27(2): 200–203.

Friend, M. and L. Cook. 1992. "The New Mainstreaming: How It Really Works." *Instructor* 101(7): 30–36.

Friendly, M., J. Beach, and M. Turiano. 2003. *Early Childhood Education and Care in Canada, 2001*, 5th edition. Toronto, ON: Childhood Resources and Research Unit, University of Toronto.

Fromberg, D.P. 1987. "Play," in *The Early Childhood Curriculum: A Review of the Current Research*, ed. C. Seefeldt. New York: Teachers College Press, 35–74.

Frome, P. and J. Eccles. 1998. "Parents' Influence on Children's Achievement-Related Perceptions." *Journal of Personality and Social Psychology* 74(2): 435–52.

Fulghum, R. 1989. *All I Really Need to Know I Learned in Kindergarten*. New York: Random House.

Gerber, S. 2000. "Preparing Experienced Educators for Collaboration and Consultation within Inclusive Schools." A paper presented at the International Special Education Congress, University of Manchester, July 24–28.

Gesell, A. and F.L. Ilg. 1943. *Infant and Child in the Culture of Today: The Guidance of Development in Home and Nursery School*. New York: Harper and Brothers.

Gestwicki, C. and J. Bertrand. 2003. *The Essentials of Early Childhood Education*, 2nd edition. Toronto: Nelson Thompson.

Gilliam, W., E. Zigler, and V. Leiter. 2000. "A Critical Meta-Analysis of All Evaluations of State-Funded Preschool from 1997 to 1998: Implications for Policy, Service Delivery and Program Evaluation." *Early Childhood Research Quarterly* 15: 441–73.

Girard, K. and S. Koch. 1996. *Conflict Resolution in the Schools: A Manual for Educators*. San Francisco: Jossey-Bass.

Glascoe, F. and H. Shapiro. 2008. Introduction to developmental and behavioural screening. *Developmental Behavioral Pediatrics Online*. Available at www.dbpeds.org/articles/detail.cfm?TextID=%205. Accessed April 12, 2008.

Goelman, H. 2008. "Three Complementary Community-Based Approaches to the Early Identification of Young Children at Risk for Developmental Delays/Disorders. *Infants and Young Children* 21(4): 306–23.

Goleman, D. 1989. "The Roots of Empathy are Traced to Infancy." *New York Times* (March 28): 20–21 (Section B).

Graue, E. 2009. "Reimagining Kindergarten: Restoring a Developmental Approach when Accountability Demands are Pushing Formal Instruction on the Youngest Learners." *The School Administrator* 66(10):10–15.

Greenough, W., J. Black, and C. Wallace. 1987. "Experience and Brain Development." *Child Development* 58: 539–59.

Gullo, D. 2000. "The Long Term Educational Effects of Half-Day vs. Full-Day Kindergarten." *Early Child Development and Care* 160: 17–24.

Hackman, J., 1976. "Influences on Individuals," in *Handbook of Industrial and Organizational Psychology*, ed. M.D. Dunnette. Chicago: Rand-McNally, 1455–1525.

Hannon, J. 1999. "Talking Back: Kindergarten Dialogue Journals." *The Reading Teacher* 53(3): 200–203.

Haskins, M., J. Liedtka, and J. Rosenblum. 1998. "Beyond Teams: Toward an Ethic of Collaboration." *Organizational Dynamics* 26(4): 34–50.

Healey, J.M. 1987. *Your Child's Growing Mind*. Toronto: Doubleday.

Hertzman, C. 1999. "The Biological Embedding of Early Experience and its Effects on Health in Adulthood," in *Socioeconomic Status and Health in Industrial Nations: Social, Psychological and Biological Pathways*, eds. N.E. Adler and M. Marmot New York: New York Academy of Sciences, 85–95.

Hertzman, C. and J. Frank. 2006. "Biological Pathways Linking the Social Environment, Development and Health," in *Healthier Societies: From Analysis to Action*, eds. J. Heymann, C. Hertzman, M.L. Barer, and R.G. Evans. New York: Oxford University Press, 35–37.

Hertzman, C. and L.G. Irwin. 2007. "It takes a child to raise a community: 'Population-based' Measurement of Early Child Development." Vancouver, BC: Early Human Learning Partnership.

Hertzman, C. and M. Wiens. 1996. "Child Development and Long-Term Outcomes: A Population Health Perspective and Summary of Successful Interventions." *Social Science and Medicine* 43(7): 1083–95.

Hirsh-Pasek, K., and R. Golinkoff. 2008. "Brains in a Box: Do New Age Toys Deliver on the Promise? in *Child Development in a Changing Society*, ed. R. Harwood. Hoboken, NJ: Wiley Press.

Ho, S. 2000. "Decentralization and Parental Involvement: In an Asian Educational System." Paper presented at the biennial meetings of the American Educational Research Association, New Orleans, LA.

Hohmann, M., D. Weikart, and A. Epstein. 2008. *Educating Young Children: Active Learning Practices for Preschool and Child Care Programs*. Ypsilanti, MI: High/Scope Press.

Holton, D. and D. Clark. 2006. "Scaffolding and Metacognition." *International Journal of Mathematical Education in Science and Technology* 37(2): 127–43.

Housden, T. and R. Kam. 1992. "Full-Day Kindergarten: A Summary of the Research." Carmichael, CA: San Juan Unified School District.

Howland, J. 2003. "Into the Province of Shared Endeavor." *Independent School* 62(3): 12–17.

Ipsos Reid poll, released October 27, 2009. Available at www.ipsos-na.com/new-polls/pressrelease.aspx?id=4567.

Ivarie, J. 1995. "Strategies for Managing Conflict in the Collaboration Process." Paper presented at the

Annual Meeting of the Council for Exceptional Children. Indianapolis, IL.

Janus, M. , 2006. "Measuring Community Early Child Development." *The CAP Journal* 14(3): 14–16.

Janus, M., J. Lefort, R. Cameron, and L. Kopechanski. 2007. "Starting Kindergarten: Transition Issues for Children with Special Needs." *Canadian Journal of Education* 30(3): 628–48.

Janus, M. and D. Offord. 2007. "Development and Psychometric Properties of the Early Development Instrument EDI: A Measure of Children's School Readiness." *Canadian Journal of Behavioural Science* 39(1): 1–22.

Jehn, K. 1995. "A Multimethod Examination of the Benefits and Detriments of Intragroup Conflict." *Administrative Science Quarterly* 40(2): 256–82.

Jensen, E. 1998. *Teaching with the Brain in Mind.* Alexandria, VA: ASCD.

Johnson, J. 1993. "Language Development Component: All Day Kindergarten Program 1991–1992. Final Evaluation Report." Elementary and Secondary Education Act, Chapter 1. Columbus, OH: Columbus Public Schools Dept. of Program Evaluation.

Johnson, L. and J. Mathien. 1998. "Early Childhood Services for Kindergarten-age Children in Four Canadian Provinces: Scope, Nature and Models for the Future." Ottawa, ON: The Caledon Institute of Social Policy.

Johnson, M.H. 2001. "Functional Brain Development in Humans." *Nature Reviews/Neuroscience* 2: 475–483.

Kaiser, A., G. Mahoney, L. Girolametto, J. MacDonald, C. Robinson, P. Safford, and D. Spiker. 1999. "Rejoinder: Toward a Contemporary Vision of Parent Education." *Topics in Early Childhood Special Education* 19(3): 173–76.

Kamerman, S. and J. Kahn. 1997. *Family Change and Family Policies in the West.* New York: Oxford University Press.

Karweit, N. 1992. "The Kindergarten Experience." *Educational Leadership* 49(6): 82–86.

Katz, L.G. 1998. "What can we learn from Reggio Emilia?" in *The Hundred Languages of Children: The Reggio Emilia Approach—Advanced Reflections*, 2nd edition, eds. C. Edwards, L. Gandini, and G. Forman. Greenwich, CT: Ablex, 27–45.

Katz, L.G. 1995. *Talks with Teachers of Young Children: A Collection.* Norwood, NJ: Ablex.

Kershaw, P., L. Irwin, K. Trafford, and C. Hertzman. 2006. *The British Columbia Atlas of Child Development* 1st edition. Vancouver, BC: Human Early Learning Partnership.

Kirkman, B. and B. Rosen. 1999. "Beyond Self-Management: Antecedents and Consequences of Team Empowerment." *The Academy of Management Journal* 42(1): 58–74.

Knudsen, E. 2004. "Sensitive Periods in the Development of Brain and Behavior." *Journal of Cognitive Neuroscience* 16(8): 1412–25.

Kohen, D., J. Brooks-Gunn, T. Leventhal, and C. Hertzman. 2002. "Neighbourhood Income and Physical and Social Disorder in Canada: Associations with Young Children's Competencies." *Child Development* 73: 1844–60.

Korabik, K., G. Baril, and C. Watson. 1993. "Managers' Conflict Management Style and Leadership Effectiveness: The Moderating Effects of Gender." *Sex Roles* 29(5–6): 405–421.

Kuhn, T. and M. Poole. 2000. "Do Conflict Management Styles Affect Group Decision Making? Evidence from a Longitudinal Field Study." *Human Communication Research* 26(4): 558–90.

Kuo, C. 2009. "The Factors of Design on Playing Equipment in Young Children Schools by Viewpoint of Young Children Behavioral Development." *Education* 129(4): 755–69.

Ladd, G., and J. Price. 1987. "Predicting Children's Social and School Adjustment Following the Transition from Preschool to Kindergarten." *Child Development* 58: 1168–89.

Lai, M. and N. Law. 2006. "Peer Scaffolding of Knowledge Building through Collaborative Groups with Differential Learning Experiences." *Journal of Educational Computing Research* 35(2): 123–44.

Lam, S., P. Yim, and T.W. Lam. 2002. "Transforming School Culture: Can True Collaboration be Initiated?" *Educational Research* 44(2): 181–96.

Laverick, D.M. 2008. "Starting School: Welcoming Young Children and Families into Early School Experiences." *Early Childhood Education Journal* 35: 321–26.

Lazarus, P. 1983. "Kindergarten Children's Communication Competence: Findings from an Ethnographic Study." Paper presented at the Annual Meeting of the American Educational Research Association. Montreal, QC.

Lillard, S. 2005. *Montessori: The Science behind the Genius*. New York: Oxford University Press.

Limbos, M., D. Joyce, and J. Roberts. 2010. "Patterns of Use of the Nipissing District Developmental Screen by Physicians in Ontario." Available at www.cfp.ca/cgi/content/full/56/2/e66. Accessed November 7, 2010.

Littleford, J. and J. Brand. 2010. "Working with Early Childhood Educators: A New Partnership for Educators." *ETFO Voice* 12(4): 32–34.

Lu, M.G. 2006. *Introduction of Young Children's Education.* Taipei : Wu-Nan Press.

Mahoney, G., A. Kaiser, L. Girolametto, J. MacDonald, C. Robinson, P. Safford, and D. Spiker. 1999. "Parent Education in Early Intervention : A Call for a Renewed Focus. " *Topics in Early Childhood Special Education* 19: 131–40.

Maslow, A.H. 1954. *Motivation and Personality*, 2nd edition. New York: Harper & Row.

Mathien, J. 2001. "Children, Families, and Institutions in Late 19th and Early 20th Century Ontario," (master's thesis, Ontario Institute for Studies in Education, University of Toronto).

Maxwell, K. and S. Eller. 1994. "Children's Transition to Kindergarten." *Young Children* 49(6): 56–63.

Maynes, N., L. Julien-Schultz, and C. Dunn. 2010. "Modeling and the Gradual Release of Responsibility: What Does It Look Like in the Classroom?" *Brock Education Journal* 19(2).

Maynes, N., L. Julien-Schultz, and C. Dunn. 2010. "Managing Direct and Indirect Instruction: A Visual Model to Support Lesson Planning in Pre-Service Programs." *The International Journal of Learning* 17(2): 125–40.

McCain, M. and F. Mustard. 1999. "Early Years Study." Toronto, ON: Government of Ontario.

McGrath, J. 1991. "Time, Interaction and Performance (TIP): A Theory of Groups." *Small Group Research* 22(2): 147–74.

McGrath, W. H. 2003. "Ambivalent Partners: Relationships Between Mothers and Teachers in a Full-Time Child Care Center," (unpublished doctoral dissertation, University of Pennsylvania).

McLoyd, V. 1998. "Socioeconomic Disadvantage and Child Development." *American Psychologist* 53(2): 185–204.

Miller, A. 2001. "What are the Various Kinds of Kindergarten Schedules?" Clearinghouse on Early Education and Parenting. Available online.

Miller, A., W. Valasky, and P. Molloy. 1998. "Learning Together: The Evolution of an Inclusive Class." *Active Learner: A Foxfire Journal for Teachers* 3(2): 14–16.

Miller, D. 2002. *Reading with Meaning.* Portland, ME: Stenhouse Publishers.

Miller, S., E. Replogle, and H. Weiss. 1995. "Family Support in Early Education and Child Care Settings: Making the Case for Both Principles and Practices." *Children Today* 23(4): 26–29.

Mitchell, C, and L. Sackney, L. 2001. "Building Capacity for a Learning Community." *Canadian Journal of Educational Administration and Policy* 19 Available at www.umanitoba.ca/publications/cjeap/issues19.html.

Morris, J. and R. Steers. 1980. "Structural Influences on Organizational Commitment." *Journal of Vocational Behavior* 17(1): 50–57.

National Center for Education Statistics (NCES) 1999. "Early Childhood Longitudinal Study: Kindergarten Class of 1998-99." Washington, DC: U.S. Department of Education, Institute of Education Sciences. Available at www.nces.ed.gov/ecls/kindergarten.asp.

National Institute of Child Health and Human Development. 2003. "Does Amount of Time Spent in Child Care Predict Socioemotional Adjustment during the Transition to Kindergarten?" *Child Development* 74(4): 976–1005.

National Institute for Early Education Research. 2004. Available at http://nieer.org. Accessed July 31, 2011.

Nevin, A., J. Thousand, P. Paolucci-Whitcomb, and R. Villa. 1990. "Collaborative Consultation: Empowering Public School Personnel to Provide Heterogeneous Schooling for All." *Journal of Educational and Psychological Consultation* 1(1): 41–67.

Ontario Legislative Assembly. The Day Nurseries Act. Revised Statutes of Ontario, 1990 (reprinted 1998). Amended by The Services Improvement Act effective January 1, 1998. c. D-2 Amended by: 1997, c. 30. Sched.C:1999, c. 12. Sched. E, s.2 1999, c.12, Sched. G, s. 21: O. Reg. 500/00:2001.c. 13, s.14.

Ontario Legislative Assembly. Ontario Regulation 262, 1990. Amended 1998, 1999.

Ontario Ministry of Education. 2007. "Early Learning for Every Child Today: A Framework for Ontario Early Childhood Settings." Available at www.children.gov.on.ca/htdocs/English/topics/earlychildhood/early_learning_for_every_child_today.aspx. Accessed July 31, 2011.

Ontario Ministry of Education 2010. "The Full-Day Early Learning–Kindergarten Program" (draft version). Toronto: Queen's Printer for Ontario.

Ontario Ministry of Education. 2010. "Every Child, Every Opportunity: Practice of Interaction." Available at www.ontario.ca/en/initiatives/early_learning/ONT06_023401. Accessed February 25, 2010.

Ontario Ministry of Education 2010. "Parents in Partnership: A Parent Engagement Policy for Ontario Schools." Toronto: Queen's Printer for Ontario.

Ontario Ministry of Education. 2010. "Growing Success: Assessment, Evaluation, and Reporting in Ontario Schools." Toronto: Queen's Printer for Ontario. Also available at www.edu.gov.on.ca.

Paley, V. 2001. *In Mrs. Tully's Room: A Childcare Portrait.* Cambridge, MA: Harvard University Press.

Parkay, F., B. Hardcastle-Stanford. 2000. *Becoming a Teacher*. Toronto, ON: Allyn & Bacon.

Parkay, F., B. Hardcastle-Stanford, J. Vaillancourt, and H. Stephens. 2009. *Becoming a Teacher*, 2nd Canadian edition. Toronto, ON: Pearson.

Parten, M. 1933. "Social Play among Preschool Children." *Journal of Abnormal and Social Psychology* 28:136–47.

Paul, P. 2008. *Parenting, Inc*. New York: Times Books.

Pelletier, J. and C. Corter. 2005. "Toronto First Duty: Integrating Kindergarten, Childcare, and Parenting Support to Help Diverse Families Connect to Schools." *Multicultural Education* (Special Issue on Families and Multicultural Education) 13(2): 30–37.

Piaget, J. 1930. *The Child's Conception of Physical Causality*. New York: Harcourt Brace & Co.

Pianta, R. and M. Kraft-Sayre. 1999. "Parents' Observations about their Children's Transitions to Kindergarten." *Young Children* 54(3): 47–52.

Porath, M. 2009. "Fostering Social Expertise in Early Childhood." Early Child Development and Care 179(1): 93–106.

Prochner, L. 2000. "A History of Early Education and Child Care in Canada, 1890–1966," in *Early Childhood Care and Education in Canada*, eds. L. Prochner and N. Howe. Vancouver, BC: UBC Press, 11–65.

Rahim, A., N. Magner and D. Shapiro. 2000. "Do Justice Perceptions Influence Styles of Handling Conflict with Supervisors? What Justice Perceptions, Precisely?" *International Journal of Conflict Management* 11(1): 9–31.

Rathunde, K. and M. Csikszentmihalyi. 2005. "Middle School Students' Motivation and Quality of Experience: A comparison of Montessori and Traditional School Environments." *American Journal of Education* 111(3): 341–71.

Reedy, C.K., W.H. McGarth. 2010. "Can You Hear Me Now? Staff–Parent Communication in Child Care Centres." *Early Childhood Development and Care* 180(3): 347–57.

Resnick, M., R. Gueorguieva, R. Carter, M. Ariet, Y. Sun, J. Roth, et al. 1999. "The Impact of Low Birth Weight, Perinatal Conditions, and Sociodemographic Factors on Educational Outcome in Kindergarten." *Pediatrics* 104(6): e74.

Reynolds, A.J., J.A. Temple, D.L. Robertson, and E.A. Mann. 2001. "Long-Term Effects of an Early Childhood Intervention on Educational Achievement and Juvenile Arrest." *The Journal of the American Medical Association* 285(18): 2339–46.

Rimm-Kaufmann, S., R. Pianta, and M. Cox. 2000. "Teachers' Judgments of Problems in the Transition to Kindergarten." Early Childhood Research Quarterly 15(2): 147–66.

Robinson, F., W. Croxall, P. Kenny, and D. Klingspon. 2010. *Fostering Human Development and Empowerment: A Conceptual Bridge Between Vision and Action.* North Bay, ON: The Human Development and Empowerment Group.

Rothenberg, D. 1995. "Full-Day Kindergarten Programs." Available at http.//ceep.crc.uiuc.edu/eecearchive/digests/1995/drkind95.html.

Rubin, K., G. Fein, and B. Vandenberg. 1983. "Play," in *Socialization, Personality, and Social Development*, eds. P. Mussen and M. Hetherington. Vol. 4 of *Handbook of Child Psychology*. New York: Wiley, 698–744.

Rybczynski, M. and A. Troy. 1995. "Literacy-Enriched Play Centers: Trying Them Out in 'The Real World.'" *Childhood Education* 72 (1): 7–12.

Santamaria, L. and J. Thousand. 2004. "Collaboration, Co-Teaching, and Differentiated Instruction: A Process-Oriented Approach to Whole Schooling." *International Journal of Whole Schooling* 1(1): 13–27.

Saracho, O. and B. Spodek. 1995. "Children's Play and Early Childhood Education: Insights from History and Theory." *Journal of Education* 177(3): 129–48.

Saye, J. and T. Brush. 2002. "Scaffolding Critical Reasoning about History and Social Issues in Multimedia-Supported Learning Environments."

Educational Technology Research and Development 50(3): 77–96.

Schneider, B. 1987. "The People Make the Place." *Personnel Psychology* 40: 437–53.

Schore, A.N. 1997a. "A Century after Freud's Project: Is a Rapprochement between Psychoanalysis and Neurobiology at Hand?" *Journal of the American Psychoanalytic Association* 45(3): 807–40.

Schore, A.N. 1997b. "Early Organization of the Nonlinear Right Brain and Development of a Predisposition to Psychiatric Disorders." *Development and Psychopathology* 9: 595–631.

Schore, A.N. 2001. "Effects of a Secure Attachment Relationship on Right Brain Development, Affect Regulation, and Infant Mental Health." *Infant Mental Health Journal* 22(1–2):7–66.

Schulz, L., and E. Bonawitz. 2007. "Serious Fun: Preschoolers Engage in More Exploratory Play When Evidence is Confounded." *Developmental Psychology* 43(4): 1045–50.

Schulz, L., A. Gopnik, and C. Glymour. 2007. "Preschool Children Learn about Causal Structure from Conditional Interventions." *Developmental Science*, 10(3): 322–32.

Schweinhart, L.J. 2004. "The High/Scope Perry Preschool Study through Age 40." http://highscope.org/Research/homepage.html. Retrieved April 2010.

Schweinhart, L.J., H.V Barnes, and D.P. Weikart. 1993. "Significant Benefits: The HighScope Perry Preschool Study through Age 27." Ypsilanti, MI: High/Scope Press.

Schweinhart, L., J. Monte, Z. Xiang, W. Barnett, C. Belfield, and M. Nores. 2005. "Lifetime Effects: The High/Scope Perry Preschool Study Through Age 40." Ypsilanti, MI: High/Scope Press.

Shore, R. 1997. "What have we learned?" in *Rethinking the Brain: New Insights into Early Development*. New York: Families and Work Institute, pp. 15–27.

Shores, E. 1998. "A Call to Action: Family Involvement as a Critical Component of Teacher Education Programs." Tallahassee, FL: Southeastern Regional Vision for Education.

Singh, K. and L.M. Shifflette. 1996. "Teachers' Perspectives on Professional Development." *Journal of Personnel Evaluation in Education* 10(2): 145–60.

Siraj-Blatchford, I., K. Sylva, S. Muttock, R. Gilden, and D. Bell. 2002. "Researching Effective Pedagogy in the Early Years." Research Report 356. London: Department for Education and Skills.

Skrtic, T. 1987. "The National Inquiry into the Future of Education for Students with Special Needs." *Counterpoint* 4(7): 6.

Somech, A. 2008. "Managing Conflict in School Teams: The Impact of Task and Goal Interdependence on Conflict Management and Team Effectiveness." *Educational Administration Quarterly* 44(3): 359–90.

Stanovich, P. J. 1996. "Collaboration – The Key to Successful Instruction in Today's Inclusive Schools." *Intervention in School and Clinic* 32(1): 39–41.

Statistics Canada. 2002. "PALS 2001: A Profile of Disability in Canada, 2001." Ottawa, ON: Ministry of Industry. Available at www.statcan.ca/english/freepub/89-577-XIE/info.htm. Accessed January 18, 2008.

Sylva, K., C. Roy, and M. Painter. 1980. *Childwatching at Playgroup and Nursery School*. Ypsilanti: MI, High/Scope Press.

Tabors, P. 2004. *One Child, Two Languages: A Guide for Preschool Educators of Children Learning English as a Second Language*. Baltimore, MD: Brookes Publishing.

Thomas, M., and M. Johnson. 2008. "New Advances in Understanding Sensitive Periods in Brain Development." *Current Directions in Psychological Science* 17: 1–5.

Thompson, S., J. Maxwell, and S. Stroick. 1999. "Moving Forward on Child and Family Policy: Governance and Accountability Issues." Ottawa, ON: Canadian Policy Research Networks.

Thousand, J., R. Villa, A. Nevin, and P. Paolucci-Whitcomb. 1995. "A Rationale and Vision for Collaborative Consultation," in *Controversial Issues Confronting Special Education: Divergent Perspectives*, 2nd edition, eds. W. Stainback and S. Stainback. Baltimore, MD: Brookes Publishing, 223–32.

Tinsley, B., C. Markey, A. Ericksen, A. Kwasman, and R. Ortiz. 2002. "Health Promotion for Parents," in *Handbook of Parenting: Practical Issues in Parenting* 2nd ed., Vol. 5, ed. M.H. Bornstein. Mahwah, NJ: Lawrence Erlbaum Associates, 311–28.

Tjosvold, D. 1999. "Bridging East and West to Develop New Products and Trust: Interdependence and Interaction between Hong Kong Parent and North American Subsidiary." *International Journal of Innovation Management* 3(2): 233–52.

Tjosvold, D., C. Hui, and Z. Yu. 2005. "Conflict Management and Task Reflexivity for Team In-Role Performance and Extra-Role Performance in

China." *International Journal of Conflict Management* 14(2): 141–163.

Tomlinson, C. 1999. *The Differentiated Classroom: Responding to the Needs of all Learners*. Alexandria, VA: ASCD.

Toohey, K. and E. Day. 1998. "Communities of Participation in Learning ESL." Paper presented to the Annual Meeting of the Teachers of English to Speakers of Other Languages. Seattle, WA.

Trehearne, M, et al. 2000. *Kindergarten Teacher's Resource Book*. Scarborough, ON: Nelson Education, 409–14.

Tucker-Drob, E.M., M. Rhemtulla, K.P. Harden, E. Turkheimer, D. Fask. 2011. "Emergence of a Gene x Socioeconomic Status Interaction on Infant Mental Ability Between 10 Months and 2 Years." *Psychological Science* 22(1):125–33. Epub 2010 Dec 17.

Turkheimer, E., A. Haley, M. Waldron, B. D'Onofrio, and I. Gottesman. 2003. "Socioeconomic Status Modifies Heritability of IQ in Young Children." *Psychological Science* 14(6):623–28.

Turnbull, A.P., V. Turbiville, and H.R. Turnbull. 2000. "Evolution of Family Professional Partnership Models: Collective Empowerment as the Model for the Early 21st Century," in *Handbook of Early Childhood Intervention*, eds. S.J. Meisels and J.P. Shonkoff. New York: Cambridge University Press, 630–50.

Turnbull, A.P. and H.R. Turnbull. 2001. *Families, Professionals, and Exceptionality: Collaborating for Empowerment*, 4th edition. Upper Saddle River, NJ: Prentice Hall.

Umek, L., and P. Musek. 2001. "Symbolic Play: Opportunities for Cognitive and Language Development in Preschool Settings." *Early Years* 21(1): 55–64.

Van Lier, L. 1996. *Language and Languages: Study and Teaching*. New York: Longman

Villa, R., J. Thousand, and A. Nevin. 2004. *A Guide to Co-Teaching: Practical Tips for Facilitating Student Learning*. Thousands Oaks, CA: Corwin Press.

Vygotsky, L.S. 1978. *Mind in Society: The Development of Higher Psychological Processes*. Cambridge, MA: Harvard University Press.

Vygotsky, L.S. 1987. "Thinking and Speech," in *The Collected Works of L.S. Vygotsky*, vol. 1, eds. R. Rieber and A. Carton, trans. N. Minick. New York: Plenum, 39–285. (Original works published in 1934, 1960.)

Webb, S., C. Monk, C. Nelson. 2001. "Mechanisms of Postnatal Neurobiological Development: Implications for Human Development." *Developmental Neuropsychology* 19(2): 147–71.

Weiss, C., J. Cambone, and A. Wyeth. 1992. "Trouble in Paradise: Teacher Conflicts in Shared Decision Making." *Educational Administration Quarterly* 28(3): 350–67.

Werf, G. van der, B. Creemers, H. Guldemond. 2001. "Improving Parental Involvement in Primary Education in Indonesia: Implementation, Effects and Costs." *School Effectiveness and School Improvement* 12(4): 447–66.

Wilms, D. 2002. *Vulnerable Children: Findings from Canada's National Longitudinal Study of Children and Youth*. Edmonton, AB: University of Alberta Press.

Wilson, B. 1996. *Constructivist Learning Environments: Case Studies in Instructional Design*. Englewood Cliffs, NJ: Educational Technology Publications.

Wolfe, P. 2001. *Brain Matters: Translating Research into Classroom Practice*. Alexandria, VA: ASCD.

Wood, D., J. Bruner, and G. Ross. 1976. "The Role of Tutoring in Problem Solving." *The Journal of Child Psychiatry and Psychology* 17(2): 89–100.

Wood, D., L. McMahon, and Y. Cranstoun. 1980. *Working With Under Fives*. Ypsilanti, MI: High/Scope Press.

Yang, S.C. 1998. "The study on young children's creativeness and playing behaviours in conventional playing courts." Taipei: Psychological Publishing.

Yelland, N. and J. Masters. 2007. "Rethinking Scaffolding in the Information Age." *Computers and Education* 48(3): 362–82.

Zenger, J. 1994. *Leading Teams: Mastering the New Role*. Homewood, IL: Business One Irwin.

Zornoza, A., P. Ripoll, and J. Peiró, J. 2002. "Conflict Management in Groups that Work in Two Different Communication Contexts: Face-to-Face and Computer-Mediated Communication." *Small Group Research* 33(5): 481–500.

Index

Note: Entries for figures and tables are indicated by "*f*" and "*t*," respectively.

F